Editing the Organizational Publication

by Edmund C. Arnold

with the assistance of
Kathleen Anne Loomis

Lawrence Ragan Communications, Inc.
Chicago

First printing June 1982
Second printing May 1983

Copyright 1982
by Lawrence Ragan Communications, Inc.

Library of Congress Catalog No.: 82-060043
ISBN 0-931368-09-X

Lawrence Ragan Communications, Inc.
407 South Dearborn Street
Chicago, IL 60605

Contents

The Editor

1	as Executive	1
2	as Communicator	17
3	as Production Manager	40
4	as Writer	65
5	as Copyreader	82
6	as Typographer	120
7	as Art Director	148
8	as Newspaper Designer	184
9	as Magazine Designer	199
10	as Newsletter Producer	220
11	as Circulation Manager	238
12	as Contractor	246
	Glossary	264
	Index	281

Chapter 1
The Editor

☑ as Executive
☐ as Communicator
☐ as Production Manager
☐ as Writer
☐ as Copyreader
☐ as Typographer
☐ as Art Director
☐ as Newspaper Designer
☐ as Magazine Designer
☐ as Newsletter Producer
☐ as Circulation Manager
☐ as Contractor

Glossary
Index

Any editor wears many hats; an organizational editor wears a couple more.

Every editor is a communicator, an executive, a writer, a copyreader, a typographer, a researcher. An organizational editor must also be a diplomat and an advocate.

Any editor must most of all be a communicator. That means deciding the areas that will be covered by a publication, assigning staffers to provide that coverage, setting standards for reporting and writing. The editor must be an administrator, directing the work not only of the staff but of typesetters, printers, and other craftspeople; the editor must administer a budget, for accounting becomes a more pressing duty year by year. (Every aspiring journalist should take at least one accounting course.)

The editor must be a writer—indeed, wants to be a writer—for that is one of the most satisfying aspects of the job. The editor must be a copyreader, the last authority on accuracy, style, and consistency. The editor must be a typographer, packaging the content of a publication in a way that will assure it being read, or directing the work of a graphic designer. The editor must be a researcher, seeking feedback from the reader.

All these functions must be carried out simultaneously and constantly, and that's enough to keep practically anyone busy on a 25-hour daily schedule.

The organizational editor must do all these. . .plus a few important more. The organizational editor works within a closed political and economic organism. The editor must be a trusted company representative, familiar and comfortable with the economic goal of the organization. The editor must be privy to top management's objectives and decisions, yet retain rapport with the workers, be their collars blue, white, or pink.

The organizational editor must be a diplomat. For editors work with creative people—who often may be described, without fear of libel, as prima donnas. Many organizations depend greatly on volunteers who cannot be held to the constraints of a commercial operation. The editor must deal with news sources who are suspicious of the press in any of its forms...but are never in doubt as to their own importance. The organizational editor must cross all kinds of departmental lines which, although invisible, are as zealously guarded as the Sino-Russian border.

Obviously there isn't a simple blueprint for the execution of all these diverse and demanding responsibilities. Indeed, the person who can accomplish all these tasks to perfection has yet to appear on the human scene. So this book seeks to synthesize the knowledge and experience of hundreds of editors who have collectively solved these problems.

Editors, like their publications, come in a wide and interesting variety. So do their objectives, their techniques, their resources, and their unique problems. But the differences are more apparent than real and this book addresses itself to the basics that are common to them all. For the new editor there are tricks of the trade that are brand new. For the experienced editor there may be a new idea here and there; but the major value will be a systematic review and reevaluation of familiar knowledge, a checklist for evaluating standard operational procedures. The very title of this book suggests the breadth of the field and definitions are in order.

An "organizational publication" is one published by an organized, well-defined group to carry communication which it thinks or knows will not be carried by any other publication.

The group may be a commercial one; indeed this area is often referred to as "industrial journalism." But while industry and commerce have been associated with this form of communication for more than a century, nonprofit organizations have had an even longer history of such journalism. It's highly probable that most organizational editors today are not affiliated with industry or a "company" as such.

Educational institutions—from school districts to universities—are broadening their communications programs; health-service groups are expanding theirs at an even faster pace. Community groups—from the Art League to the Little League and from Save the Whales to Save the Taxpayer—are using periodicals. Comparatively new, but increasing constantly in numbers, are the publications of governmental units, especially at the city level. Labor unions use journalism skillfully. Purely social organizations have discovered the value of purposeful communication.

Audiences, too, vary greatly. Originally organizational publications were directed to employees or members. They soon expanded to include stockholders, customers, dealers, legislators and other governmental officials, and often the general public. Many organizations have a whole stable of periodicals, each directed to a specific audience. Most seek to reach all audiences with a single publication.

So already we have enough diversity to populate a three-ring circus. The kinds of "publications" vary almost as much.

"Publication"—at least in this book—refers to periodicals, communications issued at regular, even if infrequent, intervals. And "publication" refers to printed matter, although this may not exactly conform to common usage. Often law decisions consider broadcast matter as being "published"—and many organizations use oral communications most effectively. This book will stay strictly with printed matter though "publications," for our purposes, do not include annual reports—although these may technically meet our definition—nor booklets, brochures, fliers, etc., that most organizations issue from time to time and even quite regularly.

(Actually, all these products of the printing press against which we have so arbitrarily slammed the door are to a large extent covered in this book. For the principles of communication—verbal and nonverbal—are applicable to all the printed matter that comes off the presses.)

This book will consider *magazines, newspapers,* the new hybrid *magtabs,* and *newsletters.* As the same principles apply to each of these, the editor of any one is urged to consider all the others. Common principles often will be stated only once to avoid monotonous repetition although they apply to other publications as well as the one being scrutinized at the moment.

Put them all together, they spell, not "Mother," but "organizational publications," a jawbreaker, sometimes abbreviated to the "voiceless, bilabial, plosive" *OP.* Sometimes one might wish that a term that comes trippingly off the tongue, "house organ," would not be anathema to so many editors today.

Technically it's an accurate term: Periodicals are described by Mr. Webster as "organs" and they are produced by and for a "house." In the 50s it was still a good term that editors themselves used without pang or apology. But since then the term has become pejorative—if not actually riot-inciting. Some observers feel that "organ" has too much physiological connotation, especially sexual. But that seems a bit far-fetched in today's permissive society. It's more logical to assume that the term was abandoned in the embarrassment of recalling the content of a typical "house organ" a quarter of a century ago. In too many instances, such a publication was woefully amateurish. It was filled with such earth-shaking intelligences as to who had bowled a 300 game, whose child graduated from kindergarten, and who had a silver wedding anniversary. In between were lists of service awards, recipes, press releases from the advertising department. And, of course, The President's Message, soul-stirring in its inspiration.

God was in His heaven and all was right with the world—at least that part of the world that the periodical ostensibly covered. Never was heard a discouraging word about inflation, absenteeism, competition, layoffs, and other things that go bump in the industrial night. Close your eyes and they'll all go away...that was the editorial motto.

The editor often—probably usually—had little if any journalistic training in the heyday of the house organ. Immediately after World War II it became fashionable for companies to have such a publication. Objectives were misty, if benevolent, and editors were given no specific goal. Often editors were chosen because they had written such interesting letters to servicemen on distant battle fronts. Or they were amateur poets or novelists. Or they were almost ready for retirement and this was a graceful transition into the rocking chair. Or they simply happened to be in the Personnel department which had, by coin-flipping, been charged with producing the house organ. The average age of the editor was probably 50 percent higher than it is today.

Today's organizational editor is young, more often a woman, well-educated and usually with at least some training in journalism. Today's editor takes a professional approach to the job and—an interesting and encouraging phenomenon—seriously expands and sharpens professional skills. Workshops and seminars are constantly being conducted on all levels—local to national—by both nonprofit and commercial groups and are well attended.

That old "house organ," while it still exists here and there, is no longer typical and its name had to be replaced. But because the multisyllabic "organizational publication" is such a cumbersome term, it won't be used too frequently in this book. Nor will the inelegant "OP." We all assume that this is the particular breed of journalism that we're talking about.

The journalistic duties of any editor are examined in detail in the following chapters. But we must first consider the unique responsibilities of the organizational editor.

First of all, such an editor must share the goal of the organization. If it is a commercial group, that goal is making a profit. The editor must be sure—as much in the viscera as in the brain—that this is an honorable pursuit that benefits many people. Recognizing the flaws of this system—and all economic systems fall short of Utopia—the editor chooses to retain the baby while throwing out the bath water.

An organizational publication is unabashedly published to enhance the well-being of its sponsor: to increase productivity of employees, to persuade the voters to approve a bond issue, to encourage savers to invest capital so we can buy more machinery for our employees to use, to create a favorable image of our group in the public mind so we can resist encumbering legislation or regulation.

The organizational editor accepts that responsibility without apology. It is neither dishonorable, dishonest, nor fattening to perform such journalistic chores.... if they are done according to basic journalistic ethics.

Organizational journalism is advocacy journalism and in many ways the editor is like an advocate in the courtroom. An attorney presents the client's case as forcefully and persuasively as possible. He doesn't give the opponent's side because there is a counsel there who will do just that. When each case has been offered, the jury makes up its mind.

The organizational editor does the same. He or she presents the organization's case as persuasively as possible but always accurately and truthfully. For we know that the other side of the case will be presented just as skillfully; and ultimately the jury—the reader, the public—will render the verdict. No matter how noble or how small an organization, there is always another group that views its activities from a different viewpoint.

The editor operates under a "diplomatic passport," using avenues that are not open to all employees, many that are closed even to people higher on the organizational totem pole. This status is usually not formalized and that's all to the good. Some editors, seeking to have their status spelled out, have found that some practices that are acceptable while being overlooked, cannot be condoned when put in writing.

Many editors have found the truth of an old Army proverb: "It's easier to get forgiveness than to get permission." Instead of asking for an OK on a proposed course of action, the editor just goes ahead and does it, as unobtrusively as possible. Success will never be challenged and if someone does blow the whistle on what some may regard as rash, the editor who throws himself on the mercy of the court usually emerges unscathed.

Because the editor is constantly working outside the chain of command, with people who are not direct superiors, that relationship must be handled delicately.

The editor must always give the impression that, whatever the formal table of organization shows—he or she is really working for the chief executive officer. The mantle of the top executive's patronage is an admirable suit of armor.

Because editors rarely have authority over most of the people they must work with—even staff members are often volunteers who can't be bossed around—they have to attain their goals by diplomacy. Here the editor uses political techniques. And the greatest of these is to do favors for people. It will help if you like people and actually get pleasure from doing things for them. But even if such favor-doing is less than soul-lifting, it is an essential in persuading people to work with you. Favors given are readily converted into favors received. And in any organization—the bigger, the more definitely—we can accomplish more outside the usual formal channels, when people do things for other people, especially those they like, rather than just fulfilling a job description.

(It's worth noting that the editor's ability to skip many links in the chain of command is a major benefit of the job. A young employee in the accounting or sales departments won't have contact with the top executive for many years, if ever. But a young editor will have access to the front office immediately. As management is always looking for young talent to bring up, the person who comes to the chief's attention obviously has a big advantage. That's why organizational journalism can be the job of entry to many completely disparate fields.)

The editor must seek acceptance as a competent professional. This status is not easily achieved; it must be earned over a long period. Absolute reliability is essential. As readers accept and trust an editor, so does management. Absolute loyalty is essential. This doesn't mean being a yes-man; the good editor is a good lieutenant. Once a decision has been made, the editor executes it at the highest possible level of performance. But until that decision is made, the lieutenant will argue vigorously and cite hard evidence for the professionally best choice.

The editor must have absolute confidence in his or her own capability. That must be stressed in every dealing with peers and superiors. "You're the expert on the technical content of this story," the editor will tell the engineer. "But I'm the expert on writing. I won't mess around with your blueprints; you don't mess around with my words." A deprecatory smile takes the bite out of such a statement without losing the import.

Some editors believe that professional acceptance can be hurried, that it can be "bought" by investing time and effort in an accreditation program. Unfortunately, this is not so. Accreditation may raise the status of an editor among fellow editors and that may rub off onto nonjournalistic peers. But the mere act of accreditation is almost an artificial one. Plumbers and accountants can be tested for professional status. But how would one attempt to accredit a Michelangelo or a Shakespeare? Creative people just can't be measured by an implacable yardstick.

The editor must understand the organization's overall communications program—ought, even, to play a strong role in establishing it. And then the editor must be realistic and see clearly how the publication fits into the larger program. Even while making the periodical part of the greater program, the editor must use the other facets of the program to strengthen the publication.

Often the editor is charged with duties well beyond publishing. He or she may write special publications such as the annual report. The editor is frequently a speechwriter as well as the writer of press releases and a liaison with the local media. Editors often handle bulletin-board communications and just as frequently write copy for a telephone hotline or closed-circuit TV.

If the editor does do any or all of these communications chores, it is easy to link them with the publication. Writing a speech for the chief executive, for instance, enables the editor to "cover" the speech for the publication without travelling across the continent to hear it or wrenching the printer's deadline to include it.

(We might note the necessary technique in covering a speech before it is given. The phrase "in a speech prepared for delivery in San Diego Monday" is insurance against the most horrendous of journalistic gaffes: reporting something that never happened. The CEO may miss a plane and a podium, might even go to That Great Board Room in the Sky in the interval between the writing of the story and the time it comes off the press. So we can't say "Chairman Smith, in a speech at San Diego, said...." If it isn't said we're guilty of false reporting. But the speech *was* prepared for delivery, whether that happened or not, and that we can say with absolute accuracy, come hell, high water, or grounded flights.)

Whether the editor or someone else prepares the broadcast news the acceptance of the publication can be enhanced by just adding, "More details on the situation will be covered in the issue of 'Company Bugle' coming out Thursday." Bulletins, posted or circulated, can also note that greater coverage will be given by the periodical.

Whatever the organizational program, the publication is just a part. The editor must always be part of the team.

Finally, the editor must be well endowed with good old-fashioned common sense. As this book will stress, there is no "right answer" to an

TABLOID PAGE in op format uses compact typography. Nameplate and box in lower left are in red, lower right picture is duotone. This is publication of the Graphic Arts Union, Washington, D.C.

8 EDITING THE ORGANIZATIONAL PUBLICATION

VERTICAL FORMAT is used by "The Word" for Manville Forest Products, West Monroe, Louisiana. Page consists of two 8½x11 units, a size growing in popularity.

editor's problems. Nor is one proffered here. Rather, a set of guidelines is suggested. If you follow them you will never go wrong. But if you want to illuminate the journalistic firmament with the lightning of genius, you must master the "rules" so well that you can break or bend them with good results.

Communication, while demanding skill to reach its highest level, is still not an esoteric exercise in witchcraft. Any intelligent person can do more than a passable job of it. Editors must ultimately follow their instincts, their gut reactions. But that instinct must be sharpened by conscious and conscientious study of proven techniques. The greater this reinforcement, the better the chances that instinct will provide the best solution to a problem.

A basic decision is what kind the publication should be. Newspapers come in two standard sizes. A *broadsheet* is the format most used by dailies; the page is about 16x21 inches, give or take an inch or so in either direction. *Tabloids* are just half that size, usually about 11½x15 inches. Growing in popularity is a sheet 11x17, a little longer and narrower than a tabloid. The page is twice as big as an 8½x11 standard letterhead and so does not cut to waste.

The major distinguishing feature of magazines is that they are bound, usually with metal staples, occasionally by a thin strip of glue in the *gutter*, at the fold. Magazines are in three common sizes. Those in the size of *Life* are about 10½x13 inches; the most common is *Time*-size, 8½x11, and the smallest is the size of *Readers' Digest*, 5½x7½. These, too, may vary a few picas in either direction. The magtab is basically a tabloid folded so what would be the front page of the newspaper becomes the front and back covers of an apparent magazine.

Sometimes *magapaper* is used as a synonym for magtab. More often, though, this imprecise word is applied to publications with tab-sized pages but with distinctly "magazinish" layout style.

Then hybrids rear their interesting heads. Many publications in tab newspaper form are treated like magazines in content and form. Many smaller publications are small newspapers rather than regular magazines.

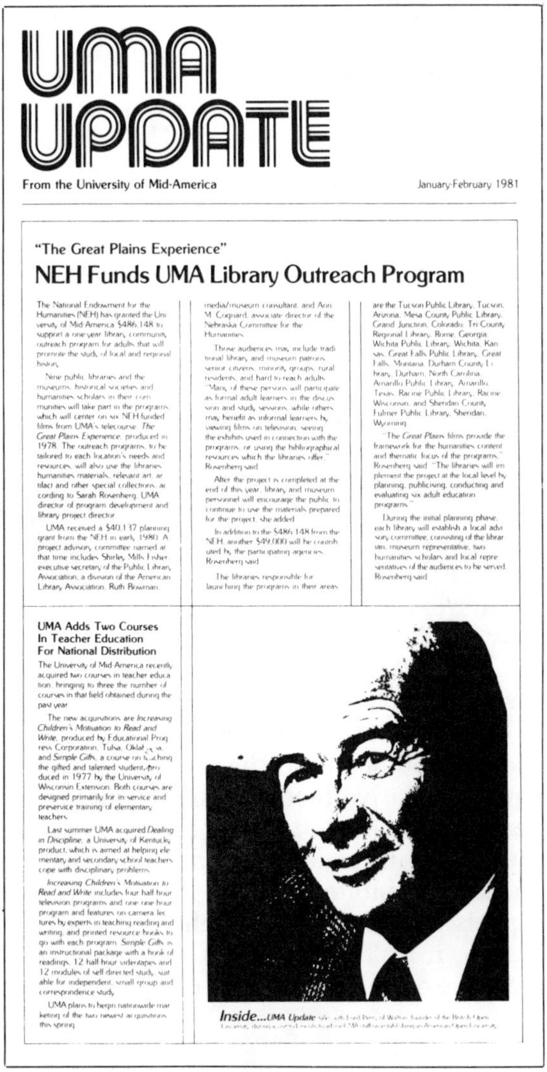

UMA UPDATE

From the University of Mid-America — January-February 1981

"The Great Plains Experience"

NEH Funds UMA Library Outreach Program

The National Endowment for the Humanities (NEH) has granted the University of Mid-America $486,148 to support a one-year library community outreach program for adults that will promote the study of local and regional history.

Nine public libraries and the museums, historical societies and humanities scholars in their communities will take part in the programs, which will center on six NEH-funded films from UMA's telecourse, *The Great Plains Experience*, produced in 1978. The outreach programs, to be tailored to each location's needs and resources, will also use the libraries' humanities materials, relevant art, artifact and other special collections, according to Sarah Rosenberg, UMA director of program development and library project director.

UMA received a $40,137 planning grant from the NEH in early 1980. A project advisory committee named at that time includes Shirley Mills Fisher, executive secretary of the Public Library Association, a division of the American Library Association; Ruth Bowman, media/museum consultant; and Ann M. Coqnard, associate director of the Nebraska Committee for the Humanities.

Those audiences may include traditional library and museum patrons, senior citizens, minority groups, rural residents, and hard to reach adults. "Many of these persons will participate as formal adult learners in the discussion and study sessions, while others may benefit as informal learners by viewing films on television, seeing the exhibits used in connection with the programs, or using the bibliographical resources which the libraries offer," Rosenberg said.

After the project is completed at the end of this year, library and museum personnel will encourage the public to continue to use the materials prepared for the project, she added.

In addition to the $486,148 from the NEH, another $49,000 will be contributed by the participating agencies, Rosenberg said.

The libraries responsible for launching the programs in their areas are the Tucson Public Library, Tucson, Arizona; Mesa County Public Library, Grand Junction, Colorado; Tri-County Regional Library, Rome, Georgia; Wichita Public Library, Wichita, Kansas; Great Falls Public Library, Great Falls, Montana; Durham County Library, Durham, North Carolina; Amarillo Public Library, Amarillo, Texas; Racine Public Library, Racine, Wisconsin; and Sheridan County Fulmer Public Library, Sheridan, Wyoming.

"The *Great Plains* films provide the framework for the humanities content and thematic focus of the programs," Rosenberg said. "The libraries will implement the project at the local level by planning, publicising, conducting and evaluating six adult education programs."

During the initial planning phase, each library will establish a local advisory committee, consisting of the librarian, museum representative, two humanities scholars and local representatives of the audiences to be served, Rosenberg said.

UMA Adds Two Courses In Teacher Education For National Distribution

The University of Mid-America recently acquired two courses in teacher education, bringing to three the number of courses in that field obtained during the past year.

The new acquisitions are *Increasing Children's Motivation to Read and Write*, produced by Educational Progress Corporation, Tulsa, Oklahoma, and *Simple Gifts*, a course on teaching the gifted and talented student, produced in 1977 by the University of Wisconsin Extension. Both courses are designed primarily for in-service and preservice training of elementary teachers.

Last summer UMA acquired *Dealing in Discipline*, a University of Kentucky product, which is aimed at helping elementary and secondary school teachers cope with disciplinary problems.

Increasing Children's Motivation to Read and Write includes four half-hour television programs and one one-hour program and features on-camera lectures by experts in teaching reading and writing, and printed resource books to go with each program. *Simple Gifts* is an instructional package with a book of readings, 12 half-hour videotapes and 12 modules of self-directed study, suitable for independent, small group and correspondence study.

UMA plans to begin nationwide marketing of the two newest acquisitions this spring.

Inside...UMA Update

VERTICAL FORMAT in unusual proportion is used by "UMA Update" of the University of Mid-America, Lincoln, Nebraska. Dimensions are 9x18. Nameplate, in Novelty letterform, and all rules are in rich blue.

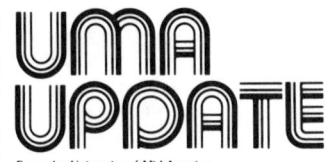

10 EDITING THE ORGANIZATIONAL PUBLICATION

MAGTAB FORMAT is used by "Timberline" of British Columbia Forest Products Limited of Vancouver. Magazine covers (at left) are visible in mailing, then publication unfolds to show conventional tabloid page. All inside pages are tab size, 11½ x17. Note that nameplate is used on both "front pages." It—and heavy horizontal rules—are in bright green.

Occasionally a publication will be in an unusual format. Square pages appeal to some avant gardists; some publications are designed as small envelope stuffers to be sent out with monthly statements, most often for utilities. Other periodicals have unusually tall and skinny pages. Any departure from the three basic sizes, though, usually entails extra costs because the paper *cuts to waste*. Even though the publication uses only a portion of the standard page, it must pay for the whole sheet, no matter how much of it is wasted.

The hard-to-pin-down *newsletter* is defined as precisely as seems possible in Chapter 10.

To a large extent, the page size will be dictated by the budget. But there are other factors that will be discussed in succeeding chapters. An equally decisive factor is the frequency of publication. This poses a vexatious problem. Ideally, the more frequently a publication appears, the greater its reader acceptance and the more effective it is. Appearing weekly, a publication can soon become habit-forming; the reader expects and anticipates each issue and goes looking for it if, for any reason, it isn't delivered. A few companies publish daily papers and these are eminently successful.

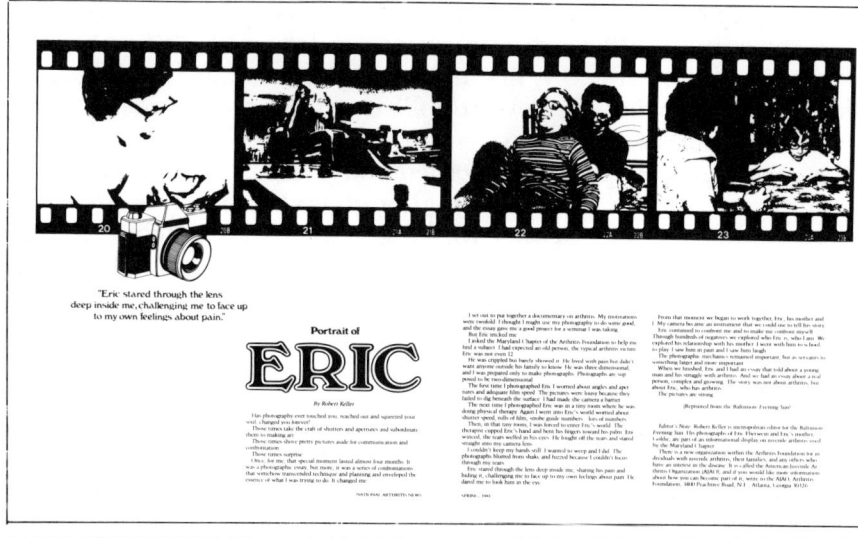

MAGAPAPER FORMAT uses tabloid-size page—this is 10¾x15—but design is often that of magazine. This is spread from "National Arthritis News," Atlanta, Georgia. Headline and blurb are in denim blue.

Manipulating the budget to give us sufficient frequency with an adequate number of pages is definitely a monumental project. Here postage costs become an important factor especially as postal rates increase with alarming frequency. At present rates, it is less expensive to mail out a 24-page publication than two 12-pagers. So the pressure is always to reduce mailings.

A monthly seems to be more habit-forming than a semi-monthly or biweekly. A quarterly is the least frequent publication that can be considered a periodical. Because a quarterly has more flexibility for issue dates, the editor has more choices for designating it. Most commonly, issues are labelled Winter, Spring, Summer, and Fall. This allows publishing any time in the appropriate three-month span. A more flexible system is to number each issue within a year: 1990-1, 1990-2, 1990-3, etc. If, then, for any reason an issue must be skipped—not an unheard-of occurrence in organizational journalism—there will be no glaring gaps. For Issue 2 can be Fall just as readily as Spring or Summer.

Many editors run a one-person show. Their managerial problem—and not a slight one by any means—is to discipline their own time. While many editors—as creative persons—dislike regimenting themselves, others find that a strict schedule which they force themselves to follow makes for greatest productivity. The trouble is often with people the editor can't control; they constantly interrupt. A machine operator can pick up immediately after an interruption; the creative person must take extra time to get the derailed train of thought back on the tracks.

A good gambit is to designate one or two days as "going-to-press days" when the editor will brook no intrusions. A large sign, affixed to the door, has a salutary effect. While all interruptions cannot be refused, it's interesting to note that often even the CEO will hesitate to break in upon the editor on those sacred days.

Some editors just spend those crucial days working at home. Some organizations find this totally acceptable; others throw corporate tizzies on the grounds that if you ain't working in my potato patch, you ain't working. Many people expect editors to be temperamental. Often this can be used to advantage. But be sure your temperamental idiosyncrasies are well thought out; don't offend or irritate your associates.

The editor who has a staff to direct must devote a goodly part of the work week to being an administrator. Ever since Hammurabi, countless writers have imparted advice on how to be a good boss. All of them are distilled into the New Testament admonition to do unto others as you would have it done unto you. Every editor knows what he or she wants from a boss: consistency, fairness, appreciation of a good job, coaching on performing duties, willingness to listen to new ideas, chewings-out only in private and absolute backing-up of the editor in any showdown. And that's what the staff wants of the editor. Consistency is essential to a well-running department. Policy should not only be consistent, it should be written out.

The editor should have a detailed set of job descriptions and procedures. These should be based on functions that must be performed, not on the people who perform them. A story must be written by a reporter; it must be edited by a copyreader. The same person may do both jobs; several persons may do a single job. By listing functions, we increase flexibility. A new person joining the staff may combine layout and proofreading tasks which formerly were done by two people. We can always assign different people to jobs but the jobs themselves remain unchanged.

Some organizations prepare books—from starkly simple to quite elaborate—setting forth policy, style, and procedures. Useful under any circumstances, such guide books are especially valuable when the organization has publications in many, far-flung regional plants or offices. Chesapeake & Potomac Telephone and United Parcel Service have outstanding examples of such editors' or correspondents' handbooks.

Many editors say: "Ah! This is obvious; why bother to write it all down?" Of course, there's truth in the statement. But having it in writing is invaluable when you approach Personnel and ask for a new position in your department. It's equally valuable when the editor becomes incapacitated and a substitute must take over on short notice.

Recognition for doing a good job is an essential need of the human race. We put feathers in war bonnets and pin medals to heroic chests.

THE EDITOR AS EXECUTIVE   13

UNUSUAL FORMAT is that of "Currents" of Hawaiian Electric Company, Honolulu. Page is uncommon 10½x12 and is folded so that outside cover is only half of that area. Nameplate, in Shadowed letterform, is printed in soft violet.

The editor who publicly recognizes good staff work is using a proven method. By-lines are the first recognition. The editor ought to establish the practice of bestowing by-lines as a reward, not as a meaningless constant on the most humdrum story as is done in too many publications. But when this award is given only for achievement it becomes a useful public accolade.

It is essential that the editor share praise with staffers. We are all too familiar with the coach who talks up every victory as a demonstration of his genius and writes off every defeat to inept performance by the athletes.

The editor should seek status symbols for the staff. Desirable parking spots are often made available to staffers if the editor makes the case that they must be mobile to do their jobs best. Some editors issue press cards identifying staffers and asking cooperation from organizational personnel.

The publication's own awards should be displayed in the masthead.

The editor should conduct a critique just as soon as an issue comes off the press. This is a difficult job to do as none of us really likes to accept criticism of our brainchildren. (We must remember, though, that "criticism" in its original meaning is not only adverse evaluation. It is "the act of analyzing and judging the quality of work.") We also dislike making adverse evaluation of the work of our peers; we don't want to raise hackles and create friction in our jobs. It's so much easier to say "Well done!" under all circumstances. Yet that is not a kindness; to praise a poor performance is to ingrain a bad habit even deeper.

The critiquing sessions must adhere strictly to principles and to demonstrations, good or bad, of such principles. We must zealously avoid criticizing the creator even as we dissect the creation.

Each issue should be analyzed for content. C&P Telephone, for instance, categorizes content into six themes: reporting customer satisfaction, expanding and improving service, explaining economics of business, establishing the company as a good place to work, hailing good citizenship, and miscellaneous. Good balance among these themes is sought in every step of planning and execution and the critique demonstrates how well the objectives are being met both in this single issue and in the yearlong program.

The staff evaluates each portion—however small—of each page. A good scorecard has three columns, something like this:

Good headline	Adequate head	Weak head (poorly written or too long)
Strong lead	Lead does job	Lead is weak
Good paragraphing	Paragraphs average 8 lines or under	Paragraphs too long
Sentences short, declarative	Sentences average 20 words or less	Sentences too long or awkward
Caption interprets picture	Caption is adequate	Caption poorly written
Photo quality is high	Photo meets standards	Photo is cliche or poorly posed or of poor quality
Photo well-cropped	Photo cropping OK	Photo poorly cropped
Photo well-displayed	Photo adequately used	Photo too small, too large, or poorly placed in relation to story
Page carries at least x number of stories	Carries x-1 stories	Carries x-2 or less stories
Heads varied and well isolated	Heads displayed adequately	Heads not varied adequately, are too small, are bumped
Overall layout inviting and simple	Overall layout adequate	Overall layout dull and uninviting
Dominant art and dominant headline	Heads and art adequate	Page is dull, no eye appeal
Last page makes strong finale	Last page adequate not a catchall	Last page used for slopover and accumulation

Each article and photo and each page is inspected and scored by giving 4 points for each quality noted in column 1; 2 points for each in the middle column; and no points for those in the third. In addition, 5 to 25 bonus points may be added to the grand total for outstanding treatment and 5 to 20 penalty points may be deducted for particularly poor treatment. The editor establishes what the satisfactory total is. All issues then, are graded against the criteria of previous issues, not against another publication. The trend of these "quality totals" is a good indicator of the improvement, or lack thereof, over any given period.

The same company asks the editor of each of its four major publications to prepare a cost analysis of each issue using report sheets reproduced on the facing page.

The editor should always be receptive to new ideas. None should be rejected out of hand. Even the most impractical suggestion deserves to be slept on overnight. Rejections must always be accompanied by explanations. When an idea is accepted, the originator should get full credit for it. No editor loses respect or peer acceptance by giving credit to a subordinate. Quite the contrary. The editor's standing is enhanced by a reputation for bringing up young talent. Even if a staffer leaves for a new job, it can be a compliment to the editor just as the manager of a minor-league baseball team is credited with polishing-up the talent that takes a player to the big leagues.

The editor may not actually be able to do every job as well as the staffer and that need not be a problem. But the editor must know what the job entails and be able to evaluate it fairly and help the staffer do it better. You can coach a person to superior performance even though you can't do it yourself.

The editor owes it to subordinates to give periodic—maybe even daily—reports on how well the staffer is doing his or her job. This is entirely apart from the formal evaluation that many organizations require. As the staffer is acclaimed for good work, bad work must immediately—and privately—be censured. If a person is just not cut out for a particular job, the real kindness comes not by keeping him or her on it (often so long that a beneficial change becomes difficult if not impossible), but by helping find a job more compatible with the talents, interests, and temperament of the staffer.

The editor should—by action, not word—stress the responsibility of that position instead of its perquisites. The good editor is not above any task, be it interviewing the president or running proofs back to the printer. Willingness to pitch in and help at any level and any stage of production is a major contribution to high staff morale and performance.

While sharing praise, the editor should always take blame all alone. The culprit can always be confronted later and privately. But the initial rap is always taken by the editor. In many instances, it will be obvious what the editor is doing. But no person has ever lost face for standing by accepting blame for a subordinate's mistake. Usually it's just the opposite; there is admiration for the superior who protects his or her subordinates. And the staff so protected repays loyalty with loyalty.

Volunteer staffers create a whole new batch of problems. And the farther they are, geographically, from the editor's office, the more acute some of these problems become. Pity the editor in Chicago who has staffers in Anchorage and Istanbul.

The first job is recruiting volunteer staffers. This may be done by "running an ad" in the publication. Even better is seeking recommendations by former *stringers*. (This term comes from a practice by weekly papers early this century who paid rural correspondents by the inch. The writer would paste together all published material into a long "string" which was then measured and paid for.) This, of course, can't be done if an editor is assembling a network for the first time.

Often Personnel can be helpful in providing clues as to talents and willingness.

Correspondents should be briefed carefully on their duties. In most instances it's best to ask only for information which can be written or rewritten back at the office. If the stringer doesn't expect to see a story in its exact submitted form, there is no disappointment when it is rewritten, and there is satisfaction when rewriting isn't needed.

The correspondent should be rewarded for volunteer labors. The writer's name should certainly be in the masthead; the name, department, phone number, and, often, portrait, should be included in the heading if one is used, or as part of the by-line.

(To make a masthead listing meaningful, deadwood should be removed. It should be a written condition that a stringer who has not contributed for x number of issues will not be named in the masthead. As soon as contributions resume, the name is added. There should be no fanfare in either instance. This practice assures that such listing accurately honors actual workers, not those who seek an effortless notation on personnel records.)

Correspondents should be rewarded by public recognition. If at all possible, volunteers should be gathered for at least an annual meeting and banquet. If distances make this impractical, perhaps such an event can be held on a regional basis. At any rate, the stringer deserves a good dinner when the editor comes around on a field trip.

A trophy for the outstanding correspondent of the year is an excellent way to focus the spotlight of acclaim, not only on the staffer, but onto the publication itself.

Often an organization has some kind of memento—glasses, paperweights, ash trays, caps, etc.—that the editor can latch onto for the volunteer staff. Specially imprinted T-shirts are not so expensive that their cost can't be absorbed by even a modest budget.

A continuing problem is to maintain volunteers' interest. Some editors issue a regular newsletter for correspondents. This combines personal news, kudos, shoptalk, and suggestions on how to do the job more easily, productively, and satisfyingly. A national correspondent's publication, *The Reporter's Report*, published by Ragan Communications, Inc., is available for editors whose staff—or budget—is too small to warrant issuing their own newsletter. Of course, the telephone is still an excellent tie between editor and stringer. Every budget should allow sufficient funds for regular calls.

Communication is a people process. The editor who best learns how to handle people will consistently be the best communicator.

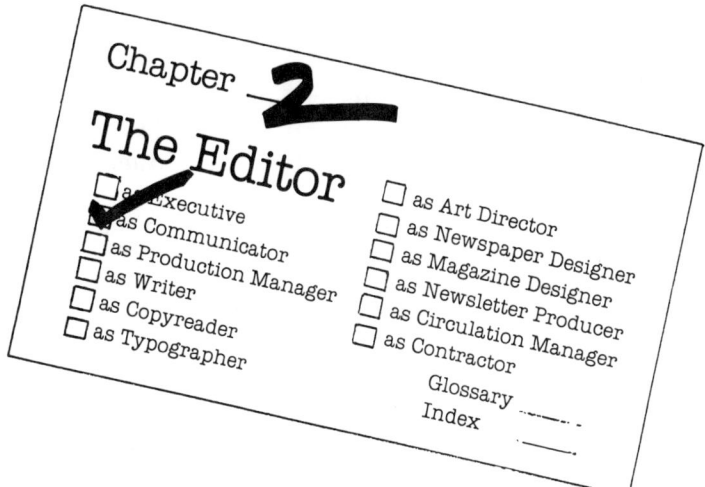

Chapter 2
The Editor

☐ as Executive
☑ as Communicator
☐ as Production Manager
☐ as Writer
☐ as Copyreader
☐ as Typographer
☐ as Art Director
☐ as Newspaper Designer
☐ as Magazine Designer
☐ as Newsletter Producer
☐ as Circulation Manager
☐ as Contractor
  Glossary
  Index

A publication is like a department store; it must carry a line of merchandise that will appeal to a diverse group of people. The editor must provide an "editorial mix" that has a similar broad appeal.

The basic content of an organizational periodical is determined by the sponsoring organization. A hospital magazine will be concerned with health-care information; a manufacturing corporation's newspaper will concentrate on the doings of the company and others in the same field.

But all publications must constantly address the eternal question asked by every reader: "What's in it for me?"

All of us are egocentric, the world revolves around us. The closer others are to us, the more they concern us. Our families, in the nearest orbit, are of prime interest, then come relatives, friends, and other people. We are interested in our organization because of its influence on us and our lives. Like the typical employee, we don't care whether the company made a profit last quarter; what we want to know is, "Will I have a job in the next quarter?" We want to have assurances that the fate of our organization will permit us to pay the mortgage, visit the grocery regularly, and live with at least a modicum of comfort.

The editor who answers that question, ". . .for me," over and over again, in many different ways, is the successful editor.

There are two kinds of organizational publications: *internal* and *external*. Internal ones are directed primarily to employees and/or members of the organization. External ones go to a wider audience, stockholders, customers, and even the general public. But these lines are not drawn sharply; sometimes internals may go to stockholders; often externals go to employees. A few organizations try to combine the two publications but this is rarely successful; if they seek two audiences, most organizations publish both kinds. IBM, which has a very broad range of internals, made its *Think* magazine a major voice to the same audience that read *Atlantic* and *Harper's*.

The difference in audiences between internals and externals changes only the editorial approach, not the editorial goal. In either instance the editor is committed to imparting information that will, ultimately, be beneficial to the organization.

Always the technique comes back to that which answers "What's in it for me?" Suppose we're editing an internal for a manufacturing company. We talk about what's happening in the factory, what new machinery or techniques are being put to use, what new products we're making, what effect our day-to-day operations have upon the employees, and their continuing needs.

An external publication for the same company would stress the benefits that our products bring to the user, our customer. We'd talk about customers who use our products advantageously, about customers who have developed applications of our materials that might well be used by other clients of ours. We'd talk about our contributions to the trade, to the economy, and to society in general.

The "tone of voice" of the two publications will vary. Internals are more "family" in flavor. In general newspaper style—which we'd probably follow in our external—almost everything is written in the third person. But in an internal we might follow the example of some successful editors who consistently refer to "our" products, what "we" anticipate for the coming year and that "you" are being urged to give to the blood bank.

Reporting Opinions

Internals may depart from general newspaper style in expressing opinions. Commercial newspapers attribute every opinion to some person. "Amalgamated is in favor of the proposed plan," said Walter J. Smith, vice-president for operations. Or: Secretary of State J. Wellington Smith said that the administration is dubious about the value of the plan, etc.

But in organizational journalism, the publication very often is the voice of a company or group which has a definite corporate opinion and this opinion will frequently come out in print. The style the publication has adopted will determine how that opinion is expressed. It may follow general newspaper style and quote an official of the organization, by name, with the opinion in quote marks. Or the publication might simply say: "We believe that the President's Social Security plan is inadequate...etc." if it is plainly evident that the "we" is the organization. Or the editor may simply attribute the opinion to the company—"Amalgamated supports the Senate version of the bill. . . ."

Another aspect of style the editor must determine is how much background information to give. Standard newspaper style is to recapitulate practically all the background information on a continuing story, so that the reader just stepping off a spaceship would have a pretty fair idea of what happened yesterday in the never-ending saga. Many organizational editors depart from this convention to some degree. Organizational communication presumes an audience with a special interest in whatever you're writing about, and very few readers fresh from spaceships. But style will determine how much common knowledge you expect from your readers, and how much you have to re-explain each time it comes up again.

If your hospital is building a new wing, for instance, you probably don't have to tell the employees the same thing every month. You don't have to repeat the exact location of the new wing, or how much it costs, or list which departments will move and which will stay in the old building—as the daily would do; just tell how the construction is coming along.

But if your readership extends far beyond the employees, and your publication is read by people who do not have a close connection with the daily operations of the organization, you will have to repeat more of this information every month.

Internals may cover events that are less than happy. We might do a story on a new quality-control program that implies, at least, that performance up to now has been less than satisfactory. We might report a bad accident in the plant or generally unfavorable news: declining enrollment in a school system, smaller contributions to charitable causes, the softening of an export market, or a decrease in gross earnings for the past quarter.

Many organizations would prefer to keep this linen—even though soiled only slightly—from public airing yet feel that the "family" ought to know about it. This is not to suggest that something printed in an internal can actually be kept a family secret. For copies of any publication will constantly go far beyond the obvious, limited audience. Yet we'd anticipate that the information printed in an external will automatically go to a much larger audience, some of which, at least, will not be entirely sympathetic to our organization's aims. Business competitors are always interested in the other guy's publications, from internals to externals to catalogs to advertisements.

If we do report "bad" news in an external, it is always with an upbeat point of view: "Hey, look at how we overcame. . . . Look how we solved this problem. . . . Look how ingenious we are. . . . Look at how we can help you prevent a similar disaster. . .etc."

Some externals run material that is barely—if at all—related to the organization's functions. But it would seem that those publications which best serve their organizations are those which keep their coverage to the primary area of organizational interest and tie—at least by implication—every story to "what's in it" for the reader: employee, stockholder, customer, or ordinary citizen.

Externals usually have a larger budget than internals. That's because their audiences are larger, often considerably so. Then the economics of printing can take over. There is a fixed preparatory cost for any printing job; it costs as much to make a plate for a run of a hundred as for 10,000; it takes as long to write an article for a dozen readers as for a thousand. So, the longer the press run, the smaller that preparatory cost is per issue. That means that full-color—utterly impractical for an internal of a few hundred copies—will cost only a couple pennies for each copy of a 100,000 circulation.

The editor must remember, though, that you can't buy excellence. A superior publication comes not from the expenditure of money but the investment of creativity, skill, and hard work. No matter what the budget, the prime requirements are still those basics of communication that apply to all publications, minuscule or gigantic.

Readers, be they of the *New York Times* or the *Well Drillers Journal*, are always more interested in "people news" than in "thing news." While we must report on things, we must also seek to translate such information into people news. Will proposed trade agreements protect or eliminate *my* job? Will the x-million-dollar expansion of our facilities make *my* job easier? Will revised insurance coverage take care of *my* dental bills?

Every periodical is to some extent an "organ of record." We must write our own small episodes of current history. So we are concerned with thing news; but we must give it as much flavor of people news as possible.

This does not mean that we trivialize all news, reducing it to a paragraph in a gossip column. But we can show how events will affect a typical employee of our organization. We can show the effect of hard news on employee morale or effectiveness. We can translate astronomical figures into numbers that ordinary people can understand: The multi-million-dollar investment in new machinery is the equivalent of buying three new automobiles for every employee. Or the profit the company made last year will give the typical stockholder the equivalent of half the return obtained from a savings account.

Above all, the organizational publication must educate the reader to the basics of economic life. Every organization, be it Amalgamated Widget Manufacturing or East Speed Zone School District, is in a competitive situation. Ultimately—although rhetoric, emotions, and side issues becloud the situation—the economic existence of our organization and eventually our country will depend on how well every individual employee outproduces an opposite number in a competitor's organization. Our readers must be educated to understand that money is merely a symbol of work and productivity. Whether we are paid $1 or

$100 for an hour's labor doesn't matter at all; our production remains the same. We must swap that production for someone else's. If we buy an hour's worth of a bakery's production for a dollar or ten times that amount, the numbers of dollars exchanged is immaterial... we swap our production for theirs.

It is when we have salted away an hour's production—with a certain monetary measurement—and want to spend it later—when a new, higher number is used in measurement—that we feel the debilitating effects of inflation.

Because general-circulation publications have failed to educate the public in these basics, it remains for the organizational publication to do so. And this we can do well because we can translate general terms into the specific experiences and needs of our readers.

Each editor will develop a personal formula for a good editorial mix. It begins as an unarticulated feeling and finally, if the editor is smart, is committed to paper (make a list!) in the form of a "charter" for the publication. This document, which defines the editor's responsibilities and prerogatives, is also a contract between the editor and an organization's executives, among whom there is often a difference of opinion about the mission of the periodical.

Magazine Content

The magazine editor can be most explicit in establishing an editorial mix. An editor whose publication served a national organization once said: "I want a piece about the whole organization, the parent company, in each issue. I also want one about one of our branches. Then I want an article about a department or a small section, and finally, one about just a single individual."

Another editor, rather more pretentiously, said: "I want an article which will make the reader say, 'Gosh! I never knew that before!' I want another that will make him say, 'I agree. I wish I had put it that way.' I want a piece that will make the reader chuckle, another that will bring a tear. There ought to be one we might call 'inspirational.' Finally, I want the whole issue to make the reader feel good, not running around snapping fingers and yodelling, but just feeling that in the world—or at least our part of it—good guys don't necessarily finish last."

We note that in both instances, these successful practitioners have directed their material to the individual readers. "What's in it for me?" "All of it is for you!"

As this philosophical mix is translated into specific articles, the editor must also keep a sound geographic mix. In some instances this will embrace the whole country, maybe even the whole world. In some cases the organization may have two or three locations within one city or a metropolitan area. In most instances departments are separated by only a wall or a hallway.

But each subdivision of the organization must get adequate coverage by articles that not only satisfy members of that subdivision but all the readers, no matter where they may be.

Certain centers produce more news than others. Washington dominates all world news; the World Series winners get more coverage than a Class B also-ran. And in any organization, "headquarters" produces much—if not most—of the issue-to-issue news. The editor must work diligently to avoid the appearance that the publication is just a one-way street from headquarters down to the rest of the organization.

An effective device is one used by some high-school editors. It can work for most other editors, with obvious modifications. The scholastic editor gets a printout of names of all students in the school. After each issue is printed, each name that appeared is checked off on the list. The object is to get every student's name in the paper at least once each academic year.

Certain students are perpetual newsmakers: the star basketball player, the president of Student Government, the girl who gets the lead in every play. (In our context this is the president, the chief executive officer, the sales manager, etc.) Other students will naturally break into print once or twice a year. Then there will be a number who never do anything newsworthy. These are the challenge: How do we get their names in print with legitimate stories?

This writer once persuaded a high school staff to adopt this plan. Some months later, on a return visit, he was challenged by a young woman who snorted, "You sure got me in a mess. I have to do a story about a girl who's an absolute nothing. She sneaks into class just before the bell; she doesn't talk to anyone; right after school she disappears. She's never at a game or a prom or a club meeting. She's just a nothing and I have to do a story on her, for heaven's sake!"

The reporter was only semi-assured that this was a real demonstration of her journalistic skills, to dig out a story.

Some months later, the same reporter was bubbling over. "Thanks for giving me the push to do this story. Now I know what a real heroine is." It developed that this nothing-girl had a bedridden mother, a father holding two full-time jobs, and five younger siblings. It was a hectic dash to pack lunches for the little kids, get them breakfasted, washed, dressed, and off to school. Earlier she had packed her father's lunch and, just before leaving, had to make sure that her mother had her whole day's needs in arm's reach. After school the student did all the housework for a family of eight. No wonder she had no time for the social joys of adolescence.

The reporter did an admirable story, using the word "heroism" in its truest sense. And the reporter had a feeling of accomplishment. This was no run-of-the-mill assignment. It doesn't take great reportorial ingenuity to cover a school board meeting or a championship baseball game. But it takes real perception to see a story in a run-of-the-mill person.

Most organizations are far too big to hope to get every employee's name in print every year. But there should be incentive to dig for the less-than-obvious stories among ordinary folks. The newsmakers we shall always have among us.

We can use such a list to make sure of regular coverage of every location, every department, every subdivision, no matter how small or obscure.

Newspaper Content

The newspaper editor has minimal control over editorial mix; events themselves dictate content. But there are some non-news features that the editor can determine.

A highly popular, most effective department is that which deals with questions from employees. More and more organizations are assigning a high-ranking official—very often the president—to answer these inquiries. The most effective columns are those where no punches are pulled. And it's refreshing to see CEOs meeting employee concerns head-on, without ignoring, dodging, or sweeping them under the carpet. In every instance, candid responses are respected by employees and there is a demonstrable raising of morale.

Many questions are directed to people in lower echelons. A technical inquiry about withholding taxes, for instance, can be answered by the Payroll Department to everyone's satisfaction. It's the sticky ones that demand attention from the only people who can do anything about it, top executives.

The newspaper editor originates soft material just as the magazine editor does. Feature or background stories are often originated by the editor. Many are just dreamed up, many come from seasonal influences, the best are by-products of straight news events.

That's why the alert editor devours daily newspapers. If there's a political crisis in a country where our company has a plant, we get a hard-news story from the vice-president for overseas on its effect on our organization. But if we can find an employee who has served in that country, maybe we can get a colorful soft-news story that explains the physical setting of this latest coup, the attitudes of the people there, some amusing anecdotes about service there, etc.

A natural disaster in a far-off corner of the world may require expert assistance that our organization can give. A man-made disaster anywhere can be occasion for reassuring our readers that proper precautions have been taken so similar calamity does not befall us.

The editor of a newsletter, although primarily charged with factual reporting, also has opportunity—limited by space restrictions—to originate material.

One-Theme Issues

The *one-theme issue* was introduced in the 60s by *Newsweek* with an historic issue devoted entirely to the many facets of black life in America. Its tremendous popularity among general-interest publications has caused many an organizational editor to try the technique. Subjects such as safety, the organization's role during a disaster, economics, etc., seem appropriate. "What does the new year forecast for us?" is a frequent theme.

This device, of course, puts all the editor's eggs in one basket. If the

LETTERS TO THE EDITOR are solicited by "Gulf Oilmanac" of Gulf Oil Co., Pittsburgh. A regular business-reply envelope is bound into magazine for mailing of form. Many replies are publishable as letters to the editor; others give good story tips. This technique also encourages questions which are then answered by top management people.

"Outlet" of Wisconsin Electric System in Milwaukee, binds in form that folds down to business-reply envelope. Questions may be asked anonymously but employee can indicate that name may be used to facilitate mailing answer directly to home.

topic is broad enough, timely enough, and addresses itself to the reader's personal concerns, the result might be a triumphal tour de force. But if the reader is uninterested, total readership is lost. In a typical issue, we know that rarely will any single reader consume every piece in the book. But should the latest news from the sales department be passed over unread, the piece about the new model of framgistics may catch that reader. So the editor must always ask whether an all-or-nothing situation is warranted by using only one theme.

It is virtually impossible to have a one-theme issue of a newspaper or magtab; the mix of current news can't be focused upon that theme. But a double spread, or even more, may be devoted to a single theme in a newspaper, and in a magtab the cover and several spreads can be given to one topic.

A major difference between organizational publications and commercial periodicals is the absence of advertising in the former. But even that difference is being erased a trifle. Many newspaper editors, and some magazine editors, run certain company announcements in the form of *display advertising*, the kind we see in daily newspapers. They feel that ads contribute to the newsiness of a paper and that many announcements are well suited to such treatment.

Growing in popularity is the *classified*-advertising section, the "want ads," that many publications run. Such advertising is a major service to the employee and its effectiveness is superlative. Want ads have high

CLASSIFIED ADS take two full pages in "Tielines" of Michigan Bell, Detroit. 11x15 page is divided into five columns, feasible because small—agate—type has shorter optimum line length. Notice that "display classifieds" are placed at bottom of page and properly build up, however slightly, to the right.

DISPLAY ADVERTISING is rare but growing in organizational publications. "IABC News" of International Association of Business Communicators, San Francisco, uses 11x16 page, taller than conventional commercial publication, whose depth is shown by arrow above ad at left. Magazine format customarily runs advertising at outside of page. For newspapers, best technique is to pyramid ads upward to right on all pages.

readership; even people who aren't looking for a used baby buggy or a vacation cottage to rent will avidly read column after column of want ads.

The editor's major concern is establishing the categories under which these reader ads will be displayed. Basically there are two groups: something is wanted, something is offered. Scrutiny of past issues will determine how finely each of these headings must be broken down. The more the merrier is the general approach although we don't want categories so fine-tuned that they are used only once a year or never have more than a single ad under a heading.

With very rare exceptions, want ads are free. A few publications ask a minimal fee to discourage frivolous ads; real "income" is inconsequential. But there may be a problem of reporting such revenues, small as they are, and perhaps paying some applicable tax. This is a nuisance that far exceeds the few dollars that want ads might earn.

A very few organizational publications even accept paid display advertising. This probably began with airline magazines. These magazines, at the beginning, were purely organizational, provided as an antidote against boredom for passengers when planes were much slower than they are now. Emphasis was on entertainment although there was material that familiarized the reader with the particular airline publishing the magazine. Then hotels and car rental agencies, knowing that the passenger might need their services at the end of the flight, asked for the opportunity to reach this captive audience, almost at the point of purchase, with their advertising messages. This was a genuine service and the magazines began accepting such ads. Results were excellent for the advertiser and the kinds of services offered were expanded. Today such magazines can hardly be classed as organizational and their ad volume would make many, more obviously "commercial," magazines envious.

In the late 70s, as inflation and recessions cut into the budget of organizational publications, a few genuinely organizational publications accepted paid advertising. Again it was advertising which came in "over the transom," unsolicited, from businesses that were located close to the plant or building or offered services or goods of particular interest or need to employee-readers.

Editors who do accept paid advertising report that it has had no adverse effect on readership. There is always a danger, though, that commercial newspapers in the area will be annoyed at what they call "amateur competition." Especially if the organization is located in a small town, where loss of such advertising revenue would be more noticeable to the regular newspaper, this might have adverse effects on public relations.

Editorials are carried only infrequently in organizational publications. Because these are the corporate voice of the organization, they might well become factors in legal cases and so clearance procedures are strict. So comments on controversial issues are most commonly carried as messages from the president or high corporate officer.

Although editorials in daily papers often treat noncontroversial subjects—productivity, blood-bank support, well-dones, and even the innocent pleasures of a new season—organizational publications often present such topics in the editor's personal column. Such columns, commonplace in commercial periodicals, are becoming more frequent in organizational ones. With the disclaimer that views presented there do not necessarily reflect the position of the organization, such columns can provide the comment that readers like.

A useful device for all concerned is a department headed "When They Ask You. . . ." Members or employees are always being asked about the doings of the group. Sometimes inquiries seek only information; usually they are prosecutorial: "Why are your rates so high?" "Why didn't they treat my Johnny better in your hospital?" "What do you want to save those whales for, anyway?" Columns that suggest answers—by giving pertinent facts—enable the cross-examined to defend themselves. Such answers are beneficial to the organization and this technique doesn't give the impression of employees parroting a party line.

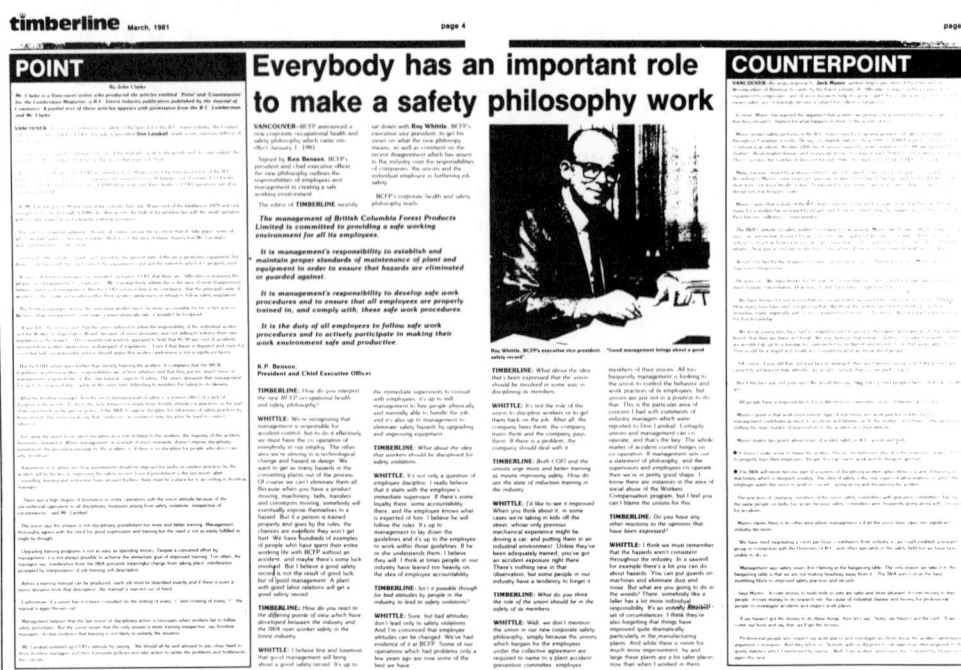

OPINION PAGES are rare in organizational publications, but "Timberline" of British Columbia Forest Products, Ltd., Vancouver, handles controversial issues which create high readership. Here strongly debated issue is presented in "Point" and "Counterpoint"—reprinted from a national trade journal—at outside of this double spread. Company's position is given in center portion. Heavy rules are in Kelly green. Page size: 11½x17.

Once the editorial mix of planned features has been established—and anticipating a large percentage of unplanned reportage in a newspaper and the commonplace news sections of magazines—the editor must establish the *progression* of the publication, the order in which material is presented.

Magazine Progression

Typical progression in a magazine goes like this:
The cover, usually a full-page picture, sometimes with *appeals* or *posters* or variously named lines of type that tout inside-page articles.

If the magazine is *self-covered*, with the front page of the same paper as the rest of the *book*, it is numbered page 1. If a *stock cover* of heavier paper encloses the book, its four pages are all referred to as covers: front, back, inside front, and inside back.

With self-covers, page 2 usually carries the *masthead* (discussed in

TABLE OF CONTENTS of "Mt. Lebanon" is illustrated with miniatures of inside-page illustrations. Page is 8x11, in black and white. Magazine is unusual in that it is joint publication of Mt. Lebanon, Pittsburgh suburb, and Mt. Lebanon School District. Advertising is accepted and circulation is free to everyone in community.

TABLE OF CONTENTS of "The Stater" uses small pictures but does not tie them specifically to stories. Published by the state of North Carolina, magazine has unusual format, almost square, 8½x9½.

Chapter 7) and the *table of contents*. Sometimes the editor's personal column runs here, often a message from the president does. With stock covers, the masthead and table usually run on page 1 of the book itself (which would be page 3 of a self-covered magazine). Often this is the only copy that runs on that page.

It can be debated—and frequently and vociferously is—that the table of contents is unnecessary in a typical organizational magazine. It seems logical to assume that the reader will leaf through as many as 24 to 32 pages of a magazine to see what's available and not have to be coaxed inside by the table.

A good way to test the argument is to ask: "How many people do I think will read an article because it's listed in the table of contents? How many people do I think would fail to read a story because it was not listed?"

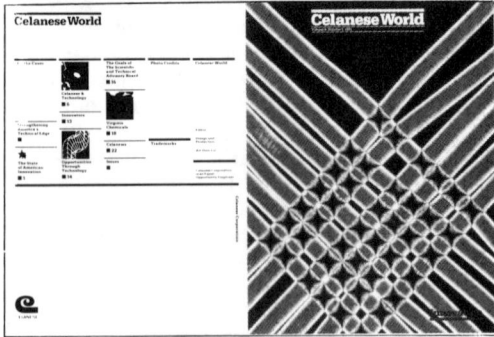

TABLE OF CONTENTS for "Celanese World" of Celanese Corporation, New York City, runs on back cover. Small pictures are in full color as is front cover.

The size of the table can, and does, vary considerably, usually because of the pressure of space. Treatment of the table is discussed in Chapter 9.

Pages 4 and 5 in self-cover, 2-3 otherwise, is the first good double spread available. Here we should display our strongest article.

Always articles should start on a spread. The first time readers see an article is the best time to capture their attention. Each time readers skip over a story, perhaps intending to return to it later, the chances of that return are diminished. So the first crack we get at them is when we ought to let loose our heaviest artillery. It is illogical to begin an article with one page, then waste the following double spread either because the readers have already been captured or because they have once rejected our advances and are apt to spurn our second attempt.

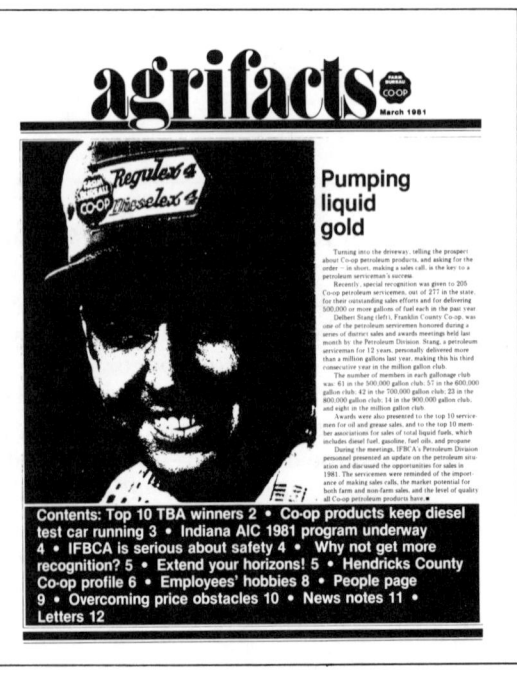

TABLE OF CONTENTS for "Agrifacts" of Indiana Farm Bureau, Indianapolis, runs on cover of magapaper. It resembles appeals used on conventional magazines but is a complete listing instead of just highlights of contents.

It is useful to alternate long and short articles. The availability of color is another factor in placing articles; sometimes color will run on only half—or fewer—of the pages.

After the articles usually comes the news section. And regular features often run here. Much depends, of course, on the length of those features. If they take a whole page, they may well be run in the front of the book, especially if that enables the next article to start on a double spread.

The important thing is not where the contents appear but that they are consistently in the same relative position to establish their familiarity and the habit of reading them.

The last page of editorial content—the inside of a stock cover or the back of a self-cover—is a most important one, for the reader should be left with a feeling of satisfaction, already anticipating the next issue. So this should be the spot for material that will undeniably fill that need. It might well be the editor's own column or that of some other writer. It may be a regular feature such as a personality sketch—if it's not a back-scratching obeisance only to the top brass.

The back cover is too often wasted. Whether stock or self, this is valuable space that ought not be left blank. Usually the mailing indicia run there and the rest of the page must be designed around this area. (Stock covers often "wrap around," the picture on the front cover continuing onto the back.) Self-covers have a tendency to become a catch-all to take care of previously overlooked nits-and-lice items; this should be avoided.

It's been said that a magazine should end like a symphony, with a well-rounded chord; it should not be like a bagpipe running out of wind. So this last hurrah should not be the typical accumulation of small items that have failed to find a place earlier in the magazine.

Newspaper Progression

Newspaper progression is quite simple because the editor usually has fewer categories of material to work with. The front page is, of course, devoted to the most transient, unplanned events.

Page 2 is often the equivalent of the commercial paper's editorial page. The masthead is usually here—although this position is certainly not mandatory. The message from the CEO takes the place of the regular editorial. Letters to the editor customarily run on this kind of a page, no matter where the page itself runs. Questions directed to management are most appropriate here, and many editors will run a cartoon just as the daily editor runs an editorial cartoon on such a page.

A logical progression will group news into broad categories: companywide, branches, departments, social events, sports, personnel news such as retirements, promotions, etc.

If any such grouping comprises only a "column," it would carry a standing heading and could run on the same page with another category. Some editors like to run these regular features in column 1 of each page; others run them on the outside columns. This technique assures consistent placement but it does cut down the room for maneuvering in creating a pleasant pattern for the rest of the page.

If the publication goes through the mail "peeled"—not in an envelope or wrapper—room for mailing indicia is necessary. This often creates a dilemma. Because this mailing area is far from attractive, it is often placed on the back page and the paper is folded. This makes sure that, once it is unfolded, the front page is unmarred. But before that unfolding, the reader sees nothing very attractive at all. The best way of solving this problem depends on the amount of space required for mailing information, which in turn depends on the method used for affixing the address. Some systems can't draw a very fine bead and require a large area to aim at; others are more precise in placement and can get by with a minimum blank space.

If a large area is required, it can well go at the bottom of page one. A strip is just marked off for this purpose and above it the regular page pattern is created. The area alongside the labelling space can be used for the masthead, for the indicia themselves will take up no more than 40% of this across-the-bottom strip.

Sometimes the mailing area runs sideways at the foot of column 1 or of the right-hand column. In some cases only half the column-width is required and body type of a news story runs at a very narrow line-length alongside the indicia.

Before any commitment is made, though, the editor should check with the mailing department to determine which placement is most efficient. Some machines work best when the folded edge of the paper is inserted in the labelling device; others prefer the open end of pages.

Of course, if distribution is done in-house, this problem just doesn't exist. But there is still the question whether a tabloid newspaper should be folded or left flat. As there is no definitive evidence as to which is better, we would consider that when the would-be reader sees a whole unfolded page that there is more "bait" to lure him or her into picking up a copy than when only the top half is visible on a folded copy. If papers are placed in containers, their size is a factor.

The editor of a paper of which some 20,000 copies are distributed in-plant recently spent several thousand dollars to replace baskets which held folded tabloids with new ones that allowed full-page display. The investment was economically justified, the editor reports, by the increase in pick-ups.

Magtab Progression

The magtab cover is normally all art and refers to an inside story.

The back cover carries the mailing indicia, if that is required, and in any case should have strong, attractive content. A good use for the back cover is as a bulletin board. In fact, one editor makes this back page a photo of an actual corkboard with pieces of paper held in place by pushpins and thumbtacks. Bulletin material is then printed on these "slips."

When the magtab unfolds, it becomes a newspaper and should use newspaper progression.

The referred-to story, pronounced "reefered," the one that the cover picture alludes to, can appear on the second or third tabloid page. Note that the first full tabloid page is numbered 1. The mag covers, front and back are unnumbered but occupy the last page of the tabloid.

Covers

Magazine covers must be functional and their primary function is to lure the reader into picking up the book and then to open it to inside pages.

The cover must, of course, identify the publication and this in itself will lure the reader who has, over a period of time, found the content to be of interest and value.

The nameplate is best kept in one position to enhance identification. If the magazine is published frequently, we might hope that more intense recognition would allow the nameplate to be moved around to harmonize with the art. But if frequency is less than monthly, no such recognition has built up and a constant placement of the nameplate is necessary. If appeals are used, their handling—and usually position, too—must be consistent.

SALON COVER of "The Log" is not related to a specific inside story. Full-color picture shows handsome wood engraving of trademark of International Paper Company, Portland, Oregon. Page: 9½x13½.

SEASONAL COVER of "Echo" of Polysar Ltd., Sarnia, Ontario, is striking in black and white. Nameplate in Outline letters is in light blue-green. Page: 8½x11.

Appeals, also called *billboards* or *teasers*, are small headlines which advertise inside articles. These may duplicate the heads on the stories or paraphrase them. Like the table of contents, billboards are a topic of debate, many editors believing that a magazine of no more than 32 pages doesn't benefit from teasers.

If appeals are used at all, they should be nowhere near the number used on commercial magazines. Most effective is the single one that refers to the article illustrated or connoted by the cover art.

Cover art is most effective when it heralds a strong inside feature. But often this art stands independent of any other content. This is the *salon cover*. On rare occasions the cover may be all-type, made up completely of appeals. Even rarer, but effective, is to start the lead story on the cover in type far larger than regular body type, continuing in normal body type on page 2 or 3. This must be used most infrequently, though, lest the magazine look be lost, replaced by that of a sensational tabloid.

When color is available, it can be a strong identifier as well as a lure for the reader. *National Geographic* would probably be recognized by its yellow cover, even without a nameplate, and *Time* uses a vivid red as a trademark.

The use of color, on the cover or inside, is largely determined by the budget.

There is a way to use full color on a Spartan budget: preprinted covers. These are purchased stock covers printed with a full-color picture and blank on the inside pages and sometimes on the back. The nameplate of the magazine is surprinted locally on the front cover, and the back and insides are printed in customary fashion.

Preprinted art must be of general interest and is frequently seasonal. At Christmas, for instance, the editor has a choice of Santa or angelic tots or stockings-hung-with-care. Thanksgiving, Easter, and the Glorious Fourth are occasions for interesting art. While a great variety is available, editors who use such covers are always a bit uneasy that some other magazine may appear at the same time with the identical cover. Chances of your readers receiving such a duplicate cover are negligible, though, and certainly not worth losing sleep or hair over.

Surveys and Polls

As a sender, the editor is intensely interested in the action and reaction of the receiver, the reader. As information is gathered about the acceptance and credibility of the publication, the editor also gathers data that are valuable to the organization in general and its management.

The best way to find out what the reader thinks, not only of your publication but of things in general, is to go to the reader. Editors ought to eat in the cafeteria, lunch rooms, and greasy spoons where employees eat. The editor should get onto the work floor as much as possible. The editor ought to be a spectator—if not a player—at the bowling alleys, softball diamonds, and other places where employees gather.

Although it is rarely admitted, editors customarily are removed from their readers. An inspection of your own activities, on and off the job, and the people you normally associate with will quickly demonstrate how far you are from "the grass roots" of your particular organization.

A daily editor, Rolfe Neill, raised the *Philadelphia News* from a nondescript tabloid to an important newspaper that is fiercely admired by a strong middle-class readership. Neill spurned downtown restaurants to eat at pizzerias in South Philadelphia, chili palaces in Camden, and assorted eateries in factory districts. There he listened avidly to determine what his potential readers were talking about and what topics raised the highest interest. But his favorite device was to ride busses. He'd place a copy of his *News* on an empty seat and sit right behind it. Then he'd watch to see how a person would pick up the paper and leaf through it, note how much time was spent on every page and every story and, in general, observe the reader's reaction.

As he became aware, firsthand, of his reader's interests and concerns, he made the *News* their primary source of information in meeting those needs and in a remarkably short period brought the once-ailing newspaper to enormous popularity with its blue-collar readership.

Of course, there are surveys and polls that can be a tad more accurate in their findings. But it must be cautioned that research studies, popular as they are, can easily be misinterpreted.

Most people know at least the rudiments of polling. First, the sample must accurately reflect the "universe" that it seeks to typify. If you're surveying your company's employees and 47% of them are women, then 47% of your survey sample must be female. The sample can also be broken down by age, occupation, income, ethnic or racial group, etc. Each new qualification we impose on the sample makes it more complicated. So we must determine what of such data is really pertinent. The difference between a woman's and a man's interest in an organizational publication may be important as the editor plans its content, but whether the respondent is Democrat or Republican probably has no bearing at all.

In making a readership survey, we must decide how precise it needs to be. The larger the portion of the "universe" which we sample, the more accurately the results will mirror the opinion of the total population. But we will undoubtedly be satisfied with less than perfect reliability (if for no other reason than the staggering costs of achieving such a result). The question is, how much less do we want?

This is measured by the *reliability tolerance*—if that figure is 10%, for instance, it means that the result discovered by the survey may be as much as 10% away from the actual truth, higher, or lower. If 80% of the readers like classified ads in a survey with a 10% reliability tolerance, in reality anywhere from 70 to 90% of the population hold a similar opinion.

The editor should determine what reliability tolerance is required. Then, from charts readily available at any library, it can be determined how big a sample must be taken for the universe being tested.

If the survey is to be conducted by mail, we must be aware that normally only about 50% of the questionnaires will be returned. So, if you need 400 returns, you must send out at least 800 survey blanks.

Participants in the survey must be chosen at random. If you need to find out how 2,000 readers react, you need about 700 responses for a 3% (plus or minus) reliability. That means you must question, roughly, every third person. If your universe is the employees of a company or members of an organization, which most often is what the editor works with, you obtain the master list from Personnel or the secretary of the organization. You go down the list, checking off each third name. To assure a perfectly random selection, choose your starting point by pure chance, drawing straws, rolling dice, or pulling a slip of paper from a hat to determine whether you start with the first, second, or third name on the list.

Suppose you start with the second name. Then the fifth, eighth, eleventh, and so on, names make your sample. If for some reason a checked name is not suitable—you know Charlie Jenkins is off on a long vacation-recuperation—you go to the next name and keep counting by threes.

Perhaps it's important to duplicate a certain male-female ratio in your sample. Say you need 175 female responses and 525 from males. You go through the list, checking off every eleventh name. Write the name down if it's female; if not go to the next woman's name. If you run out of female names before you get 175, start again at the top of the list. Then you do it all over again with men's names, this time counting off every fourth male. Do this for each subdivision your survey needs.

There are some apparently random samplings that will not give reliable information. You can personally ask questions of every third person you meet in the hall or the parking lot or the washroom. The results will say no more than "a certain number of people said so and so." You can't count on any valid relationship between those answers and what your entire group of employees thinks, though you may get one by sheer accident.

Printing a questionnaire in the publication itself, while a popular and harmless pastime, is no more accurate. Primarily, your poll will show only what fairly regular readers think. There will be no note taken of the periodicals that go into the wastebasket unread. The effort required to clip out the survey form and return it to the editor will also shut off the reader who doesn't feel strongly enough, pro or con, to go to that great exertion.

The truly accurate poll can be conducted by two methods. By personal interviews, you can make sure that every question is answered—indeed, that the respondent is actually taking part. If there's a flat refusal to answer, the poller can immediately go to the next name on the list. And you don't have to build in a big cushion for lost responses; if you need 400, you interview 400 people and stop.

A major value of face-to-face polling is that the interviewer can ask open-ended questions and get reader reactions that are not asked for, or asked precisely enough, in the formal questions. And by the inflection and choice of words, the reader often conveys far more between the lines than is actually spoken.

These interviews take time and there is a danger that the respondent won't state views as readily as might be done on a "secret ballot."

Questionnaires mailed out for a so-called "self-administered" survey do give the protection of anonymity. They also give time for the reader to consider the answers and perhaps be more accurate than a quick reply off the top of the head.

The cost of mailing, not only the first questionnaire but the follow-up that often is required, can be considerable and this becomes a budgetary factor in choosing methods.

In any case, the wording of the survey form is of highest importance. Many a survey is as loaded as "Have you stopped beating your wife?" We're all familiar with those mailed out by political candidates: "Are you in favor of God, motherhood, apple pie, and the American way of life or are you going to vote for that irresponsible, venal, corrupt, and

INFORMAL READERSHIP POLLS use forms bound into publication. "HFH Review" of Henry Ford Hospital of Detroit, has form that folds into business reply envelope. "Employee Newsletter" of Patrick Henry Hospital of Newport News, Virginia, uses a half-page gatefold which is to be deposited in box at time clock.

cretinous moron, my unworthy opponent?" Questions must be neutral, with no hint whatsoever as to what is "the right answer."

The simplest question to answer and to tabulate is one that asks for just yes or no, true or false, agree or disagree. Shadings of attitudes can be determined by having the respondent rank items in order from the best to the worst. Similarly, the respondent can give a grade from 1 to 10 to various statements or items.

In all instances, there should be a category of Don't Know, Not Sure,

None of the Above, or Undecided. For there are always a substantial number of people who can't or won't make up their minds, and ignoring them may invalidate the survey.

In all instances the questions must be interesting and the survey short. Pretesting it on a small group will show weakness in phrasing.

Mailed-out questionnaires should be sent with a covering letter signed by the highest possible organizational executive. This gives an importance to the project that encourages participation.

If, in about three weeks you haven't received a 50% return, a second mailing is required.

A detailed, comprehensive guide on this subject is available from Ragan Communications. The book, called *How to Conduct a Readership Survey* and written by W. Charles Redding, offers organizational editors and communications managers step-by-step guidelines to conducting valid readership or audience surveys.

A major finding of any survey is what your readers like and dislike, and the editor can take steps to adjust content to those wants. But all interpretation must be leavened with editorial common sense. A new religious magazine was once launched after a most intensive pre-publication research to determine what the reader wanted. The first issue provided exactly what the survey called for. Response was enthusiastic and that enthusiasm continued for ten months. But when it came time to renew subscriptions, results were absolutely dismal. What the reader had asked for was dessert and pastries—short anecdotes, humorous pieces, lots of "pretty pictures" in full color, many cartoons. When the editor failed to provide the meat and potatoes of substantial articles and hard information, the reader was dissatisfied. For the editor must realize that readers don't actually know what they want or need; they rely on the editor to provide a balanced menu.

Polls and research—scientific or informal—can be useful tools in determining such a menu. But in the final analysis, an editor proceeds as much—or more—by instinct as by science. The best tactic is to feed as much hard, factual material as possible into the brain for the making of both rational and instinctive decisions. Then, when instinct speaks, the editor should trust it.

Chapter 3

The Editor

- [ ] as Executive
- [ ] as Communicator
- [ ] as Production Manager
- [x] as Writer
- [ ] as Copyreader
- [ ] as Typographer
- [ ] as Art Director
- [ ] as Newspaper Designer
- [ ] as Magazine Designer
- [ ] as Newsletter Producer
- [ ] as Circulation Manager
- [ ] as Contractor

Glossary
Index

The steps in creating a publication are many and disparate. The editor performs many different jobs, sometimes several at a time, during this long and intricate process. The better the procedure is organized, the more successful and happy the editor is.

Yet, despite good organization, the editor of a newspaper cannot escape the whims of fate. No editor can foresee a volcano spreading ash throughout the organization's building, an Arab embargo that changes organizational lifestyle, the death of a leader, or any of the events that make the news budget. Newsletters and the news section of a magazine are just as dependent upon the turn of events. But the feature section of the magazine, far, far more than the feature material of a newspaper, can be determined by the editor. So we plan as much as possible and perfect our procedures to handle the unexpected. Now let's go through the steps of getting a magazine into the hands of the reader. (We'll then look at newspapers and, in Chapter 10, newsletters.)

Contents Chart

The editor should begin planning on an annual basis because many stories are seasonal and cyclical and each issue must harmonize with all other issues.

A good device is to make a large chart to hang on the editorial wall and divide it into 13 months if you have a monthly publication; some editors prefer to use 13 sheets of regular typing paper. The larger these charts, the better, so the editor can see at least the major items without needing a spy glass.

The chart shows the last issue, the current one, and the next 11 months and the current month as it comes up next year. As an issue is complete—

say January's of this year—the December sheet is thrown away and a blank for next January is added.

On the chart are listed story ideas for each month. Those which must run in that month are written in red. Suppose the editor gets an idea: "In March let's do a piece on our Accounting Department." Then a second thought: "No, let's do that in April. Everyone will be working on income tax returns then and will be more aware of the need for and problems of accounting." But looking at the chart, the editor notices, in red, that in June, Peter Applegate will mark his 35th year in Accounting. So: "Let's combine a story about Pete with an overall view of Accounting. We can tell two interesting stories in human terms." Some magazine editors will show a page-by-page chart for each month, often including minute detail of photography and layout.

Either right on the chart or in a separate date book, the editor keeps a *future book*. (This is especially important for a newspaper editor!) Every upcoming event that the editor learns about is noted in the future book. Most ideas come from the current issue of our publication. If we did a piece on an annual meeting in April, we know that next April we'll do the same. But it goes down in the books because we don't trust our memory. (It's surprising how often the most professional staff will overlook an important event.) So the editor goes through the current issue, noting future events suggested therein. Reporters are urged to contribute items for the book. These may be the obvious; they may be less transcendental but worth noting, usually personal items. New futures are being added constantly.

The monthly chart may be expanded to include a progress chart. In vertical columns we can note when and to whom a story was assigned, when it was turned in, edited, sent out for and received clearances, sent to the typesetter, proofs received and returned, and, perhaps, pasted up. At a glance the editor can see where an incipient bottleneck may be lurking and take preventive action before it turns into a crisis.

Beginning editors often think this is too much putting-down-on-paper. Quite the contrary! An essential of good editing is the old admonition: "Make a list!" The more we commit to paper, the more brain cells we can put to the real thinking demanded by an editorial job.

Another useful tool is the odds-and-ends book, which lists information that is at the tip of your tongue but you just can't think of it. . .and that happens usually when you're in an awful hurry or amidst a genuine crisis.

Such items may be: What kind of paper are we printing on? Whom do we call at the printer's when our proofs are late? Who's the person who can speed our clearances by bending a little organizational protocol? What's the home phone number of our correspondent 867 miles away in our West Inhabited Zone plant? What's our postal permit number? The et ceteras go on and on.

Proper spacing is essential to a good publication. If preprinted pasteup sheets are not used—or even if they are—a *page spec* chart can be a handy tool that gives basic format specifications. This is handy as a wall chart. A *spacing chart* shows the proper amount of white space between elements. Another useful "list" to make is a chart showing the *readability range* of every font of body type as determined by formulas given in Chapter 6. Show not only the line-lengths in picas but also by typewriter characters so you can write approximately line for line. If you have a word processor but type is not set automatically from it, it's helpful to note the margin settings that will give you the visual image that most closely approximates a typeset line. Then you can immediately gauge how long your copy is. Also give the setting that will give the approximate length for each of your headline styles. Then you won't have to count characters each time you write a head.

Actual work on a magazine may begin six months ahead of publication—or even before that. If the writer is far away and you must exchange many letters during the gestation of the story, a good time cushion will protect your sanity. Many stories will be *evergreen* or *anytime* (often abbreviated to *time*) that can run in almost any issue instead of demanding use at a specific time. They go into the *bank* until needed.

PRODUCTION CHART shows progress of every story for publication. An additional column is frequently used to show when story was first written. Note that president's message and retirements and service awards do not require clearances.

THE EDITOR AS PRODUCTION MANAGER 43

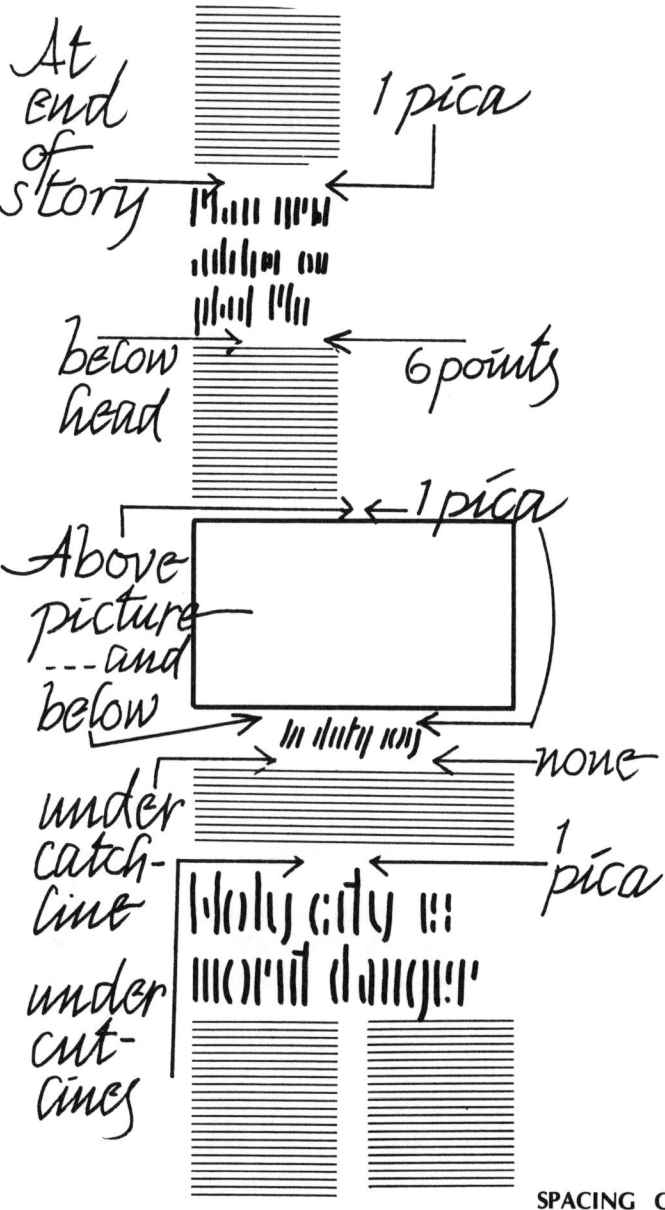

SPACING CHART gives all specifications necessary to maintain consistency. Chart is not—and need not be—to scale. It may be expanded to show spacing for bylines, sandwiches, breaker heads, etc.

Clearances

The most important steps—writing the article and editing it—will be covered in the next two chapters. Now, in most instances, the organizational editor has a peculiar requirement: clearances.

This is, without argument, the most vexatious part of an editor's job. Clearance procedures and numbers vary with the organization. The bigger the organization, usually the more—and more nit-picking—the clearances required.

The editor should accept clearances, not only as necessary evils, but as a useful backstop. On daily newspapers, the copyreader used to be a veteran who had worked his way up from a reporter's beat. When a story cleared his desk, the reporter knew that embarrassing errors would be purged. For the old pro knew that the Big Fire was in February of 1898, not October; that Oak Street becomes Talleyrand once it crosses West Main; that the Rev. Edmund Greevey spells his name with a *u*, not an *o*. It was a great assurance to have this infallible ally.

So in organizational journalism. Usually the persons giving clearances are experts in their field. The engineer knows that it was an Nx-712, not 711, that made the flight to the moon; the sales manager knows that Roland Wortley covers South Iowa, not South Dakota. More important may be clearances from the Legal or Patents Department. Legal may know—as the editor does not—that a lawsuit is pending and that a certain apparently innocent statement in the magazine may be construed as a concession to the plaintiff's case. Patent attorneys know those technicalities that can give a competitor a leg up. The editor should be grateful for this protection against unknowing errors. It's when the reviewer leaves his or her field of expertise that problems set in.

The eternal procrastinator leaves a mangled schedule on the bloodied floor. And the eager beaver wants to demonstrate to the world and the boss just how zealous an underling can be. The same characters complicate approval of proofs, too.

A column by the author in *The Ragan Report* drew the largest response and endorsement of any piece in his series. Because it is so pertinent, it is reprinted on the opposite page. The techniques it suggests are equally useful in obtaining original copy clearances as well as approval of proofs.

The copy is finally sent to the typesetter. This may be in an in-plant print shop, it may be an outside supplier. It doesn't matter, production steps are identical.

MEMO:

"My one single problem which most concerns me," writes a respondent, "is to prepare printed jobs for management people who have no journalistic backgrounds and attempt to supervise my job assignments. What do I do?"

And here, Gentle Reader, we have one of the ironies of American corporate life. A businessman takes the advice of his accountant, attorney, time-and-motion expert and the elevator operator's mother-in-law. But let a communications person—anyone from editor to advertising director to PR man—throw out a suggestion and it's like throwing out a Christian into the den of lions.

Everyone, but everyone, is an expert in communications. An engineer whose only polysyllabic vocabulary is "sine, cosine," is a literateur in the final analysis. A patent attorney who thinks Zane Grey is American literature, inserts an apostrophe before every final s in the copy. A joker who stutters when he answers the telephone complains about the rhythm of the balance sheet and wants a more Elizabethan (Elizabeth Taylor, that is) flavor to the footnote on page 9.

Unfortunately, the idiots—as the poor—are always among us. More frequently they are a rung or two above us. We can't avoid them (it would be a lonely world if all the idiots were removed) so we must learn to live with them.

The first thing is to translate everything possible into $ and ¢. This is usually the most telling criteria for these incorporated Mickey Mousers. Have that financial data at your fingertips. If Maximus T. Bloughard insists on green paper for your Christmas issue, have a sample of Novatone Heather, 80-pound substance ready to show him.

"Oh, yes," you interject, "I thought you'd like something like this. Your favorite shade of green as I recall. But, alas, this will add $196.47 to the bill and I'll need to ask you to authorize this request for a budget exception."

How salutary a phrase. . ."budget exception"!

The next defensive ploy is the deadline.

Before any job, make a pact with the president's secretary. "Shall we say, then, that I'll have the material for Mr. Bigg's attention on February 12?"

To this she can only say yes.

Now when Phinella Hayersplittier starts suggesting rewriting the Old Testament, gently interject the deadline with the president into the conversation. "I'd like to do this, Ms. H," you gently submit, "but I'll get in dutch with the Big Man. Would you give a buzz to his secretary and get me an extension. You carry more weight with him (she sure does, 225 pounds) than I do."

MEMO:

Filthy lucre rears its head here again. Arrange with your printer (who at heart is as much an anarchist as any editor) that on a certain date, overtime rates set in on your job. He need not be too intent on levying said rates. But it is very handy to explain to one of the hierarchical vultures that his or her suggestion will get us past March 11... "and that's the overtime rate date, you know."

Another moment of extreme vulnerability for an editor is when he must show proofs.

The saving device here is the photostat. Never submit the original printer's proof. Always give a photocopy to the harpies. This has several benefits.

First of all, photocopier paper isn't pleasant to write on. Its surface is too glassy.

Secondly, each person is proofing only one, personal copy. There's no chance for one-upmanship. This is a major factor in extensive author's alterations.

Sales Manager J. reads the proof first. He makes a few obvious corrections, simple typos. Then he bucks it on to Personnel Supervisor W. She has no obvious corrections to make. But. . . .

"I'll show that smart-bottomed Jack Jones that I'm as sharp as he is. Hand me my red pencil and let me at it!"

And, because there aren't any typographical errors to mark, she changes "red" to "crimson" and "fire" to "conflagration," etc. and you're stuck with two extra days and a hundred bucks worth of AAs.

There's another factor in a communal proof. Otherwise placid and peaceful executives are like a school of pirhanas. They get drunk on blood. As they see the wounds of previous proofreaders' marks, our heroes become as maddened as the carnivorous fish. Each correction is a stigmatum, discharging the intoxicating serum; the fewer previous "corrections," the less the blood lust.

One editor I know affixes a memo to each proof:

"Please read this proof before _____. At that time your corrections will be combined on the master proof of Mr. President. Because of budgetary considerations, you are reminded that our printer goes into overtime rates _____ and that each alteration in this proof costs $3.73."

If you combine the various "corrections" onto the master proof yourself, you can always leave one out. "I noticed that Mr. Bigg had approved this statement (He hadn't; he had merely not disapproved!) and I was sure you wouldn't want to contradict him," you might observe casually.

MEMO:

Or you may just—most sincerely—plead human error on your part. But chances are you have to do neither. Most alleged "corrections" are mere gambits in the executive-wing game and are forgotten before you even send the proof back to the composing room.

Another important tactic of editorial self-preservation is: "Never ask for permission."

An Army editor once told a general, "It's easier to get forgiveness for something you've done in this division than it is to get permission to do it." That applies to most divisions. That applies to most commercial armies, too, I've found.

Do it. If it succeeds, praise your bosses. (One of them must have, back last Spring or a year or so ago, have said something that could be construed as the embryo for any brilliant idea ever hatched.) If it doesn't work, ask forgiveness.

Finally, collect character witnesses.

Every time you win a contest, make very, very sure that your officers' ranks are made aware of that. Pass along—and keep for your files—kind words from practitioners in your field. Display your plaques and certificates prominently and proudly.

You are your own best character reference. The capable editor has an air about him or her that comes only from self-confidence. That comes only from complete mastery of your subject.

I know that this little screed sounds sophist and cynical. It wasn't meant to be. Each ploy given here is a legitimate one. It may be a wee bit childish to you. But when you're playing with 3-foot-high people, you play dolls and Fish, not Monopoly and contract bridge.

Proofreading

The first type the editor sees is the *galley proof*. These are long narrow strips of paper, only a little more than one column wide, photocopies of the original phototype. The galley is read and corrections and changes are noted on it in one of the most important steps in publishing: *proofreading*.

The function of proofreading is to purge the printed page of error, factual or mechanical. The very act of printing words gives them an authority that spoken or typewritten words do not carry. Printed words become the accepted, definitive information; anyone in doubt about the accuracy of any statement will ultimately seek the final authority: It's right here in the book! We owe it to our readers that only absolutely accurate information be given the imprimatur of authenticity by printing.

Since 1450, when proofreaders first were Ph.D.s who of their own knowledge could attest to accuracy, a system of proofreading has developed with a set of symbols for easy, fast, and unmistakable corrections. These are similar to those used by copyreaders (discussed in Chapter 5) but they are not the same. It is useful that we make the distinction lest we compound errors in attempting to correct them.

Typographic errors (*typos*) are mechanical ones: The writer or the typesetter has hit the wrong key, transposed characters, or fumbled fingers generally. If done by the typesetter, these errors are corrected at no cost to us. But if we must correct our own errors or—worst of all!—if we make changes in error-free type, the printer will charge those costs to us. . .and very hefty costs they can be. (Some people estimate that to change a single line may cost as much as $4.) All these are *author's alterations* (*AA*).

The typesetter is instructed to "Follow the copy. . .out the window," if necessary. If the manuscript says "Columbus discovered America in 1493" and the type says "1493," the typesetter's job has been done properly. To correct this error is an author's alteration and will be charged against said author's account. But these errors of act must be corrected, of course, to make our printing authoritative, no matter who pays for the change.

The AAs that should be avoided are the second guesses. The writer has said that "Cigarets and cigars are bad for your health." The editor or writer or somebody, coming across this phrase in the proof decides that it should be the airlines' term, "smoking material." So one or two lines of type must be reset.

(To correct errors or make changes in phototype, it is usual to set the entire line. This *correction line* is then pasted over the original *error line*. To paste over a single letter, to change "hart" to "hurt," would be a picky job that would demand great care, and probably time, placing a tiny piece of paper in the proper position. If our phrase "smoking material" ran in two lines, two correction lines must be set.)

The worst AA is one that adds characters to a line of type. Original copy says "pity." To make this more elegant, the proofreader says "commiseration." Now look what happens: In the four spaces where "pity" had appeared, we must cram 13 characters of the fancy word. The typesetter can put "com-" or, in a loose line, "commis-" in the original gap; but the rest of the new word must go into the next line. Often we keep moving letters from one line to the next until the extra characters can be tucked into the widow line. Often several to many lines must be reset to change a single word.

Such AAs are rank extravagances and should not be tolerated. Any word that passed scrutiny by the writer, the editor, and perhaps a third copyreader, is good enough to withstand changes in type.

There are two methods of proofreading, *guideline* and *book*. By the guideline method, the error is circled, a line leads from it to a margin, there the correction is written. By the book method, two unconnected marks are used for each error. One—the *intratype mark*—is made at the site of the crime. The other in either adjacent margin, instructs how to correct the error.

On galley proofs, where most errors are detected and corrections may be many, guidelines may intersect or block out other material, thus confusing the typesetter. So for galley proofs, the book method is most useful. By the time type is in page form, errors should be quite few. And, because much of the type is at a distance from a margin, guidelines are necessary on *page proofs*.

We shall look at the book method now, noting that the same symbols may be used for both methods.

The basic intratype symbol when something has been omitted is the *caret*, an upside-down V. Within the type we write the caret to show exactly where something must be added. In the margin, either the right or left but always on the same horizontal line, we write what must be inserted. A word or letter is written there. To avoid similarity of hastily written letters, the *a*, *u*, and *w* are underscored, the *o*, *n*, and *m* are overlined. If a space is to be added we write #.

Punctuation marks are circled to keep them from disappearing; the period, especially, may be taken for a fly speck unless we call the typesetter's attention to it. To distinguish *superior characters*—those that are above, instead of below the line of type—we use an inverted caret within the type and, in the margin, we cup the character to be inserted in the same inverted caret. Superior characters include the apostrophe (which we don't want confused with a comma); single and double quo-

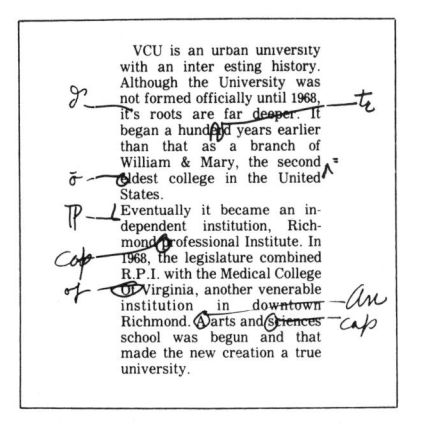

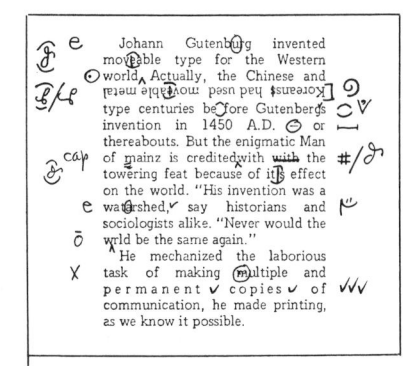

GUIDELINE METHOD of proofreading is shown in example at left. At right, book method of proofreading is demonstrated.

50 EDITING THE ORGANIZATIONAL PUBLICATION

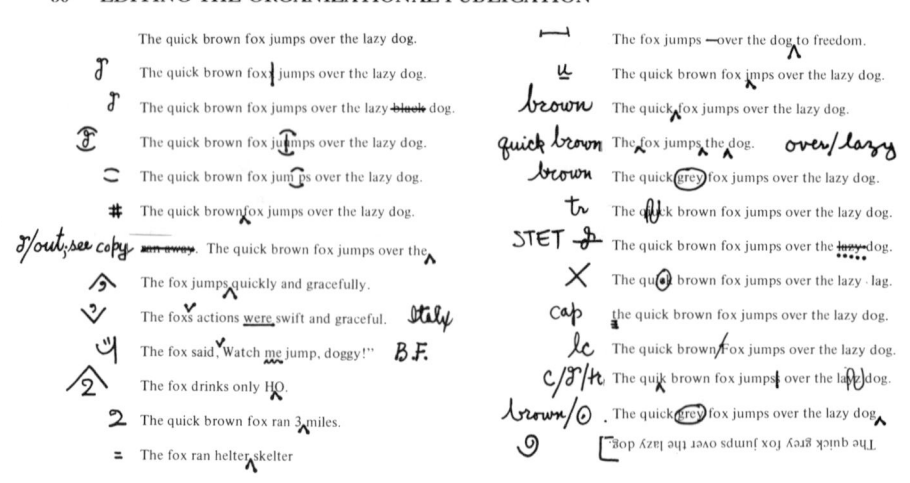

PROOFREADER'S MARKS

tation marks; and, especially in technical copy, exponents such as the ² in "pi r squared."

Similarly, when we have an *inferior character*—such as the number in "H₂O," we tent the marginal character in a caret. Note then, if it's supposed to be "132 miles" and type makes it "13," we insert a caret right after the "3" and in the margin write just "2." If we want to change "HO" into the formula for water, we write a regular caret between the letters and, in the margin, write "2" tented in a regular caret.

To take out an unwanted character, we draw a vertical line through it and in the margin write the *delete* sign which looks like a medieval handwritten *d*, short for the Latin peremptory "delendo," "throw this out." If, however, the deleted letter is in the middle of a word, "judgment," we not only draw the line through the first *e*, at the top and bottom of that stroke, we make a little half-moon, the *closeup* sign. If we use only the delete sign, the correction will be "judg ment." We must push these two portions together, "judgment," and the closeup sign does just that. In the margin, the delete mark is also cupped in the closeup sign.

If we want to take out a whole word or phrase, we cross them out with a horizontal line and write the delete sign in the margin. In this case we don't have to use a closeup sign.

We sometimes use the closeup mark alone. If the type says "press room" and we want to make it one word, we link the two in the type with closeup marks top and bottom and in the margin also write a pair of closeups. The result: "pressroom."

If we must add a hyphen, we write a caret in the copy; the marginal notation is = . This distinguishes it from a dash, whose sign is a long horizontal stroke with serifs at each end.

A common error, on the typewriter as on the typesetter, is a transposition. "Christams," for instance (a horrendous and recurring curse of this writer). The transposed characters *a* and *m*, are joined by an S lying on its side (*a lazy S* the Wild West brand was called). The marginal notation is "tr," for "transpose." We use the same device to transpose words.

To change a lowercase letter to a capital, we draw three tiny horizontal lines under the letter and write "cap" in the margin. Converting a capital to lowercase requires a diagonal slash through the letter and, in the margin, "lc."

To indicate where a paragraph indent should be made, make a big L at the proper spot and, in the margin, write a *paragraph mark*, a backward, two-stemmed cap P.

To change a Roman word to Italics, underline it in the type and write "Ital" or "Itlx" in the margin. To change Roman to boldface, underline the word with a jagged line and write "BF" in the margin. To change a word from Italics or bold to regular Roman, circle it and write "Roman" in the margin.

The basic intratype mark to change one element to another is to circle the letter or word in the type and in the margin write what it should be changed to.

Sometimes the typesetter will omit a line or even a paragraph when several of these units begin with the same word. If the omission is too great to write in the margin, put a caret at the point of nonappearance and in the margin write "OUT; see copy"—short for "So much is left out you'd better look at the original copy and add what was omitted."

Sometimes the proofreader makes a correction that isn't a correction. Say the type refers to "George Washington and William Jefferson in Colonial history." The proofreader pounces on the error and changes "William" to "Thomas." Then, many lines later, the writer again refers to "William," this time noting that he was Thomas' favorite cousin. "Omigosh! How do I undo my stupid 'correction' which ain't a correction!" (Proofreading is often done with a pen that can't be erased or, if in pencil, erasure may take the phototype right along with it. So erasing is not the answer.)

Instead, the proofreader writes a line of dots under the intratype correction and with a horizontal line, crosses out the marginal notation and, above it, writes *STET*. That's short for "stetare," "let it stand," as it first was.

On rare occasion, the proofreader will have doubts. Suppose we don't know whether the author actually meant "bays and girls" or "boys and girls." We circle the *a* in "bays" and write an *o* in the margin. Around this character we draw a long box and divide it in two. The *0* is in the right half; in the other portion we write "Qu Au," "query the author." This is like saying, "Hey, Author! I think you wanted it to be 'boys and girls,' didn't you?" If the author agrees, the query is crossed out. But if the author really wanted "bays," the original correction would be underlined with dots, the whole marginal notation crossed out and STET written in the margin.

We customarily query the author on apparent errors of fact and query the editor ("Qu Ed") on matters of style.

Sometimes there is more than one error in a line. Each error must have an intratype symbol and a marginal one. Marginal marks are separated by a slash. Be sure the marginal signs are in the same left-to-right order as the errors they correct.

Never leave it to the typesetter to figure out what you want. Many inexperienced proofreaders simply circle the error and say "Surely the printer knows that 'dag' should be 'dog'!" But the typesetter doesn't necessarily know that; perhaps the original copy did read "dag." And we must remember that the typesetter is working against a strict time pressure and doesn't read the type at all but simply follows our instructions. The system of symbols developed over the centuries has proven to be the best method, the quickest, and most unmistakable way to correct errors and assure accuracy of printed matter.

The growing proliferation of *word-processing equipment* and *video display terminals* (VDTs) enables the writer actually to "set type," while typing the original story. This may be either by an in-plant typesetter or by creating magnetic or paper tape that can be taken to a commercial typesetter for the actual composition. This process is of inestimable benefit; for now the editor has complete control over this important function. Writing on a VDT is infinitely easier than beating a conventional typewriter. Corrections and changes can be made simply and easily and even the most intricate restructuring of an article is painless. If the "manuscript" is correct, the type will be, too.

So with editing on "the tube." The onerous and monotonous—but oh-so-important—proofreading process need not be repeated once the galleys are set.

Dummies

While the typographic errors are being corrected, the editor or designer will *dummy-up* the magazine. This is preparing a blueprint that the printer will follow in preparing copy for the *platemaker*.

We may use a *sketch dummy* or a *pasteup dummy*. Either can be used for any publication although most magazine dummies are pasteups and many newspaper dummies are sketches.

For the pasteup dummy, a photocopy is made of the actual type, body, and headlines. The editor uses a *grid sheet* the exact size of the printed page with columns indicated. Each element is pasted in position with the proper spacing. Pictures are indicated by rectangles in the size

THE EDITOR AS PRODUCTION MANAGER   53

PASTEUP DUMMY, left, is converted to page of "Preservation News" of National Trust for Historic Preservation, Washington, D.C. Standing heads at top and lower right are clipped from old copies. On finished page, these elements are in bright green.

of the reduced photo (found by *picture scaling* as discussed in Chapter 7).

This method gives the best instruction to the printer's pasteup workers. The editor knows exactly where a leg of type will bend into the next column. If a horrendous widow occurs, the editor can take remedial action. If after filling a whole page or 2-page spread, we wind up with one extra line of type, the editor can decide where to cut a line to make room instead of leaving it to the printer who actually doesn't have the information necessary to do a proper job of cutting.

The newspaper editor—or anyone who uses a sketch dummy—works in a scale model of the actual page, usually on an 8½ x 11 sheet. The columns are printed or hand-drawn and alongside is the scale in inches, numbering from the top. Only written symbols tell where elements go in the final assemblage. Headlines are indicated by code and *slug line*, that word or phrase that identifies the story through all the processes. The editor writes "1-3-24 Smith" and marks off a space of 1 inch in one column which the head will occupy. As we shall see in Chapter 8, this code means that the head is 1 column wide, 3 lines deep, and in 24-point type. Three lines are 72 points, or 1 inch deep. "Smith" is the key word in the head SMITH NAMED/ NEW MANAGER/ FOR INDIANA.

Then we write a big asterisk to note the start of the body type. The story itself is indicated by a straight line running vertically down the center of the column. The *empty sweep* as the eye moves, unreading,

54   EDITING THE ORGANIZATIONAL PUBLICATION

from one point to another, is shown by a diagonal connecting the spot where reading stops in the first column and where it continues in the next. The place where one leg of type ends is marked by a horizontal line across the column; so is the end of the story except that a straight line showing body type is ended by an arrowhead.

Pictures are shown by a rectangle enclosing a diagonal cross. The slug for the picture and its size are written in this box. It may be "2 x 4½" (2 columns wide, 4½ inches deep) or "2x27" which means "2 columns wide by 27 picas deep." We may write "picas" where they are used; but usually the numbers indicating picas are so large that we know they don't mean inches.

Room must be left and indicated for the captions but they don't need a slug line; it will be the same as for the picture.

A box is shown by a rectangle drawn with a ragged line. Now we indicate the depth, usually in picas, and slug of the head and story that run in the box. As head and body carry the same slug line, we need write it only once.

If there is any other instruction to the pasteup worker, it's written in the margin.

The sketch dummy should be drawn carefully; and the point of wrapping type to another column, the end of the story, or the depth of art must be noted precisely.

Sketch dummies can be used for magazines although this is rather rare except in the news section.

SKETCH DUMMY, right, is converted into page, above. From "Emhart News" of Emhart Corporation, Hartford, Connecticut.

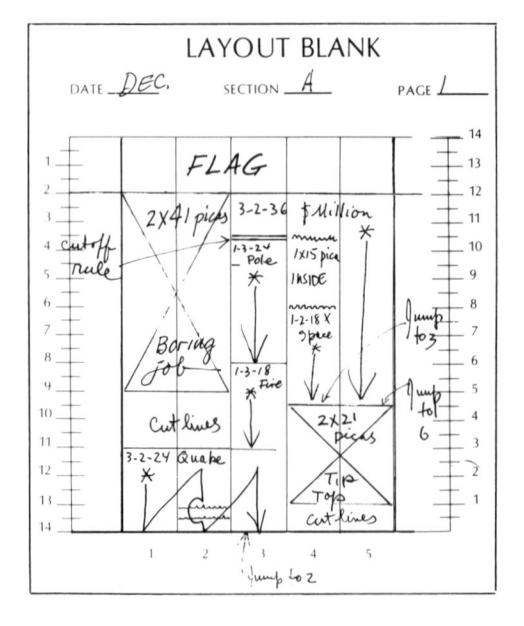

Copy Control

Newspaper pages often must be dummied before type is set. This requires an accurate system of *copyfitting* and a good *copy log*. Copyfitting calculates how much space a given piece of copy will fill when typeset.

Space is measured by the *column-inch*, an area one column wide and 1 inch deep. Note that a column-inch thus may vary greatly from one publication to another. A newspaper with 11-pica columns would have 66 square picas in a column-inch; in a magazine with 15-pica lines, its column-inch would be 90 square picas.

The easiest method is to adjust your typewriter margins so that a line of typescript will produce two lines of typeset material. If that's too wide for your paper, set the line-length so that one line of copy will make only 1½ lines of type; in that case you simply count the typewritten lines, multiply by 1½ and you know how many lines of type you have to work with. Typing at line-lengths that produce one line of type from one line of typescript is a nuisance; you have to hit the return key too often. And it's difficult to fill such short lines closely without excessive hyphenation, another deterrent to smooth typing and smooth narration.

Headlines are readily converted. Multiply the number of lines by the point size and divide by 72, the number of points in an inch. If it's a

MOCKUP for "Meidinger News" of Meidinger Corporation of Louisville, Kentucky. Note that greeking—simulation of body type—is done by drawing parallel lines of approximately x-height of proposed body type. Paragraph indents are shown and lines are ragged at right. Illustration is made by office photo-copier. Dummy is same size as finished publication, 8½x11.

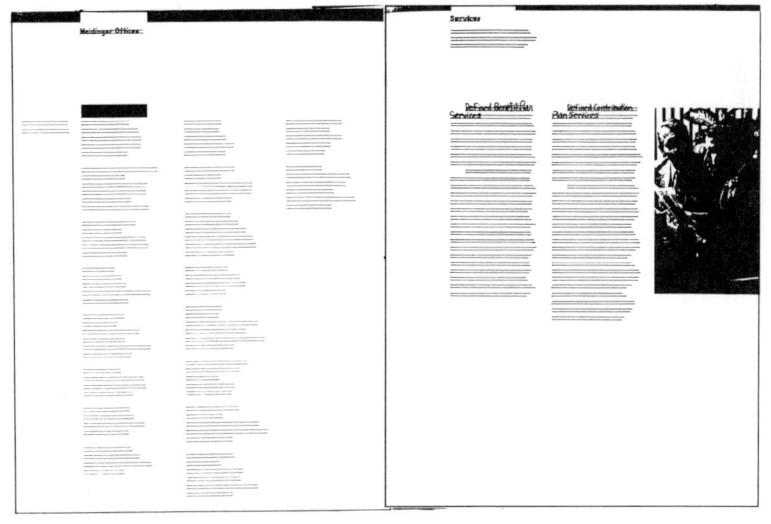

multicolumn head, multiply the depth of the head by that number. A 1-column head will take, let's say, 1 inch; the same type two columns wide will take 2 column-inches (in conversation, simply 2 inches).

As any story is copyread, any head written, or any art sent to the platemaker, its slug line and column inches are recorded in the copy log, one printed or done by hand. We mark on a printed log—or write on an informal one—the total column inches available in the issue. We have a 4-column tabloid with columns 15 inches deep. That's 60 column-inches per page. Multiply that by 8, the number of pages, and we have 480 column inches for the whole paper. We know that the constants will take, let's say, 15 column-inches, so we subtract that from the total; we have 465 inches available for fresh material.

We process a story and determine it will take 4½ inches. In the log we write: "ELECTION, 2-2-36, 4½ inches" and in the left margin write, 460½, the new amount of space left. Then we write "HEAD," 2 inches, and in the margin, 458½. Or we may combine the space for the head and story and make just one entry.

Pictures are noted in the log as "FIRE, 3x5" and 15 inches are subtracted from our running total. As that number—the unfilled area—grows smaller, we may have to begin worrying about getting in all the stories we must. Let's say we have only 20 inches unfilled but we know we have to run a story—which we can't get till the last minute—on the new insurance plan. That will take about 15 inches, we presume, and there will be a picture of a retirement party tonight that will take at least another 10 inches. We're 5 inches over.

A quick check of the log shows us an evergreen story that we can hold for the next issue. Or we note that a piece on softball can be cut by several inches or a picture can be cropped more tightly or made a column narrower. The log has allowed us to adjust unhurriedly rather than under the pressure of deadlines.

The dummy sketch or pasteup becomes the guide for making the *mechanical* or *pasteup*. This is the same size as the final print, the impeccable copy from which the printing plate will be made by photography.

Preparing the mechanical is one of the normal services performed by the printer. But more and more frequently, editors are preparing their own pasteups whether the type is set in-house or commercially. This do-it-yourself process can be a blessing. But there is also enough bane in the procedure that it warrants a second look before long-range commitments are made.

The advantages are obvious. The editor has constant supervision over the minor adjustments that must often be made, especially on newspaper pages. It saves time; your publication need not stand in line behind who knows how many others. It saves money, at least out-of-pocket money, for this process can be done while working around other

MOCKUP of 16-page tabloid, "California Local Government," Sacramento, was prepared and printed for presentation to potential advertisers. Body type is transfer greeking; photographs are indicated by Ben Day rectangles. Small insert shows greeking in same size.

assignments and during what often might be almost spare time. The disadvantage is that it requires a skill that hasn't necessarily developed with that of writing and editing. It requires patience and a frame of mind that refuses to consider this as scut work.

There should be a space in your office devoted to pasteup. A *light table* is the ideal, a slantable drawing board is the next, a flat work surface of any kind can do. This area should be kept free of other work; if you have to spend several minutes clearing off a tabletop to make room for pasting-up, your enthusiasm is apt to wane.

You should have preprinted *pasteup sheets.* These may be store-bought, in sheets approximately 16x22 with 1-pica-square grids. Or you may have them printed to your own format, with lines showing the edge of the paper sheet, the margins, and the columns. Horizontal lines at intervals of about 6 picas provide horizontal alignment. All printing is done in the light-blue ink that is invisible to the camera lens. If other guidelines are needed, they're drawn in with a blue pencil.

Galleys of cold type are cut with a razor blade with a 6-point margin on each side. This enables you to align the left edge of the strip of type along the vertical column rule with the excess paper extending into the alley. Using such a margin saves us from the horrors of our blade slip-

MEMO:

PRODUCTION CHECK LIST

PLANNING

- Assume nothing as to quantity, quality, contents, instructions, color, past performance, etc.
- Follow up on all oral and written instructions.
- Be sure to cancel all instructions, written or oral, if they are not to be followed.
- Schedule every operation. Schedule time for "follow-ups."
- Use well-designed forms for estimates and orders. Keep duplicated.
- Watch for halftones next to solids of large areas running same color.

PAPER AND INK

- Before selecting paper find out if printer has stock on hand suitable for at least two issues. He should order well in advance.
- Check light-weight papers for opacity before specifying.

COPY AND COMPOSITION

- Typewrite copy on one side of the paper. Double space.
- Be sure all revisions are made on manuscript before type is set.
- Check to see if any or all copy on the dummy is correct. This applies to headlines especially.
- Mark type size, measure, and face plainly.
- When checking proof, see what you are checking against. Get the previous proof, see dummy, look for pencil marks, pen notations, notes attached. Question all doubtful points.

MEMO:

- In marking corrections on proofs, mark them on galley or page proofs rather than in dummy.
- For reverses, body type without fine hairlines, or fine serifs, works best.
- Do not have run-arounds set until blueprints of pictures are received.
- Watch out for bad spacing between lines and words.

ARTWORK

- Check all artwork approved before sending to platemaker.
- Make list of artists and photographers and their phone numbers. Classify as to ability in: figure drawing, still life, posters, lettering, wash drawings, retouching, etc.
- Protect all art work before sending out.
- Shading sheets can be used to give tonal effects to original artwork instead of platemaker using Ben Day.
- When several line drawings are to be made at the same time, arrange for scale of reduction of artwork to be the same for all, and place together on same mount.
- If reduction is to be great, have line drawings kept open, free of closely spaced or fine lines.
- Plan for contrast in photographs or wash drawings when halftones are to be run on soft or cheap stock.
- Check to see whether regular or glossy photos are preferred, or which is more suitable for reproduction.

ping as we trim the galleys and digging into the type itself. If there is a shadow cast on the negative, it is easier to opaque it out along the margin rather than painstakingly paint around letterforms.

If your headlines come in a single strip, measure between the primary letters to get consistent horizontal spacing. Maintain this spacing even if there are no descenders or ascenders in a given line of type.

Standard spacing between head and story, picture and type, etc., must be rigidly adhered to.

It's useful to do your pasteup dummy on sheets like this. (And remember, you should make a detailed dummy even if you, yourself, are going to do the pasteup.) Very carefully mark the position of each element on the dummy. Then, if adjustments are necessary, you can make them—or at least decide where to make them—before you start pasting-up. This reduces or eliminates the need to work with single lines that tend to get lost, stick to your eyebrows, or curl up in obstinate contrariness.

The "paste" used in pasteup used to be rubber cement, a veritable invention of Satan himself. Today we use wax. Regular paraffin is melted and applied to the back of the paper. This can be done by a simple hand applicator or, best, by running the paper through a small machine. (The cost of a waxer is minor and it's a good investment. So is a simple, sharp wheel that runs down and slices off the edges of galleys.)

Wax will stick the phototype to the pasteup board but won't stick to your fingers. If an element is misplaced, it can be peeled off and repositioned with ease.

While the wax holds material reasonably firmly to the grid, it is not as solid as rubber cement and the pasteup must be handled carefully so nothing falls off or is pushed out of place.

Line art is simply pasted into position but halftones require previous preparation as we shall note in Chapter 9. *Veloxes*, or *PMTs*, photographs made up of halftone dots instead of modulated grays, are pasted into position. If *screened negatives* are used, they are *stripped in* by the platemaker. Two techniques may be used. We can simply draw onto the pasteup grid the proper rectangle and later cut a window out of the negative, following those lines. Or we can paste a piece of black or dark red paper (red photographs like black) into position and thus create a blank clear window. Screened negs are pasted so they show through the windows.

Two requisites are essential during the entire pasteup process and yet they are ignored all too often: Use the T-square constantly; wash your hands frequently.

With scores of printed guidelines, it seems they should be adequate to align type. Yet even the keenest eye will tend to let type run uphill—especially at the end of the day when fatigue is setting in. Often the random pattern of ascenders and descenders create optical illusions that distort the horizon. The T-square—and a transparent plastic *90-degree triangle*—should be used to check alignment of each piece that is pasted down.

Immaculate fingers are essential to prevent the smudges that later will require opaquing and to enable you to handle photopaper without it sticking to your fingers. A wise paster-upper will wash hands at least once per column and some do it more frequently. If this seems overdoing it, remember that cleanliness is next to godliness. So do it for your soul, if not for your publication.

If you are pasting up typewritten material, it ought to be done on grid sheets that will be reduced about 10 percent in making the plate. Such reduction sharpens the type and increases readability.

If it's convenient—though often it isn't—a photocopy may be made of the pasteup in your office. Or the platemaker may photograph the pasteup and use the resultant page negative to make a photocopy, variously called the *blue line, brown line,* or *silver line*. These copies, or the original pasteup itself, are read as the *page proofs.*

The main purpose of the page proof is to make sure that headlines and stories as well as pictures and captions have been properly joined up. It is a fairly frequent error to find the wrong head on a story, especially when they are both on the same general topic. And it's too easy to attach the wrong caption to a picture, especially when you have several pictures of all the same size and sometimes even on the same broad subject. Similar charts or graphs can easily be transposed.

But we also search out typos on the page proof and, though it may be more difficult and costly to make corrections at this stage, we still do it to purge our pages of error.

For the page proof we use the guideline method of proofreading. The error is circled and a line leads out to the margin where the correction is shown by the same symbols used for the book method. We use guidelines here because there may not be a nearby margin in which to write the instructions.

If the original pasteup is the page proof, we should not write on it, of course, but lay a piece of tracing paper over the grid and make corrections there.

Another function of the page proof is to check the *imposition*. Several pages are printed on a single piece of paper, a *signature*. If this is folded once, we have four pages. Folding it once more, and opening the fold at the top, gives us an 8-pager. Sometimes 16-page signatures are printed. The final proof allows us to check that, after folding, each page will be in proper sequence.

When proofreading has assured that all errors have been corrected and that imposition is correct, a page negative is made. Into it are stripped the screened negatives if they are used and from it is made the printing plate. But only after one more job has been performed: *opaquing.*

Sometimes pasted-on material may cast a shadow, especially if edges curl or the paper is rather heavy. Fingerprints, smudges, and flecks of dirt sticking to adhesives oozing from under pasted-on matter must be removed. Tiny imperfections that would cause black specks on the printed sheet may result during the development of the negative or because dust particles have fly-specked the enlarger or other photo equipment. These flaws—which show up white on the black negative —must be painted out by using a very fine brush and a peculiarly colored red paint. If a large area must be opaqued, we may use paper or acetate in either amber or orange, both of which appear black to the camera.

This is the opaquing process; it demands skill, patience and time. . . and consequently costs money. We want to minimize the need by pasting-up and handling the mechanical very carefully.

One law, which should be as strictly enforced as that of the Medes and Persians, is that all pasteup material must be *camera-fresh.* Often there is a temptation to clip one or more of the constants from a previous issue and paste that up. But each reproductive process makes the printed image a trifle fuzzier. If we use printed material, the image will not be as crisp as we demand. If the printed material has itself been produced from clipped matter, the fuzziness is increased exponentially. So we must insist that no one obtain a temporary convenience by grabbing nearby printing rather than walking a few paces to get fresh material.

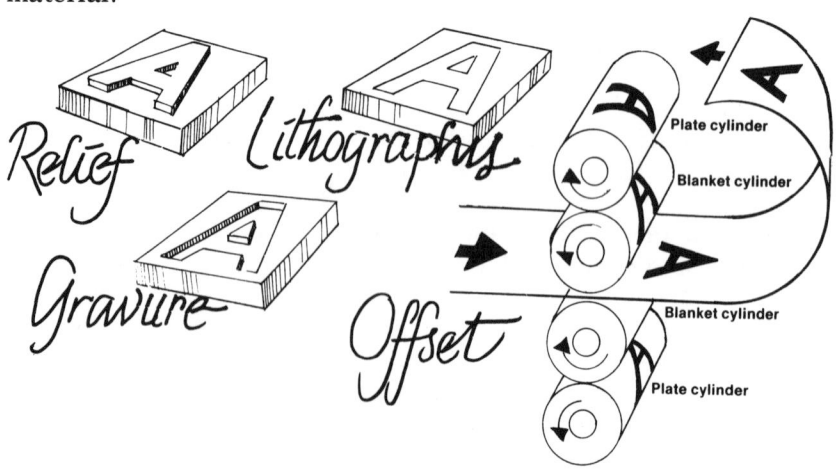

PRINTING METHODS USED FOR PUBLICATIONS. Relief or letterpress produces printed images from raised, 3-dimensional "hot metal" characters. Intaglio, known commercially as rotogravure, lays ink on paper from recessed images. Planography or offset lithography carries the image on same plane as bearing surface. Ink transfers to rubber blanket and from there is "set off" onto paper.

Offset

From the page or signature negative is made a plate for *offset printing*. Actually, this is offset *lithography* ("writing by stone"), a process that was invented in 1798. An actual slab of limestone was the printing plate. Working on the theory that oil and water won't mix, the printer put an oily or greasy image on the stone, by hand. He sloshed water to wet the stone while the oily image repelled the water. Then, when an ink roller was passed over the stone, the oily ink was attracted to the greasy image but not the wet stone. When a piece of paper was pressed upon the stone, the ink transferred onto the paper and became a *lithograph*.

Today the basic lithographic process of oil-and-water is the same, although practically all the details have changed. The stone has become aluminum; the plate is wrapped around a cylinder instead of being flat; the image is placed photographically upon the plate instead of by hand. And the image is transferred off the plate not directly to the paper, but indirectly: It is printed first onto a rubber blanket on a second cylinder, and then is *set off* (or offset) from the blanket onto the paper.

Sheet-fed offset puts one piece of paper at a time through the press; in the *web-fed* process printing is done onto a single strip of paper that feeds off a roll and is cut into a signature or pages only after it has been printed.

Letterpress

A very few publications are still printed by *letterpress*, the first, classical printing method. Also called *relief printing*, this method works like the familiar rubber stamp. Characters are raised from the bearing surface; they are inked by rollers and then deposit that ink when they come in contact with the printing paper. Originally the printer used 3-dimensional metal type—that invented by the great Johann Gutenberg in 1450—but today *plastic plates* do the job. They're made by the same photographic processes as offset plates.

Stencil Printing

The editor of a newsletter may also use a pasteup dummy, which will, of course, be fairly simple. More frequently the editor will write the story in exactly the form it will take in the finished product. When the page has been filled, it must either be retyped for camera copy or as a Mimeo stencil. Minor adjustments can be made in this final step.

In either technique, it is essential that the typewriter be thoroughly cleaned before retyping starts. And the type elements should be recleaned at least once for every page.

For Mimeographed newsletters, the nameplate can be printed by offset. Usually this is in a color other than black. Sometimes a new color is used every issue with up to four colors used alternately for the nameplate. Depending on the number of copies duplicated, usually it's most advantageous to have a full year's supply of such headed paper printed up at one time.

No matter what kind of publication or what kind of reproducing process is used, each of these steps is important and, although the editor may not do the actual work, he or she must know how it ought to be done so that proper standards can be attained. Otherwise the editor is often taken advantage of by craftsmen who insist that something is "impossible" when actually it's only inconvenient or demanding.

BROADSHEET PAGE is used by Southwire Company of Carrollton, Georgia. Company buys 15x22-inch page in "The Daily Times-Georgian" every Tuesday to carry company news. This is an excellent public relations program that acquaints community with company activities.

Chapter 4
The Editor

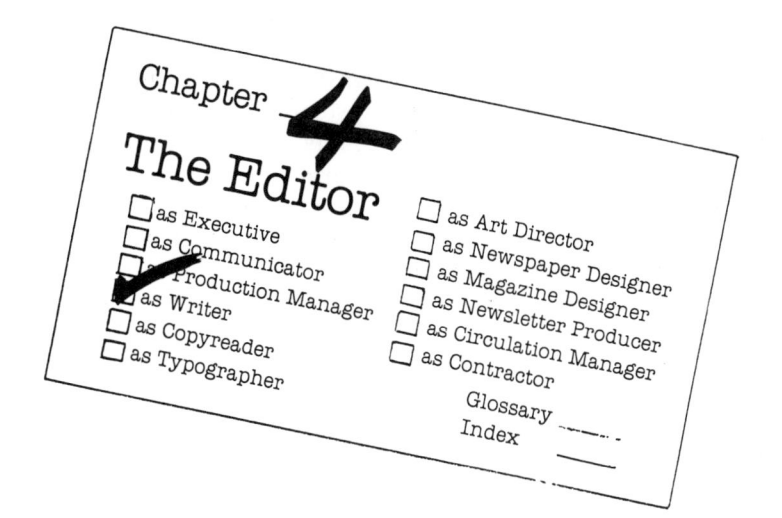

- [ ] as Executive
- [ ] as Communicator
- [x] as Production Manager
- [ ] as Writer
- [ ] as Copyreader
- [ ] as Typographer
- [ ] as Art Director
- [ ] as Newspaper Designer
- [ ] as Magazine Designer
- [ ] as Newsletter Producer
- [ ] as Circulation Manager
- [ ] as Contractor

Glossary
Index

In the athletic world, there are only a few player-coaches who not only practice but must teach their craft. In the communications world, practically every editor must perform those two functions.

On even the largest organizational publication, the editor does some writing; on most of them, the editor does much writing. All editors, no matter if their "staff" consists only of occasional, volunteer contributors, must set standards and coach the staff to attain them.

All this while, editors, as all serious writers do, must seek to improve their own writing skills.

We assume that the editor-writer knows the fundamentals of the craft: grammar, sentence construction, and—oh, how important—spelling. We shall leave those nuts-and-bolts instructions to the countless books on the subject. Here we shall concentrate on those aspects of writing that editors must convey by their coaching duties.

Newswriting

Organizational publications handle two kinds of basic information, hard news and soft. *Hard news* is straightforward reporting, usually serious and immediate. *Soft news* may be just as immediate and significant but is treated with a sugarcoating of human interest, writing tricks, and, often, humor. Hard news is objective and impersonal. Soft news is often subjective, at least to some extent. Newspapers and magazines handle both kinds of information, newsletters usually handle only hard news.

In newspapers hard news is usually written as an *inverted pyramid*. This style of story lists the facts in descending order of importance. In contrast, narrative treatment tells the story chronologically. And dramatic treatment builds the tale with flashbacks, cutaways, or other artful devices to a climax.

A conventional news story starts out with the most important element and continues by giving steadily less important details. The first paragraph (or paragraphs), called the *lead*, and pronounced *leed*, summarize what happened. The hurrying reader who absorbs only the lead, has all the salient facts. With an audience more and more accustomed to the very sketchy news coverage of the broadcast media, there is a sizable number who do read only the lead.

Another functional asset of the inverted pyramid is that it allows a story that must be cut to fit available space to be trimmed from the bottom. Then, no matter where it's cut, we know that only relatively secondary details have been lost.

Occasionally a news story will be told in straight narrative form. This is effective if the lead is strong and the writing appealing so that the reader will stay to the end. This technique is most effective when the narrative builds up to a climax. This style can clarify a series of complicated events with or without a summary lead.

The 5 Ws

Whatever the style in which it's written, a news report to be complete must give the 5 Ws. In an inverted pyramid, most, if not all, of these Ws must be in the lead.

The 5Ws are Who, What, Where, When, and Why (or How) Although this order does not necessarily imply rank by importance, it's proper that *Who* should come first. For people are always interested in other people. Indeed, it is the people involved that makes the reader interested in any story.

We're all interested in people close to us. As one editor observed, "If, when I come home tonight, my wife tells me my sister-in-law is going to have a baby, I'll be interested. But if she says, 'I'm pregnant!', I'll faint." We're also interested in famous or notorious people. Almost anything the President of the United States does is of interest to American readers; and anything that the current soap-opera queen or athletic idol does will interest a large segment of the public.

The *What* is, of course, the answer to the first question anyone asks: "What happened?" What happened may be the eruption of a volcano or the divorce of a pop singer. But unless something did happen, there is no news story, nor need for the other Ws.

When an event occurs determines whether it's news or history. Immediacy is an essential of news. While this is usually in the most immediate past, it is modified by the frequency of publication. For the afternoon *New York Post*, news is what happened in the past 12 hours; the other 12 hours is mainly the domain of the morning *Times*. For

Newsweek, the immediate is what happened in the past week; for a biweekly, "now" is in the past 14 days.

An event that happened some time ago may become immediate by its discovery or announcement. A Senate committee may uncover a peccadillo that happened months ago; suddenly it's news, the most immediate of news.

The importance of *Where* in a news story is capsulated by an old "news formula": *Interest is inversely proportionate to distance.* The shorter the distance, the greater the interest. Distance may be geographic or human. Our family is close to us, even though many miles separate its members. Viet Nam was as close as our living room during the agonizing 60s. Television breaks down mileage, too. But still, a fire in our building is of greater interest than a blaze a few blocks away; a tornado in our city overshadows one in Guatemala.

Why is always intriguing. It may be as important as why two nations have begun a war or as trivial as why a movie star is divorcing her fifth husband. How something happens or is done is often essential to our understanding.

A taut lead conveys the immediacy and excitement that grabs the reader. So the experienced reporter will often use only one or two Ws in the first paragraph and drop the others into the second or even third graf. Sometimes the "when" is omitted. This is frequently done by those periodicals which come out at long intervals. If we accept a definition that "news is anything that the reader is learning for the first time," then in a quarterly publication an event that took place 2½ months ago can be news. But often we will, instead of spelling out the time, say that it happened "recently." And where, in a daily newspaper, we'll say that something happened yesterday at 3:30 p.m., in a monthly we'd say only that it happened "in April."

The "who lead" and the "what lead" are generally the strongest attention-grabbers. "The President. . . ." or "The Pope. . . ." or "Dolly Parton. . . ." will attract at least fleeting attention. "Man walked on the moon. . . .", "General Hospital will install a $1.5 million x-ray movie system. . . .", "Fire destroyed all pension records. . . ."—any of these statements will rivet attention and whet appetites for details.

When and *where* make the weakest leads. The absolutely surest way to turn off a reader is by the "minutes of the last meeting" approach. "At 4:11 p.m. last Tuesday, employees of Transmogrified Metals, Inc., were assembled in the fifth-floor conference room. Chairman William McLeod opened the meeting with a review of last year's operations. Treasurer Sandra Gavin presented the financial report of the company. . . .and so on and so on. Then George Bewick, president, announced that the factory would be closed permanently."

Once in a great while, the exact time or place is the nub of a story. "At 2:15 a.m. Tuesday, all power will be turned off for 20 minutes as a new

68 EDITING THE ORGANIZATIONAL PUBLICATION

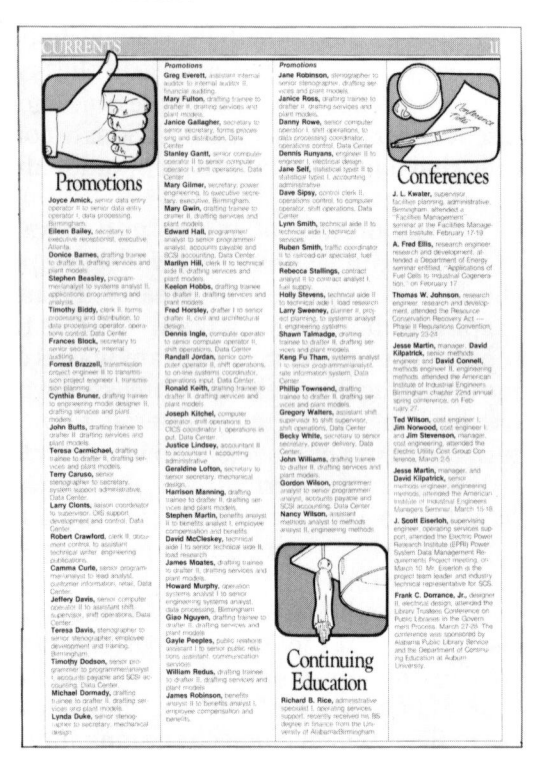

PERSONAL NEWS—staple in most organizational publications—is handled simply but made attractive by interesting ideograms in "Inside" of Southern Company Services, Atlanta.

electric supply line is connected." Here time is important and the "when lead" makes sense. Or "The employee parking lot will be barricaded 100 feet to the left of the main entrance to protect autos against possible damage when blasting occurs for the new wing of the Morrison building." Always as the lead is composed mentally, the writer must decide which of the Ws is the most important or most interesting.

Why or *how* are not widely used because reporters have discovered that these are most often not of the greatest importance.

The Ws provide an excellent checklist for the reporter gathering facts, the writer organizing a story, the editor checking it for completeness.

Soft News

Hard news, written straightforwardly in the inverted pyramid can report anything from a fender-bender to a war. Soft news—also called *features*—has just as wide a range. Most commonly identified as features are *human-interest* stories, those which are low in importance but high in interest. The fact that Sarah Alexander in Surgery raises 12-foot sunflowers won't affect the course of human events even a little bit; but it makes pleasant reading to learn that she attributes this horticultural achievement to the Elvis Presley songs she sings to the plants every evening at sundown. People like to read about people; just what they read is usually insignificant.

That's why *surveys* are so popular; people like to know what other people think. In Chapter 2 we noted requirements for scientific surveys. But we can be as unscientific as a witch doctor and still interest our readers by conducting utterly random surveys. *Inquiring-photographer* and *man-on-the-street* features are highly popular in daily newspapers and they can be as appealing in the organizational publication. The opinion of any four or five of our peers on any topic of current interest will please us. Such informal surveys need not be, and don't purport to be, an accurate cross section of our world. But we enjoy learning that one employee's favorite Christmas delicacy is Austrian gingerbread while another's is hot toddy.

Anniversaries and historical milestones make good feature material. On the 25th anniversary of our organization, we can spin a fascinating yarn from the highlights of that earlier year. The 100th anniversary of the discovery of radium can become a personal holiday for employees of a hospital that now uses that element routinely.

Interpretive reporting combines the hard factuality of straight news with the writer's personal explanation of the significance of the event. The value of such a story depends, of course, on the qualifications of the writer, either in analyzing a situation or in researching others' evaluations. This journalistic form is often poorly defined. The label is often tagged to a "think piece," the thoughts of the writer, strictly extemporaneous, off the top of the head and without authority or even accuracy. The "new journalism" of the past decade was all too often simply verbal diarrhea that belied the sanctimonious objective to "tell it like it is." Too often it was "tell it like I think it is" or, even worse, "tell it like I want it to be."

Backgrounders bring the reader up to date on events that we anticipate will reach some conclusion in the near future. Officials of our company might, for instance, ask for rezoning of our area so a research building can be erected in the parking lot and the adjacent block made available for parking. A backgrounder might tell how the company came to locate where it is, how the city's zoning was planned and

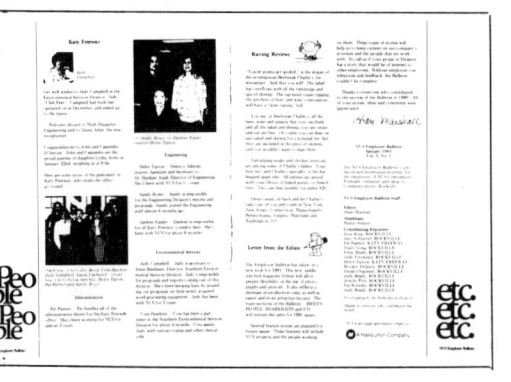

PERSONAL NEWS is carried without headlines in "NUS Employee Bulletin" of NUS Corporation, Rockville, Maryland. Marginal logos in lower outside corners of page, as well as identifying sections, make pleasant patterns.

legislated, how other expansions were handled, how successful rezoning requests were in the past, etc. Then, as the city council schedules hearings on the question and prepares to vote on it, our readers know what it's all about.

Advance stories tell about events that are going to happen, rather than those that have occurred. In many instances, advances contain background information as well.

The old "house organ" was disparaged for its "bowling, babies, and balderdash" contents. Granted that these are but side dishes to a menu of more substantial news, their value shouldn't be underestimated. *Personals* still have high readership. These short items about people in our organization have a legitimate place in most publications. Of course, the editor must have some criteria for personals. If somebody catches an 8-pound trout it might be worth a sentence or two; that someone visited his brother in Grand Rapids over the weekend is too trivial even for a column of froth.

Items a bit more substantial than simple personals are called *brights*. If our organization was hit by a flood, we can round up reports of how various departments reacted. If the summer brought severe drought, we can report the effects that it had on branches throughout the country.

We also round up very short reports by subject matter or treatment. A list of promotions, for instance, if not just a tabulation, can be a *roundup*. A group of brights or humorous items can be packaged as a roundup. The technique is a good way to handle items in sizes so small that they might be lost or overlooked if handled individually.

Organizational publications rarely use *commentary* material. As we've noted, very few carry editorials. Few carry *reviews*, critical evaluations of any of the arts. Many periodicals use a straight-news report on performances. "The General Corporation Employee Club presented its annual Musicade review. . . ." Few editors—and usually with good reason—have the audacity to evaluate performances.

Opinions are usually permitted in personal *columns*. Wherever personal value judgments are made, there must be a by-line to identify the evaluator. It's fairly common to carry disclaimers: "Opinions given on this page (or in this report) are those of the writer and do not necessarily reflect those of *MG News* or Media Generating Inc."

Often even the hardest news may be treated in at least partial feature style. Or the lead may be one other than the summary of the inverted pyramid. Whatever the technique, the aim is always the same: to give a complete and accurate account in a manner that will hold reader attention till all the information has been transmitted.

A major difference between a magazine article and a news story is the length. In a magazine we assume the reader has more time and is willing to spend it in a more leisurely reception of information. The

SHORT ITEMS are rounded-up and ornamented with colorful ideograms in "Eagle" of Anheuser-Busch Companies, Inc., St. Louis. "What's News" logo, horizontal rules, and first initial of each story are in bright blue. Page: 11x15½, on cream paper.

magazine writer is not under the intense deadline pressure of a newspaper because immediacy is not as pressing a factor for a magazine. With longer lead time, the magazine writer has more time for research, for organizing, for writing and—most important—for rewriting.

Magazine articles tend more to chronological writing although the author can use many techniques. A good article has been likened to a good movie. We open with an episode that sets the scene or the era or the mood. We tell a story, generally moving it along chronologically but occasionally using flashbacks, either to emphasize what's happening right now or to fill in background details. We build up to subclimaxes, holding and intensifying the viewer's interest. We show small details that illuminate characters or events or are just interesting in themselves.

We involve the reader, trying to place him or her in the place of a character on the screen or the printed page. We suggest—usually between the lines—"what's in it for me."

We shift from scene to scene as smoothly as possible. A movie director often uses similar visual forms to link scenes: A tree in a pastoral scene is reiterated by a tower in the following urban episode, etc. In writing we repeat phrases or words or verbal images as transition between paragraphs.

Finally we build to the climax. Usually there is a brief conclusion to pick up loose threads and to explain just what's been happening. A good magazine piece always has a strong—clarifying and resolving—closing paragraph.

Whatever the subject matter or the style of presentation, the paramount aim of the writer is accuracy and clarity. The search for accuracy is not an easy one; humans become subjectively involved in anything that interests them and the objectivity of absolute accuracy must be imposed by the writer upon the writer. At the earliest stages of reporting, the writer must learn to be wary of eyewitness accounts; for too many people don't see anything; many see only what they want to see; most see what they would like to see. Even the writer's own observations of an event will be colored by the personal filters through which we all view life.

Accuracy is most important in details. Major data tend to impose accuracy. It's rather hard to be inaccurate when we describe the eruption of Mt. St. Helens; its magnitude keeps us from calling it a tornado or a tidal wave. But whether the ash was gray or glowing when it hit the ground, whether a victim wore a ski suit or whether the clothing was burned beyond recognition, whether the road was washed out by a flooded river or blocked by a landslide—these are the kinds of details that are often misreported.

Yet it is inaccuracy of detail that infuriates the reader. "If this lousy newspaper can't even get my brother-in-law's middle initial right, or makes my address 415 instead of 417, how can I be sure it reports anything else accurately?"

One of the first demonstrations of accuracy is correct spelling. Spelling errors are not just forgivable aberrations; they are inaccuracies. The writer must spell correctly no matter how many trips to the dictionary it requires.

Grammar

In the same way, correct grammar is necessary for accuracy. If the reader wonders whom "he" refers to, information may be distorted. If a modifier can logically affect two or more words, the writer puts on the reader the burden of correct interpretation. But the writer can't transpose the sin of inaccuracy onto the reader.

Correct grammar not only contributes to accuracy, it is essential to clarity. The rules of grammar were not imposed by ivory-tower dwellers, but evolved logically in the search for clarity.

Played-by-ear spelling and faulty grammar are the indelible mark of a slovenly, undisciplined writer. Editors must purge their own writing of these mortal sins and demand the same high standards of staffers.

All of this means, of course, that at the writer's elbow must be a dictionary and a grammar book. The dictionary should be unabridged and there are many excellent editions to choose from.

An excellent grammar book is *Writers' Guide and Index to English Usage* by William Perrin. So are *Grammar for Journalists* by E. L. Callihan and *Language Skills for Journalists* by R. Thomas Berner.

The journalist needs good and constantly accessible reference material. So the desk-side library should include books like *Roget's Thesaurus*; the *Columbia Encyclopedia*, which is now available even in paperback; *The World Almanac*; and a good atlas. A good book of quotations is helpful; *Bartlett's* is the classic but there are several other good ones.

Stylebooks of the Government Printing Office and the University of Chicago are excellent basic documents although they must be modified to local usage.

Other essential reference materials are the current organizational chart and list of officers of your organization, as complete a list as possible of employees, telephone numbers of key sources of organizational information, annual reports for as long a period as available, and biographical data on as many people as possible.

The Morgue

The irreplaceable, specific reference is the publication's *morgue*, a file of its own stories. The simplest is a set of back copies and a card file listing all stories. The most complete is a set of envelopes containing the clippings from the publication, filed by subject and name.

Information can be filed under subject heads: Sales, Branch Offices, Shipping, Christmas Parties, etc. Other matter is filed under the names of the involved people. When an issue of the periodical comes off the press, the editor goes through every story and underlines the name or word under which the article should be filed. A single story will usually be filed under several headings: When the president of the company tells about plans for a new building at a branch installation, his name, expansion, research, the name of the distant community, and perhaps some other general topics would all be underlined. The same procedure is used for pictures.

With a simple card index, on the card for Research, for instance, we'd note "NEW BUILDING, Big Rapids, Mich., Dec. 12, 1981, Pg. 3, col. 2." Usually the headline and story will be readily recognized from this information. If this isn't the case, the headline might be included in the notation: NEW RESEARCH FACILITY/ PLANNED FOR MICHIGAN.

For the clipping file, the story is cut out—as many clips as are needed—and filed in a labelled envelope. This requires a lot of cutting and filing, of course, but when the writer wants information on Research, for instance, all the stories are right there. With a card index, the writer must look up each noted story in bound files of the publication.

Some morgues use envelopes of different colors to facilitate the writer's search. General topics such as Research, Pensions, etc., are filed in pink envelopes, for instance; biographical material is filed in yellow ones.

Pictures are handled a bit differently. Usually negatives—along with the clipping and contact prints of unused shots—are stored in envelopes of a distinctive color. Filing by date is best; all of the pictures shot for one issue are in one envelope. Cutlines for the picture which was used are filed, or are listed on file cards as ordinary clips, under topic headings.

Like any craftsman, a writer must have adequate tools to do the best possible job and the basic reference toolbox just suggested should be conveniently available to all writers, staff and volunteer.

Writing is a creative art that, though it can't be taught, can be learned. There are many good books which will help in the learning. The editor should be familiar with these guides, both to improve personal writing and also to help tutor staff writers. Two are worth special mention: *The Elements of Style*, a classic by William Strunk, Jr., and E. B. White, and *On Writing Well* by William Zinsser.

The ultimate textbook for the writer is writing, by anybody on any topic. We ought to read constantly. Writers can learn from any kind of material, including fiction and poetry.

Our local papers will have staff writers and columnists whom we admire and enjoy reading. Even as we absorb the information they transmit, we ought to analyze their techniques and make note how we can adopt them for our own writing. As we do so, we enhance our own enjoyment, for we get pleasure at two levels: that of every reader who receives interesting material and that of one professional appreciating another's mastery.

Writers ought to devour all the professional publications in their field. They learn about subject matter that way, of course, but they also learn—by good and bad example—how to convey that specialized matter to the reader.

As it is for any artist, though, the most important factor in attaining and maintaining excellence is constant practice. Yet this is the area where the typical organizational writer is most lax. Most of us believe that the writing we do every day on our job is sufficient to keep us sharp. Not so! We can hone our skills by writing in different styles and on different subjects than our workaday activities require or permit.

A daily "journal" becomes an invaluable self-teaching device if the writer has the self-discipline to write something every day. It may be as brief as an apt simile or a well-polished phrase. It may be a factual account of something that occurred during the day or a personal essay on a subject that intrigued us. It may be expository writing done to challenge our minds. (Try to instruct someone, without a diagram, how to tie a shoelace or how to rollerskate!) It may be fiction or poetry. The subject is not important, the self-disciplined writing is.

Most writers, unfortunately, resist even the idea of this additional writing. But the comparatively few who do use this tool are highly enthusiastic. The first month of a journal is the crucial one; the writer must compose something every day with absolutely no exception. By the end of this period, the habit is usually so well ingrained that it becomes a painless exercise. The best way is to write at the same time every day. When depends on your own daily cycle. The important thing is to write and write and write. . .and then write some more.

Pump Primers

Sometimes the most difficult writing problem occurs even before the writing does—getting started. It's been said that one of mankind's most horrifying prospects is that of putting down a mark on a sheet of empty paper, be it by a painter, a composer, an architect, or a writer. Yet a major difference between the professional and the amateur is the ability—or willingness—to work when you prefer not to work. Deadlines will not stretch to allow long waits for the muse to descend and anoint our brows. When inspiration fails, perspiration must produce acceptable writing.

Writing the first sentence of a story—worse yet, the first sentence of the day—can be an excruciating task. Most professional writers have a pet device for priming the pump.

Some writers will stop at the end of a page, preferably in the middle of a sentence. Come tomorrow morning, it's obvious what the first words on that blindingly blank piece of paper will be. Other writers think out but don't actually type out the last sentence of the day. But it will be fresh in your mind the next morning and you're off and typing. These are good devices for a continuing project that requires overnight interruptions. But starting an individual story may be more difficult.

A colleague once insisted, "Some pieces of paper just don't want to be written on." His solution to that situation was simply to roll a fresh piece into the typewriter. Or many pieces. . .until he found a friendly sheet.

When another writer was asked to comment on this technique, she said, "Be sure to throw away all uncooperative paper. I always start writing on the back of waste paper; when I strip files I keep old letters just for occasions like this. When you don't give a darn about wasting good stationery, the words come easier. And it's painless to throw away a bad start."

Unfortunately, this doesn't work for most of us. Even worse than the temporary delay is the fear that often gnaws on writers: "Has the well run dry? Is this the start of permanent writer's block?" Such doubt is self-inflating and can soon become a downright phobia.

The writer must remember that our creative, communicative processes don't wear out. The horrible historic examples of the burnt-out writer involve physical processes not mental ones. Fatigue, sickness, alcohol, drugs, or gluttony can diminish the body's ability to handle the production of the brain. But unless there is genuine mental illness, the creative wellsprings do not dry up.

So the first thing when a temporary block occurs: Don't sweat!

Forget about the story you're supposed to do. Instead, write a letter to a friend. Actually write: "Dear Dale, I'm supposed to be writing a story about a new pension plan for our company. Seems a bunch of experts came up with a new formula that will pay off more generous benefits on retirement while requiring no extra contribution by us employees. I wondered how this could be until I talked to Philip Cutsforth, an actuary in our Personnel Dept. He told me. . . ."

This "letter" will usually structure the story properly, lift the most important items to the top, present those details which the reader is most interested in. Conversion into a story is easy.

Another interesting self-starter is to reduce a story to a telegram, writing it without articles, conjunctions, and complex verb forms. Again this is often all the stimulus needed to produce a conventional story.

Still another good starter is to do the lead of a story to feature each of the 5 Ws. Who? "Michael McFarland, director of personnel, announced a new pension plan. . . ."

What? "A new pension plan will go into effect. . . ."

Where? "In five of the 12 divisions of United Conglomerate, a new pension plan. . . ."

When? "At midnight on June 30, new provisions of the company pension plan will go into effect. . . ."

Why? "To give employees a new hedge against post-retirement inflation. . . ."

Or the last lead may be based on How? "By using a complicated technique of matching investment maturity dates to expected retirements, the company pension plan can. . . ."

Few leads written to formula are usable as-is. Some require only a little polishing, others may suggest different, and better, approaches. Our "who lead," "Michael McFarland, announced. . . ." is so pedestrian it eliminates itself. But it might suggest that our Who? could be Marilyn Vuentes who actually worked out all the new numbers. Or, better yet, we might start with the ultimate Who? "Bethina Groves will find an extra $47.29 in her pension check next July. . . ."

Mental pump priming is like physical pump priming. Pour in enough water and water will come out the spout; pour information into your brain and eventually it will flow back with minimum pumping. So, when a story won't flow voluntarily, pour in more information. If you're writing about your own specific retirement plan, consult an encyclopedia and find out when pensions first were established. If you note that someone wrote the definitive treatise on pensions in 1847, look into a history book and see what else happened in '47. Don't worry about serendipity, it's an excellent idea-starter.

Teachers often use epigrams to implant ideas in students' minds. Editors might well remind their staffs—and themselves—of one formula that sets us on such a logical course of reporting that we rarely meet writing blocks:

Find out;
Sort out;
Think out;
Write out.

The good reporter generally soaks up all the information available on the subject at hand, on the principle that nobody ever had too much information for a story.

It's easy—in fact necessary—to leave out material on purpose. But when a writer has to leave out essential information because it wasn't revealed in the basic reporting process, the story suffers.

However, all writers will admit that doing additional research—like sharpening all the pencils and neatly arranging all the paperclips—can sometimes be one of those procrastination rituals that keep us away from doing our work. With experience, the writer learns to recognize the point of diminishing returns—when to stop reading through the files, fascinating though they may be, and get on with the blankety-blank story.

The reporter is the first of many *gatekeepers* in the communications process. Reporters close the gate to unessential information as they sort out the whole harvest of information they've gleaned. The copyreader, the editor, the publisher—sometimes even the corporate lawyer—close the gate, not only to a few bits of information but to phrases, sentences, paragraphs, and even whole stories. The sorting-out process, the allocation of priorities, is just about the highest mental exercise an intelligent person can perform.

As the reporter sorts out raw data, the organization of it is already taking place. The skilled reporter "composes" the story mentally, choosing the most important facet for the lead, giving priorities to the 5 Ws, weaving quotations into the account, and even composing apt and colorful phrases. Reporters on dailies usually do this as they return to their office from the scene of the event. Some of them will speak their story aloud to determine if it "reads" well.

Then the "writing out" phase becomes merely a typewriting process. Of course, creativity still works in this final stage as the writer makes last-minute changes. Actually all the processes may take place almost

Time For A Quiz

How good a reporter are you? Here's a chance to test yourself. At the right is a sample of the type of stories frequently submitted to the *Emhart News* editors. There are some glaring omissions. Can you spot them? After you've tried, read below for the answers, and a look at how the story should have been written.

Read This First →

XYZ Division Announces Receipt Of Large Order

SOMEWHERE, U.S.A. — The XYZ Division, 7 Main St., Somewhere, has announced that after long negotiations and many business trips by its top executives a "very large" contract has been signed to supply goods to China.

"This is a milestone in our company's long, proud history. We are pleased to be back in China," said XYZ President J.M. Smith Sr. "With the additional hiring required by the heavy volume of this contract with China we will have to double our workforce, perhaps even put an addition onto the plant. We will be the biggest employer in Somewhere."

XYZ is a manufacturer of chop sticks and jet aircraft. The Chinese contract is the largest in the history of the company, said President Smith. "The long-range terms of the contract mean that we have a great future. We will work closely with the Chinese to supply them with quality American-made goods. We believe this is the start of a long and productive business relationship for both parties."

The first shipment of goods to China is scheduled to be on its way by July 1. President Smith said that the Chinese have made arrangements for United States President Jimmy Carter and Chinese Deputy Prime Minister Teng Hsiao-ping to attend ceremonies commemorating the first shipment.

The XYZ Division will also open 127 offices in China. said President Smith.

Here's What Was Missing →

- How much money is involved in the contract?
- Is XYZ an Emhart company? No mention is made of Emhart.
- What kind of goods are going to be supplied to China? Chop sticks? Jet aircraft? Both?
- How many new employees will be hired? How many are there now?
- How large will the addition be? What will it cost?
- How many years does the "long-range" contract cover?
- How long did negotiations take? How many business trips were made and to where?
- If the company is pleased to be back in China, when was it previously there?
- Why is XYZ opening 127 offices in China? Who will staff them?
- Also missing: a tie-in with the recent expansion of trade by China; some history about XYZ and its product.

REPORTERS' QUIZ is given in special correspondents issue of "Emhart News," of Emhart Corporation, Hartford, Connecticut. Typical story by volunteer correspondent is analyzed and suggestions are given how to improve it. Copyrighted and used by courtesy of Emhart Corporation.

Write It This Way →

Remember To Include:
- **Who?**
- **What?**
- **When?**
- **Where?**
- **Why?**

XYZ Lands China Order; Huge Expansion Planned

SOMEWHERE, U.S.A. — Emhart's XYZ Division, here, has signed a 17-year, $100-million contract to supply chop sticks to the People's Republic of China.

The contract, largest in the company's history, is going to mean a doubling of the plant's manufacturing space, the hiring of twice as many workers, and a visit from President Jimmy Carter.

Carter is scheduled to visit the plant on July 15, along with Teng Hsiao-ping, deputy prime minister of China, to test the first China-bound chop sticks.

Construction of a $500,000 addition will begin next month, according to John M. Smith Sr., XYZ president. When completed the plant will occupy 100,000 square feet and employ 500. The doubling of the workforce will make XYZ the largest employer in Somewhere.

The XYZ Division will also open 127 offices in China to provide technical assistance to customers. Current employees will be given the first opportunities to staff those offices.

"This is a milestone in our company's history," said Smith, "and a great leap forward for the Chinese in their plans to make a greater use of Western technology." Smith noted that the U.S. and China have recently established diplomatic relations and that China plans to spend up to $65 billion on industrial expansion.

The contract calls for XYZ to supply 450,000 sets of chop sticks a year to China. This will represent about 75 percent of XYZ's annual output after the plant expansion.

Smith said that the contract was signed after 10 months of negotiations. "I made three trips to China and representatives of the China National Chop Stick Export and Import Office were here in Somewhere twice. The initial contact was made by the Chinese, who were impressed with our preeminence in chop stick technology," said Smith.

Since the XYZ company was formed in 1858, about 150 million sets of chop sticks have been manufactured, says Smith. "We actually sold several thousand in China back in the 1870s but had to cut out that market in order to meet the domestic demand," said Smith.

XYZ was acquired by Emhart in 1975.

---

simultaneously or alternately throughout all the four operations.

As the writer copyreads the typed manuscript further polishing-up may take place. Often paragraphs are rearranged, either as the writer shifts emphases a little or to make smoother transitions between grafs or scenes. For most of us, this involves scissors and paste pots; those who work on word-processing machines can make such changes with little effort.

It is the editor's responsibility to establish a tone of voice for a publication, a flavor of writing. It may be one as breathless as a fan magazine, snide as *Mother Jones*, omniscient as *Time*, militant as *Ms.*, or sophisticated as *The New Yorker*.

Best, it should be warm. That doesn't mean gushing or studiedly folksy. It means that it is obviously written for and about people by other people who care about people. This feeling can be conveyed by many styles of writing and it can be achieved even in periodicals of such highly technical or specialized nature that our first fear is that they are permanently dehumanized.

Jeffery Holmes, Director of Education, Science and Culture for Statistics Canada, puts it well: "[Organizational] writing is about people, for people: members, shareholders, employees, customers, retailers. Your reader is as individual as you are. Write for him, write for her. One trick is to take a photo of two or three target readers, enlarge, and pin on the wall above your typewriter. Write for them, not for the ceiling."

After judging a Silver Leaf writing competition for Canadian members of the International Association of Business Communicators, he said: "You can't beat simple, direct prose. A straightforward, factual account of treating cows for low milk yields scored as high with me as a poetic description of oil exploration in the Arctic wilderness. Writers who lost points were those who would not trust the facts to sell themselves and who resorted to grandiose introductions designed to impress.

"Related to those who want to impress their readers are those who want to impress the boss...usually by doing a taped interview. But a chief executive who, presumably, carries on a normal conversation while striking a million-dollar deal, seems to succumb to an attack of cliche rampant when faced with the editor of a company magazine and a tape recorder. If you are going to interview the boss, or other brass, have the guts to turn it into English before you publish. He'll probably think that that's what he said anyway. And remember that facts speak louder than puffs."

Actually, while it has many merits, the taped interview is no bright star in the crown of a writer. Simply to transcribe the tape makes the "reporter" merely a stenographer. There may be some slight creativity in dreaming up the questions and asking them in some logical sequence, yet the writer ought to play a more important role than straight man to the top banana.

The writer should create a sound narrative instead of the transcribed Q&As. There should be a description of the subject of the interview and, if it contributes to making the account more lifelike, of the setting. Direct quotes, embraced by quotation marks, have far more appeal than the stark words after "Answer." Some quotes are best in the indirect form. Many questions need not be repeated verbatim.

The writer should rearrange the interview so it flows logically from one topic to another. Often several answers can be blended into a single, more compelling statement.

This is not considered to be "misquoting," particularly in an organizational publication where presumably the interview subject and the writer are both on the same side. Especially when the subject will

CORRESPONDENTS' INSTRUCTIONS are given in special issue of "Emhart News." Regular staff of seasoned newspapermen is headed by George Thomas Chappell and maintains high quality of work by volunteer correspondents. This issue is copyrighted and used by courtesy of Emhart Corporation, Hartford, Connecticut.

review the finished product before publication, you do not risk the subsequent charge that you "manipulated" the words to twist their meaning.

The writer should explain allusions and references just as they'd be explained in a straight news story.

And always, the subject must be portrayed as a human being addressing other humans. The computer-to-computer flavor of so many taped interviews is a chilling turn-off.

Good writing is that which touches the human mind. . .and the human heart. Any style of writing that does so—even if it's that which we call "corny"—is good writing, the kind the editor should encourage on every page—indeed, in every paragraph—of the organizational periodical.

The best publication is that which is written like, anticipated like, and read like a letter from home.

Chapter 5

The Editor

- [ ] as Executive
- [ ] as Communicator
- [ ] as Production Manager
- [ ] as Writer
- [x] as Copyreader
- [ ] as Typographer
- [ ] as Art Director
- [ ] as Newspaper Designer
- [ ] as Magazine Designer
- [ ] as Newsletter Producer
- [ ] as Circulation Manager
- [ ] as Contractor

Glossary
Index

In no other stage of a publication does the editor have to combine craft and art as in the final handling of written copy. As a "copyreader," the editor must be a skilled craftsman; as an "editor," he or she must be an artist.

The copyreader has the responsibility of assuring that the manuscript is accurate, clear, and interesting while following a consistent style. The "editor" is a creative collaborator with the writer.

Let's look first at the copyreading function because it is easier to define and perform.

It includes some purely mechanical operations. The copyreader has a set of marks, similar to those of the proofreader, that assure that any and all changing of the manuscript is done so clearly that corrections are neither overlooked nor misread.

While tradition has it that the editor wields a blue pencil or a fat graphite one, in actual practice a ballpoint pen is probably the most efficient. This requires copy at least double spaced and, if your typewriter is capable, 2½ spacing is better.

All copy should be identified in the top left corner with the *slug line* (the story's label throughout production), the name of the writer, and the issue for which it's planned. If the story runs longer than a page, the bottom of each page except the last should indicate that with the notation (MORE). Succeeding pages are slugged and numbered. Often, for no obviously logical reason, pages are indicated by a plethora of numbers: 22222, 33333, etc. The end of a story is marked with a *30-mark*—the plain number 30, the same in Roman numerals, XXX, or any striking symbol like ##############. Sometimes the first page may be indicated as "1 of 4." Immediately everyone handling this copy knows that there are four sheets; should one be missing, the search can be mounted before the loss is irretrievable.

Electronic Editing

Electronic editing is coming to organizational publications much more rapidly than it did to commercial ones. Many an organizational newspaper with a circulation of, say, 2,000, has electronic tools while commercial newspapers of thrice that circulation are still using paper and pencil. This is because the organization often has word-processing and computer systems into which the editor may plug in.

Organizational editors don't seem to be quite as afraid of these electronic monsters as their daily-newspaper counterparts were a decade ago. This is smart; for the change from a typewriter to a word processor is just a change of tools, as was the change from handwriting to typewriting. The real function of the editor has not changed at all.

The basic machine for electronic editing is the video display terminal, called VDT or just "the tube." This is like a conventional electric typewriter with a few additional keys. As a story is typed, instead of producing a typewritten manuscript, *hard copy*, the machine puts the characters on a video screen. Changes can be made as readily as—and in many instances, much more easily than—with the traditional pencil or pen. A tiny square of light, the *cursor*, is moved to the point where the change is to be made; there material can be added in any quantity from a letter to a paragraph or more. Phrases and paragraphs can be shifted; the cursor indicates the beginning and end of the material to be moved and where it should go.

Simple typing errors are corrected even more easily. If the writer has typed "boy" instead of "bay," the cursor is merely moved over the offending *o;* the *a* key is struck; the correction has been made.

When the writer has finished writing and correcting a story, it is stored in the electronic memory of a computer. When the copyreader is ready to work on it, the story is called up and appears on the editor's video screen. When the editing process is complete, the editor may have the machine produce a hard copy, or it may make a *perforated tape* of paper, magnetic plastic tape, or a *floppy disk*, a pancake-sized limp phonograph record, which can then be used to actuate the typesetting machine. The hard copy may be used for conventional typesetting. In many instances there is no intermediate product; the information goes directly from the computer to the typesetting machine—even at a distant point—by *hard wiring*, a simple electric or telephone circuit. So the original writer becomes the ultimate typesetter just as the copyreader also became the proofreader.

Despite inflation, the cost of word processors is coming down steadily and more and more organizational publications may well anticipate their use in the not-very-distant future. In most instances there are distinct economic advantages that can be sold to management on a sheer dollars-and-cents basis. The advantages of saving time and increasing editorial control over the whole typesetting function may not be quite as obvious to management, but they are real to the editor and well worth conducting a campaign for.

The physical aspects of copyreading are not, of course, nearly as important as the mental ones.

The ideal copyreader should have superior knowledge of, and high appreciation for, the English language; have an inquisitive mind with a healthy skepticism; must thrive on detail; must be, in fact, a "nit picker" who realizes that it is the painstaking attention to detail that assures quality.

The Editing Process

While every copy editor will develop a personal procedure, here is a 10-step approach that is an excellent beginning. It is suggested by Dr. William Turpin, a longtime working journalist, now a professor and assistant chairman of the School of Mass Communications at Virginia Commonwealth University, who is acknowledged to be one of the very best teachers of editing in the country.

1. Read the story for content.
2. Decide what's to be done with the story, on which page it will be placed, how it will be displayed, what will illustrate it. (This step will most usually apply to newspaper stories; much earlier planning of magazine pieces usually includes such details.)
3. Make sure that the story is put together logically and that there is a natural flow from part to part, paragraph to paragraph.
4. Edit for style.
5. Edit for desired length. Ideally a story or article should be as long as it has to be. The old saying applies: "A good story should be like a bikini bathing suit. Short enough to be interesting, long enough to cover all the vital points." If possible, avoid a first editing of a piece to fill a specific hole. Leave such major surgery until its need is unavoidable.
6. Edit for accuracy of statements, claims, denials, etc.
7. Edit for the public interest. The reader is entitled to objectivity, fairness, responsibility, good taste and tone and completeness.
8. Edit the language for simplicity, clarity and correct spelling, punctuation and grammar.
9. Edit for meaning in selection of words, presenting ideas, and achieving impact.
10. Read for a final scrutiny to assure that the whole thing has properly "jelled." Often all technical requisites have been met and all individual parts are acceptable yet they fail to blend into an integrated whole.

The first two steps of copyediting are highly subjective. As we read a story we sense its qualities. Some editors say they "taste" a story; others "smell" or "feel" it. Whatever the process, it's certainly a difficult one to describe but it's true that experience enables us to do a constantly better job.

The evaluation of a story or article and its handling is also a subjective decision that, at least in part, has been addressed in Chapter 2.

In the third step, editing for organization, we ask a series of questions: Does the lead get to the point? Quickly? Does it pique curiosity, pulling the reader inexorably into the next paragraphs? Does it give all the Ws? If not, is there a logical reason for the omission? Is the lead too long or too short? Is it too wordy? (Remember that even a short lead may be wordy.) Is the lead people-oriented?

Then we consider: Does the story have a functional outline? Does it take the reader in a natural flow to an appropriate destination? Does the story give the reader a reward for having read it?

Style

To edit for style, there must be a style. *Style* is not a journalistic decalogue; there are no moral implications in it. We may say "Fayette Street, Fayette St., Fayette street, Fayette st." or even just plain "Fayette" with no fear of mortal or cosmic punishment. Any one of these variations is correct. But we choose just one form because consistency makes it easier for the reader.

Every publication must have a *stylebook*. For most of us, it is probably best to adopt the Associated Press-United Press International stylebook. Because the two major news services have collaborated on this guide and because most American newspapers use it, the style it specifies is most familiar to the reader of our publication, too. (In Canada, Canadian Press has a compatible stylebook.) The cost is low and it's realistic to provide every writer with a copy.

The editor should revise this guide to meet the specific needs of the organizational publication. Especially if yours is a new industry or interest, it probably has a vocabulary that hasn't yet been formalized by a regular dictionary. Variations of spelling and, especially, in hyphenation and capitalization are many and must be standardized.

Titles

Most commercial publications capitalize "President" only when referring to the chief executive of the United States. But some organizations prefer to cap titles of their own officers; such variations must be noted. Abbreviations that would be totally unacceptable in a general publication may well be common fare in a periodical of a technically oriented organization.

Titles can be a pesky problem for an editor. Organizations tend to use encyclopedic titles: Second Assistant Vice-President in Charge of Carbon Paper and Timeclocks," for instance. Or "Vice-President/Sales" (with or without the hyphen) or "Vice-President: Sales" (or some other punctuational aberration). Not only must spelling, capping, and punctuation follow the party line, placement of the title should be consistent. Long titles should be used after the name for clarity.

"Doctor" is a title that prickles with protocol. We award it without thinking to physicians but after that comes indecision. Should we so designate psychiatrists, psychologists, or other ists who are at least in the outer courts of the health services? Religious and academic people are routinely identified as "doctor" but lawyers, who in most cases are "doctors of jurisprudence," are never so referred to.

Editors of publications for hospitals, research institutions and the like have to designate people with doctorates in research, a title which they have earned with more than a modicum of labor and of which they are justifiably proud. Do we then designate between "Dr. Jane Jones," an M.D. intern in obstetrics, and "Dr. Sigismund Kasler," a Ph.D. Nobel laureate in cancer research? Or do we make any distinction between "doctors"?

Editors serving a constituency which includes many military people have to decide on abbreviations of rank. Those used by the services are often too cryptic for the general public. So if the editor has many nonservice readers, it would probably be best to use "civilian" abbreviations. They will be readily intelligible to military personnel, too.

Only short and common titles are used in first reference: Dr., Sen., Mayor, Lt., etc. Clerics are correctly referred to as: *the* Rev. William J. Smith rather than just "Rev."

In normal, educated American usage, we do not use "Mr." for the first designation. Some editors feel a logical need for this title. High school publications, for instance, use it to show that "Mr. James Rivers" is an adult while "James Rivers" is a student. But, unless such distinction is logical and necessary, it's best to eliminate "Mr." in first reference and use only a man's full name: William J. Smith.

More and more editors—although it is not yet a normal convention—use just the name, "Mary P. Brown," for women, too. Short titles, of course, are used the same for both sexes: "Gov. Janet Small" or "Gov. John Small."

No matter whether a title is used in first reference or not, we should avoid identification of a person with a single initial and the surname: J. Smith, S. Brown. This usage is frowned upon in America although it is used in some European countries. We use either the first name, the first name and an initial, or two initials: Sarah Brown, John Q. Smith, or L. L. Breen.

A comma usually separates the name from "Jr." or "II" or another numerical designation: Samuel Quint, Jr.; A.B. Anthony, III. The editor must determine as a matter of style whether "Jr." is capped or not. It is almost invariably abbreviated, to spell it out—James Rivers, junior—seems an affectation. A few periodicals use Arabic numerals with names, S.J. Cranston, 2nd, but most use Roman numerals for this purpose: S.J. Cranston, II.

Second Designations

Second-reference style can be perplexing. Most common newspaper style is to use only the last name for men. But some refer to "Mr. Brown" or "Dr. Grey" the second time around. *The New York Times* designates all men as "Mr." except convicted felons. This can lead to some interesting and instant demotions: "Mr. Smith was found guilty and sentenced to life imprisonment. Guards immediately took Smith to Sing Sing."

Often it doesn't seem appropriate to use the last name, with or without "Mr." In many a feature story, it's just natural to refer to a man by his first name. This usage had best be determined on a case-by-case basis rather than being written into the stylebook. We must be very careful, though, that the use of the first name isn't condescending or patronizing. We must be unusually careful with such references to young adults or members of minorities who might take such familiarity as demeaning to them.

We must be painstaking in avoiding a too-common practice by some organizational editors: The brass is referred to in second instances as "Mr. White" while employees are just "White." This class distinction is annoying and unwarranted.

Titles of Courtesy

Inevitably the editor must wrestle with a vexatious—and no-win—problem: How do we handle women's names? Especially those "titles of courtesy"—"Miss" and "Mrs.," and the recently coined "Ms."?

For years—centuries maybe—there were no such problems: Women were Miss Mary Smith or Mrs. John Brown in first reference and Miss Smith and Mrs. Brown thereafter.

But with the growth of the women's movement, there have been increasing complaints that such titles are a breach of privacy. Men's titles, it is pointed out, do not reveal marital status; why should women's?

In response, editors of all publications, general as well as organizational, have been wrinkling brows over revising the rules. Should women be given their choice of "Miss," "Mrs." "Ms.," or none of the

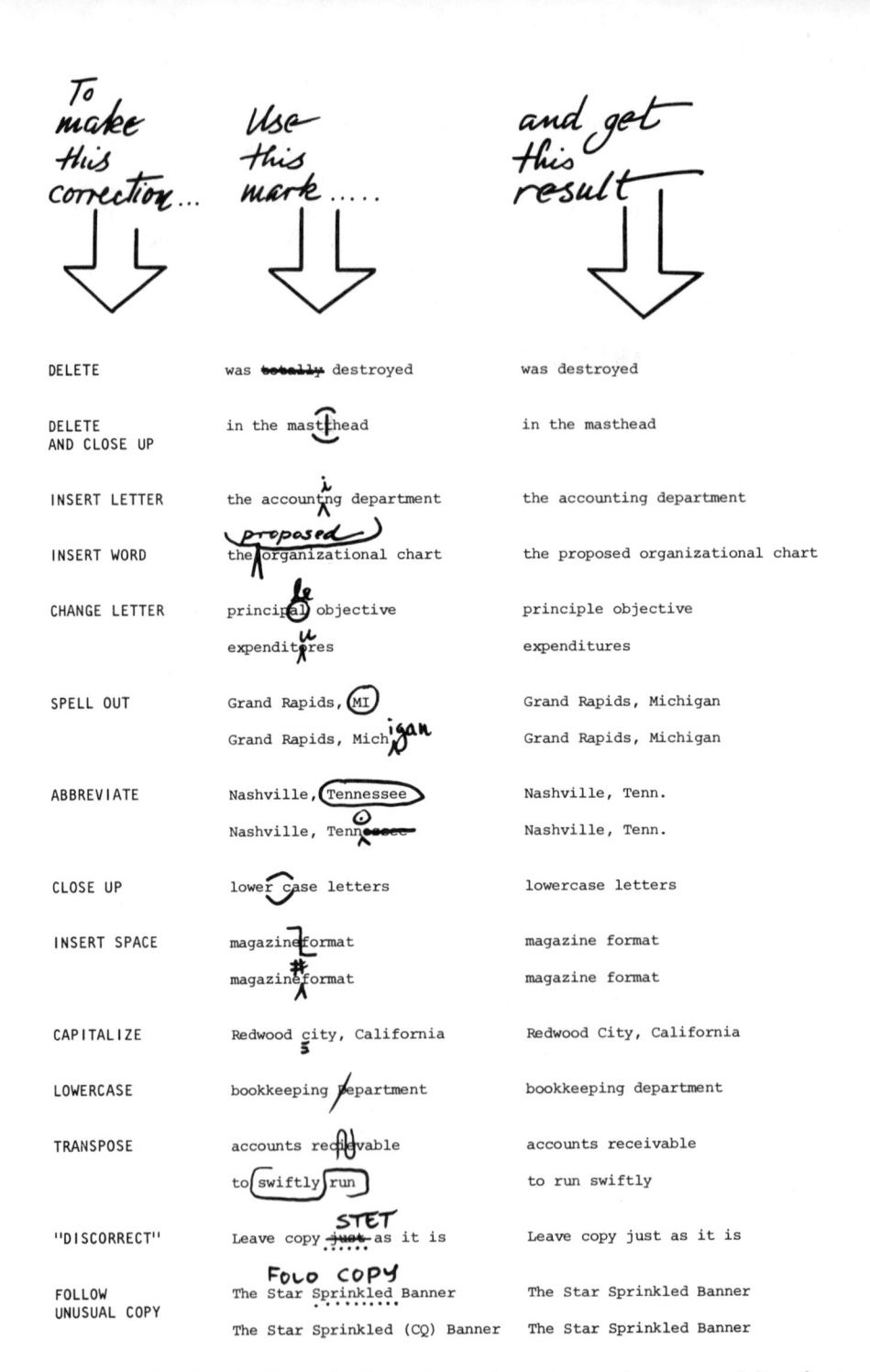

To make this correction...	Use this mark......	and get this result
DELETE	was ~~totally~~ destroyed	was destroyed
DELETE AND CLOSE UP	in the mast⌒head	in the masthead
INSERT LETTER	the accountⁱng department	the accounting department
INSERT WORD	the ⁀proposed⁀ organizational chart	the proposed organizational chart
CHANGE LETTER	princip(a→le) objective	principle objective
	expenditᵘres	expenditures
SPELL OUT	Grand Rapids, (MI)	Grand Rapids, Michigan
	Grand Rapids, Mich.^igan	Grand Rapids, Michigan
ABBREVIATE	Nashville, (Tennessee)	Nashville, Tenn.
	Nashville, Tenn⊘essee	Nashville, Tenn.
CLOSE UP	lower ⌒case letters	lowercase letters
INSERT SPACE	magazine⌐format	magazine format
	magazine#format	magazine format
CAPITALIZE	Redwood c̲ity, California	Redwood City, California
LOWERCASE	bookkeeping /Department	bookkeeping department
TRANSPOSE	accounts rec(ei→va)vable	accounts receivable
	to (swiftly) run	to run swiftly
"DISCORRECT"	Leave copy ~~just~~ as it is STET	Leave copy just as it is
FOLLOW UNUSUAL COPY	FOLO COPY The Star Sprinkled Banner	The Star Sprinkled Banner
	The Star Sprinkled (CQ) Banner	The Star Sprinkled Banner

COPYREADER'S MARKS are similar to those of proofreader but are used directly at point of change.

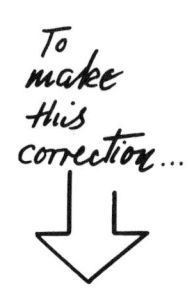

To make this correction... ⬇ *Use this mark.....* ⬇ *and get this result* ⬇

RUN IN

Also awarded 25-year pins were:

    Edgar Duclos,
    Carla Ross,
    John Cramer,
    Charles Fair and
    Robert Brown.

RUN IN

Also awarded 25-year pins were: Edgar Duclos, Carla Ross, John Cramer, Charles Fair and Robert Brown.

PARAGRAPH

⌞This reverse-L mark calls attention to a normally indented paragraph. ⌞It also shows where a new graf is supposed to start but the indention was not made in the copy.

This reverse-L mark calls attention to a normally indented paragraph.

    It also shows where a new graf is supposed to start but the indention was not made in the copy.

NO PARAGRAPH

sentence ends.⌐
⌐ W~~hile~~ *at* is now a separate graf becomes part of the previous paragraph.

OR

sentence ends.
no ¶ But no new paragraph is desired. So the two parts are connected.

sentence ends. What is now a separate graf becomes part of the previous paragraph.

sentence ends. But no new paragraph is desired. So the two parts are connected.

CONNECT MATTER

This copy is supposed to connect, ~~without any blank spaces between,~~ to the next phrase.

This copy is supposed to connect to the next phrase.

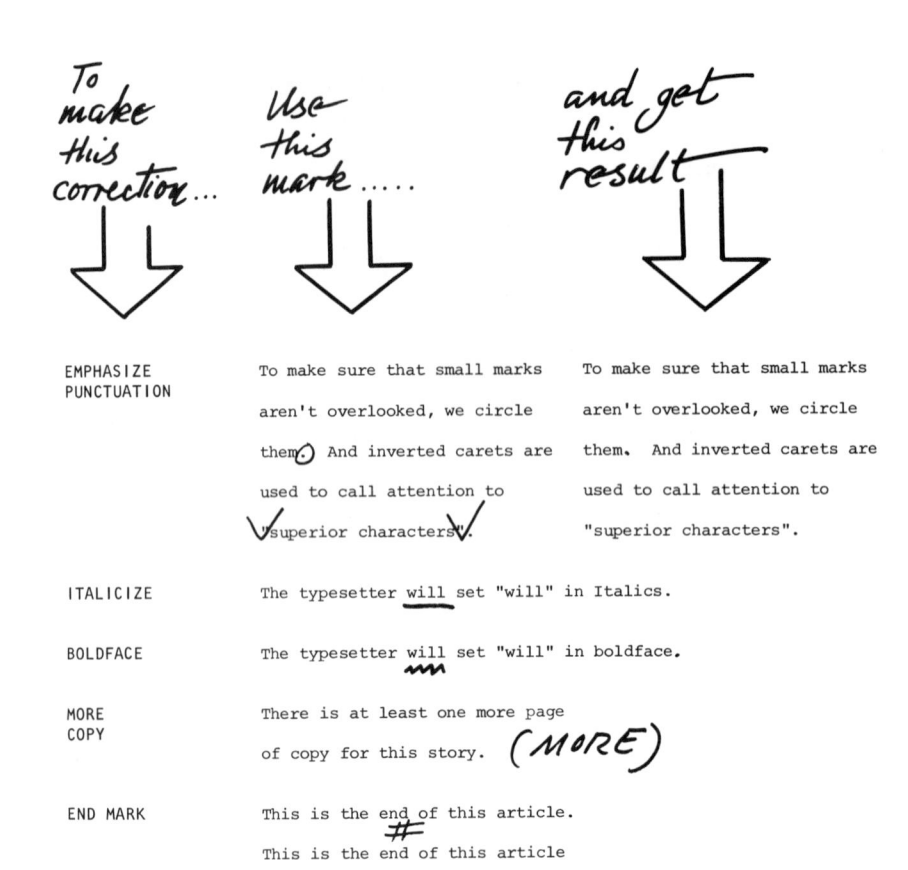

To make this correction... *Use this mark......* *and get this result*

EMPHASIZE PUNCTUATION	To make sure that small marks aren't overlooked, we circle them. And inverted carets are used to call attention to "superior characters".	To make sure that small marks aren't overlooked, we circle them. And inverted carets are used to call attention to "superior characters".
ITALICIZE	The typesetter will set "will" in Italics.	
BOLDFACE	The typesetter will set "will" in boldface.	
MORE COPY	There is at least one more page of copy for this story. *(MORE)*	
END MARK	This is the end of this article. This is the end of this article —30—	

above? How do we find out the title—if any—that a woman prefers and how do we file that information for future reference? Is there a practical way in which a woman can indicate her preference to a distant, faceless editor? Should editors worry about the sensibilities of the woman being written about and try hard not to offend her? Or should they be consistent in a chosen style, at the risk of offending people one way or the other?

That—alas!—is the one certainty in this vexatious problem: You're going to offend someone, no matter which choice you make! A recent Gallop poll showed that 83% of the women questioned "resented" the use of "Ms." Some want that title, obviously, and some want no titles.

Knowing that there will be brickbats as well as bouquets, no matter what decision is made, the editor might as well bite the bullet and live with that decision. Obviously such decisions should not be made on the spur of the moment, by whim or whimsy.

The point of view of a woman editor is given by Kathleen Anne Loomis, director of corporate communications for Meidinger, Inc., a nationwide actuarial firm:

"To most people old enough to remember World War II in person, it is almost unthinkably rude to refer to a woman by her last name alone, whether in person or in print. These same people often regard the title 'Ms.' as an unholy abomination; some may even link it with communism, moral decadence, and designer jeans!

"But to most people under 35—particularly to the young women whose 'sensibilities' are under discussion here—these opinions are nothing short of Victorian.

"In an organizational publication, much more so than in general-circulation newspapers or magazines, editors must bend over backwards to do what will least disturb their specific audiences. That means the editor must be an astute judge of which way the wind is blowing—and it may mean that absolute consistency of style should be abandoned in the interests of avoiding trouble.

"So—know the audience! The 'right answer' for the editor of a hospital magazine who often writes about older women who work in the volunteer program will probably be different than for the editor of a technical newsletter for a field in which the women are generally young, well educated, and career-oriented.

"And remember that it's never wise to offend anybody if you can help it. Even if you personally think 'Ms.' stinks, it won't kill you to use it if a woman specifically requests that title. And even if you personally think it's demeaning to advertise a woman's marital status, you're stupid to stand on principle when somebody wants *her* name printed as 'Mrs. John Doe.'

"Often it doesn't seem appropriate to use a last name alone on second reference, for women or men, with or without a courtesy title. The obvious answer is to use the first name; this is particularly common in fairly small organizations under the theory that everybody knows everybody else already. This usage seems natural in many stories, particularly features.

"And yet you may have the identical situation—for instance, an employee is going to take a trip around the world—in which you would find it natural to use the first name when said employee is a 30-year-old man, but think it better to use 'Mrs. Jones' when said employee is the 70-year-old matriarch of the family which owns the company."

The editor ought to consider the arguments of the other side. Conventional usage has evolved over many years and radical changes are not always necessarily good, the traditionalists say; editors have some obligation to maintain standards in print that are not so meticulously observed in ordinary conversation. They insist that titles of courtesy seem particularly appropriate in an organizational publication where, because we write about, for, and to those who are almost literally "members of the family," we ought to set a polite tone.

The publisher of this book, Lawrence Ragan Communications, has an interesting book, *How To Avoid Sexism* by Merriellyn Kett and Virginia Underwood, which may help an editor reach a workable solution for this problem.

Minority References

Editors must be aware of other minorities whom they may find in the audience. The many refugees from Indo-China are silent as they work their way into the American mosaic but Spanish-speaking people, long silent, are finding a voice. But even as localities vary, their demands do, too. Some prefer to be called "Hispanics," others "Latin Americans," still others "Chicanos." Editors must determine the usage best suited to their particular area and audience. So with the terms "native Americans" and "Indians."

Usage that may be acceptable for a long time suddenly becomes less than complimentary. The acceptance of the term "black" is comparatively recent; for a long time the polite word was "Negro," now anathema. Editors must be attuned to such changing needs.

Another minority—that will soon be a majority—is well-divided on its choice of titles. A recent Harris Survey asked "older adults" what they preferred to be called. Fifty-five percent wanted "mature Americans"—a rather cumbersome phrase for ordinary newswriting. Other terms, by rank of popularity, are "retired persons," "senior citizens," "middle-aged persons," "older Americans," and "golden-agers." Definitely not preferred were "aged persons" and "old men or women."

With more and more of our population getting into that imprecise age group (and not even retirement being an accurate gauge any more), all editors will be writing for a constantly expanding audience within this age group. Those whose publications carry general news or special sections about retirees will need to watch carefully for signals as to accepted usage.

One term that we can apparently eliminate is "umpteen years young." Originally used as a compliment, the term is taken by many to be condescending or cutesy. Says one "mature American": "My gawd! If a two-year-old is two years *old*, a 60-year-old damn well isn't 60 years *young*."

As always, editorial judgments must ultimately be made by the editor. Good editorial judgment is based on common sense and a common courtesy that goes beyond the niceties of mere protocol. "Know thy audience" is excellent advice.

Whatever your decision, don't ask for trouble, as so many editors have done, by advertising your "policy" on how you refer to minorities and women. Don't defend it by citing historical derivations, political philosophy, grammatical usage, or by revealing the "findings" of a poll. No matter what you say or how you phrase it, you will not please everybody. Just keep your mouth shut and do your best in the realization that as the years go by, this will probably seem like less and less of a problem.

After the copyreader has edited a story to its proper literary length, it

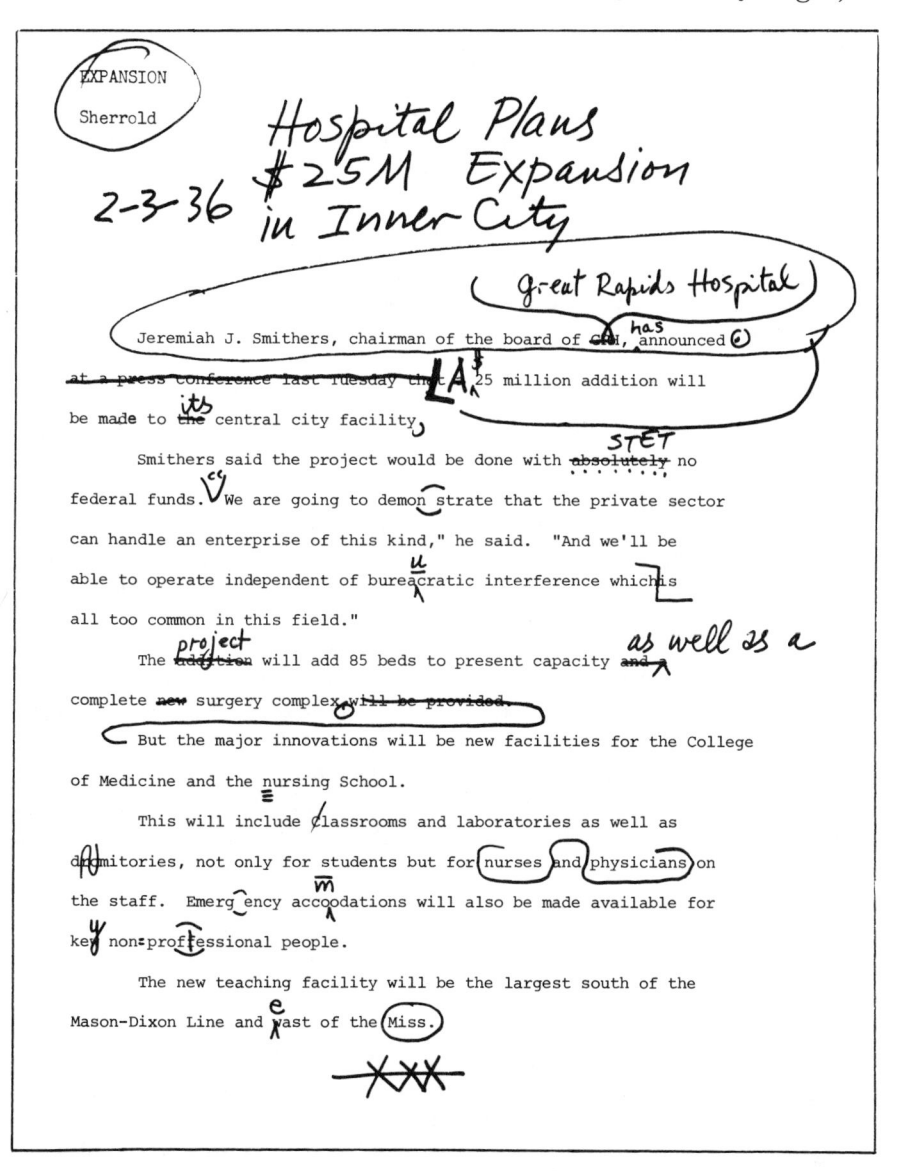

EXPANSION
Sherrold

2-3-36

Hospital Plans $25M Expansion in Inner City

(Great Rapids Hospital)

Jeremiah J. Smithers, chairman of the board of chi, has announced at a press conference last Tuesday that a $25 million addition will be made to its central city facility.

Smithers said the project would be done with absolutely no federal funds. "We are going to demonstrate that the private sector can handle an enterprise of this kind," he said. "And we'll be able to operate independent of bureaucratic interference which is all too common in this field."

The project will add 85 beds to present capacity as well as a complete new surgery complex will be provided.

But the major innovations will be new facilities for the College of Medicine and the nursing School.

This will include classrooms and laboratories as well as dormitories, not only for students but for nurses and physicians on the staff. Emergency accomodations will also be made available for key non-proffessional people.

The new teaching facility will be the largest south of the Mason-Dixon Line and east of the Miss.

xxx

COPYREAD MANUSCRIPT ready to go to typesetter. When original copy is heavily edited, it is often wise to have it retyped to speed typesetting. Note margins are narrower than normal.

is necessary to determine how long it will be in type. This entails the copyfitting function.

A headline is written for the story—a most important function of the copyreader—and it is entered in the copy log. These functions are described in Chapter 8.

Editing for Accuracy

Editing for accuracy is perhaps the most important single copyreading function. Here no formula can be suggested to simplify or even formalize the task. Some magazines, such as *Time*, have people who check literally every word in a story (not only for spelling and meaning but for shades of meaning). A tiny checkmark over the word in the manuscript shows that it has been scrutinized. Such elaborate checking is unnecessary and impractical for most organizational publications. The editor must replace this word-by-word process by assuming a highly skeptical attitude to everything written.

In a bulletin of the American Press Institute (API) an unidentified editor's rather jaundiced point of view is expressed:

"The average reporter—though not the good one—has little respect for the basic tools of his craft, the words he works with. He is impatient with distinctions in meaning. He regards as academic (a somewhat dirty word) any insistence on precision. Although he began his career because He Wanted To Be A Writer, he resists the discipline all writers must follow. As a consequence, much of his writing is full of errors ranging from small imprecisions to outrageous misuse."

These are strong words. But the copyeditor must be skeptical about everything from the spelling of "receive" to the date of the surrender at Appomattox. If there is any doubt at all about the accuracy of a statement, it should be checked against an authoritative reference. Not only the inexperienced reporter should be subjected to this double-checking, the most veteran of the old pros should also receive this discipline—and this reassurance. For a major service that the copyreader can render the writer is to be the final, infallible fail-safe protection against error.

A participant in another API seminar, explaining how to train copyreaders, said: "Suspicion is difficult to teach; but you must be suspicious in a newsroom. If your mother tells you she loves you, check it out."

If the copyreader is also the writer, it is an absolute necessity to have someone else read the manuscript even if that person is not a member of the staff. And the editor's leadership is well demonstrated by the good grace in which challenges and corrections are accepted from a subordinate or an "outsider."

Quotations

One area of "accuracy" goes beyond the simple black-and-white of true or false. That's the handling of quotations.

The Philadelphia Inquirer has an excellent guideline: "Generally direct quotations are not altered in the editing process. However, we repair minor grammatical errors in direct quotations unless those errors are pertinent to the news—or are deemed to be extremely important in reporting color. We should fix such minor errors especially in cases where they may take on undue importance and cause the speaker to look foolish. However, we should not change a quotation simply because of an error in agreement with an antecedent, for example, since such errors are acceptable in colloquial speech. Mispronunciations such as 'gonna' for 'going to,' are corrected as they are acceptable in common speech but make a speaker appear inarticulate when rendered into writing."

A *Miami Herald* reporter sums it up well: "If you are dead sure that you know what a person is saying and if that person is suffering a sort of glottal paralysis that renders his every expressed thought in an inchoate, incoherent thing, then smoothing out his quote is a mercy and not a mischief."

There are times when incorrect grammar ought not—dare not—be "corrected." This is when unique usage tells us something about the person that is colorful or pertinent. Dizzy Dean, a great pitcher turned

BLEEPING problem is explored by "Writing & Editing" of Associated Press Managing Editors Association. Page: 12x14.

baseball announcer, told his audience that "The runner slud into second base." It would be heresy to "correct" what is technically an error. And when Sam Goldwyn, the movie magnate, instructed "Include me out!" and a Damon Runyonesque character observed that "I should have stood in bed," it would be sheer madness to impose "corrections." On occasion the verbatim reporting of quotes can be punitive. A weekly editor once got a sadistic athletic coach removed from his job by repeating precisely the profane, obscene, brutal, and illiterate statements he made to players, parents, and fellow teachers. But it is rare that an organizational editor would need such a weapon. Usually such expressions will be rare and extraneous to the gist of the quotation; so we delete objectionable or even questionable words and phrases.

If the quoted person has used an indelicacy deliberately—as when Jimmy Carter promised "to whip [Ted Kennedy's] ass" or Barry Commoner's radio commercial termed his opponent's platforms as "bullshit"—we had either quote them in their precise ugliness or avoid their use entirely. Newspapers looked like prudes when they reported the projected kicking of "Kennedy's - - -" or, even worse, "a - -." Nor did their perceived IQ rise markedly when, as one prim metropolitan daily did, they referred to "Mr. Kennedy's posterior."

Quoting in dialect should be done only rarely and with a keen perception as to whether it is disparaging even by remote implication. As the managing editor of the *Houston Chronicle* observed, "We don't have enough apostrophes to handle all the sunnin' and funnin' and runnin' that goes on in the Sunbelt." So we normally add the *g* that is so often dropped in speaking. On the other hand, it seems imperative to drop the *d* from "good ol' boy" and that dialect will not normally offend our good ol' readers.

The editor's goal should always be to assure fidelity in meaning and intent, not in stenographic exactitude. Therefore many editors do not adopt the academic style of changing or adding a word in parenthesis or showing deletions by ellipses: "Mr. Jones said that that plaintiff's charges did not, despite an embarrassingly flamboyant appeal to emotion, have any demonstrable basis in fact." This statement can legitimately be changed to: "Mr. Jones said that the plaintiff's (Gregory's) charges did not. . . have demonstrable basis in fact." It can also, for most purposes substitute "Gregory's" for "the plaintiff's" and eliminate the ellipsis without violating fidelity.

We quote words and phrases that are used with unusual meanings. In the first paragraph of this chapter, for instance, the words "copyreader" and "editor" are quoted because we want to make a fine distinction between the commonly accepted meaning of the words and a more specific technical one.

Sometimes we assume that a speaker has such a distinction in mind and so we quote a word in an otherwise indirect quotation: Jones charged that the handling of the plant shutdown was "brutal."

But it is an abuse to hang quotes around words that need no such notations. It is annoying to the reader to come across: Jones said that prospects for "next year" are good. Just why "next year" should be quoted is an absolute bafflement yet this very usage appeared in a rather distinguished periodical the day before this is being written. Hospital terminology, smacking as it does of bureaucratic gobbledygook, needs to be quoted only until its meaning has been accepted by the general public. If a patient is in good or fair condition, quotes are not needed. But if it's a "guarded" condition, we do need quotes because most people are not at all sure what this word, used so peculiarly, really means.

A usage that smacks of supercilious condescension is to label a quotation with the sneering "(sic)." This Latin word means "so" and it is used (usually in parentheses) to indicate that a word, phrase, or passage which may appear strange or incorrect had been quoted verbatim. In a few cases, fraught with high significance in politics, lawsuits, or international relations, it may be necessary to note precise quotations. In most local instances, though, it seems to say: "Look how stupid the speaker is and how smart we are." Usually it's simply best to correct the error—if it really is an error. Some editors have wound up with egg on their faces because they snidely added "sic" to an absolutely correct, if little-known usage.

Dr. Turpin's seventh point—"edit for the public interest"—brings up a crucial subject: ethics. Any person who can reach the minds of many people at one time—as an editor can and does—wields tremendous power. That power—for the good of the individual who exercises it and for society as a whole—must be used with a keen awareness of ethical implications.

There is no question that the reader of any publication is entitled to the "fairness, responsibility, good taste and tone and completeness" of the Turpin yardstick. But on the requisite of "objectivity" we must make a distinction between writing for a general-circulation publication which he was describing and the admittedly advocative content of an organizational publication.

Advocacy Journalism

Readers of an organizational publication are not naive; they know that your publication is "partisan" on many subjects. Employees of a tobacco company certainly don't expect that whenever the company newspaper speaks about cigarettes it will repeat the Surgeon General's warning about involved health hazards. Nor does even the general public expect that the staff of a publication for the National Association of Manufacturers will call up Ralph Nader for his views as it writes of

NAM's legislative priorities. There are those obvious instances when your bias is expected and legitimate. Your readers know you have been hired to speak for the organization.

But advocacy journalism has ethical boundaries. When you advocate, you do it as even-handedly as possible. Says one organizational editor, "I won't lie in defense of my cause; I also try not to be shrill or snide or to whine or be a crybaby. I do give pros and cons (but then point out how the pros *clearly* outweigh the cons. ('Clearly' is an excellent word for the organizational journalist.)"

The key advice in this realistic explanation is "I won't lie."

The organizational publication may report on differences of opinion on issues where the company does not have direct stake. Here it ought to be as impartial as any commercial newspaper. There are several differing approaches to the harnessing of solar energy, for instance. While not as intense as a Russo-Sino confrontation, they are genuinely controversial. A publication for an organization interested in the subject might well explore those differences as completely as any metropolitan daily.

When claims are reported, they should be identified as that: claims, not statements of fact. Denials or counterclaims should be presented in the same story. Although organizational journalists have a different set of ethical standards than does general-audience journalism, they do have ethics that can never be ignored.

"Editing for the public interest" is best done by editing for accuracy. A true account of any situation serves the public, the reader, best. Our readers are entitled to assume that we are objective and fair and in no way is this better demonstrated than by our handling of controversy, no matter how mild it may be.

'Good Taste'

"Good taste" is perhaps the most elusive of all editorial requisites. As Supreme Court Justice Stewart once remarked about obscenity, he could not define it, but I "know it when I see it." We more readily recognize good taste when we don't see it.

One editor says, "If I wouldn't read a sentence aloud to my grandmother, I won't print it." Others use the same gauge, substituting only "Sunday School" or "my 4-year-old daughter" or whatever for "grandma."

The era of "new journalism" coincided with the dirty-speech movement and preempted many of its crudities. Our permissive society now tolerates language which a generation ago would have called for social ostracism if not horsewhipping, but many outdated oral taboos still apply to the printed word. The editor must make the fine distinction as to what is acceptable to a listener in conversation but what will offend the reader if printed.

MEMO:

GUNNING'S FOG INDEX

The simplest and easiest—and highly useful—method for determining the readability of a piece of copy is this, the Gunning Fog Index. To determine the level:

1. Use a sample of 100 or more words in figuring average sentence length.

    (Sentences that have two independent clauses separated by a semicolon are counted as two sentences.)

    Figure the average sentence length by dividing the number of words by the number of sentences.

2. Compute the percent of hard words. Count the number of words of three or more syllables (or words of two syllables or more which the reader may find unfamiliar), and divide this number by the total number of words in the sample. Omit the following from the count of hard words:
    a. Verbs that are made three syllables by "ed" or "es," like "donated" or "endorses."
    b. Combinations of short easy words, like "stockholder" or "airliner."

3. Add the average sentence length and the percent of hard words.

4. Multiply by 0.4. This result is the Fog Index of the material.

   EXAMPLE: The Fog Index computation for a 150-word letter containing 10 sentences and 15 words of three syllables or more:

Average sentence length 150 ÷ 10	**15**
Percent of hard words 150 ÷ 15	**+ 10**
	25
Fog Index Factor	**x 0.4**
Fog Index	**10**

The lower the fog index, the easier the copy is to read. Although far from infallible, this technique is useful for periodic checking of a publication. If the fog level is consistently above 10 or 12, special attention should be given to writing and editing.

Organizational life is itself a highly effective filter against bad taste. It's interesting to note that the business world—at least in its written communication—is far less crude than the general public. Profanity and the indiscriminate vocabulary of bathroom and bedroom are nonexistent in business correspondence and, hence, in its publications.

The highest technical performance of a copyreader is in editing for spelling, punctuation, and grammar. Obviously only a person who is absolutely and intimately familiar with these standards can do an adequate job of applying them to a manuscript. Even these editors may have a checklist—if only a mental one—to aid in this function.

Editor's Checklist

While each editor will compile such a list personally, here are a few items that ought to be on anyone's list:

1. *Spelling.*

If there's even the slightest of doubts, consult with Mr. Webster. Some editors—as do many writers—have a list of words that are their own albatrosses. Then, when they must use "accommodate," it's easier to glance through a list of a couple dozen habitual horrifiers than to go to the large dictionary.

2. *Comma faults.*

Are there too many or too few? This pesky little "point" (as the printer calls punctuation marks) carries far more weight of meaning than it does volume of ink. Note how the comma is vital for exact meaning in these examples:

I left him convinced that he was a fool.
I left him, convinced that he was a fool.
On the program are Collier Elliot, a former astronaut and six editors.
On the program are Collier Elliot, a former astronaut, and six editors.

The need for a comma is best tested by reading a phrase aloud, putting a marked pause at each comma, and assaying whether it makes sense.

Another device to determine the need for a comma is to insert "and" where we propose a comma.

The quick brown fox
The quick and brown fox

Here "and" doesn't sound right. It is a brown fox that is quick and we might—as German does—combine two words into a single one and refer to the quick *brownfox*.

On the other hand:
The quick agile fox

The quick and agile fox
Now "and" sounds right and it is. For the two adjectives, "quick" and "agile," each refers individually to the fox. So we write it "The quick, agile fox." This comma-testing device is one that many copyreaders swear by.

A matter of style is the use of a comma before "and" or "or" in a series. As with all stylistic rules, these must be applied consistently: Newspaper style generally drops the comma and makes it: *The newspaper is current, timely, and immediately useful. The story may sad, happy, foreboding or humorous.*

In magazines and books we more frequently retain the comma: *The newspaper is currently, timely, and immediately useful. The story may be sad, happy, foreboding, or humorous.*

Again it must be stressed that either is correct, grammatically.

While titles after a name are set off by commas—Jane Rogers, assistant treasurer of the medical auxiliary,—short titles before a name never take a comma—Mayor Jane Rogers.

If an editor wants to send the typical writer into a tizzy about the use of commas, all that's necessary is to refer to "restrictive" or "nonrestrictive clauses." But again, though the terminology is frightening, the substance is obvious. A restrictive clause (which does not take commas) is one that cannot be removed from a sentence without changing the meaning of the main clause.

"The surgeon *who did the first heart transplant* praised the work of the emergency team." Here the italicized phrase is restrictive; if we removed it the main sentence would be distorted: "The surgeon praised the work of the emergency team."

Conversely, nonrestrictive clauses can be deleted without altering the main clause: "The main building, *which had been condemned in 1977,* stood empty and vandalized before the tornado levelled it." Here removal of the italicized nonrestrictive clause leaves a perfectly understandable sentence: "The main building stood empty and vandalized before the tornado levelled it."

Commas are the chalk marks which show where the shovel may scoop out the unneeded clause. We can test the need of commas by replacing them with parentheses. If parens would make sense in any instance, they must be replaced by commas.

A complete list of comma cautions is too long for this book. (R. Thomas Berner in his book *Language Skills for Journalists* has a particularly useful section on use of the comma.) In most instances, the editor can best determine correct use by eliminating a comma, then seeing if the sentence can be misinterpreted.

The next punctuation to check is the apostrophe. This is undoubtedly the most misused of all the points. It seems that in popular usage every time an *s* ends a word, it must be preceded by an apostrophe and I wince when every day, en route to my office, I see an elaborately lettered sign on a merchant's window: SHOE'S.

Another too-common error is to use "it's" to designate the possessive. This is a logical but incorrect assumption that the apostrophe must always signal the possessive case. Put logic aside; remember that in "it's" as in "let's" the apostrophe indicates a contraction for "it is" and "let us."

3. *Agreement.*

While no one argues that subject and verb must agree in number, many of us find it difficult to find the subject—or are too lazy to look for it. So: "The objective of editors, reporters, and writers of all kinds *are* accuracy and clarity." Surrounded by plurals, that italicized "are" at first glance appears correct. A good reminder: When there are plural and singular nouns or phrases in a single sentence, subject it to unusually close scrutiny.

A good device is to read—aloud—the sentence and inject the antecedent of a term or word right after it:

"Misspelling is one of those sins *that* makes editors gray before their time." What does the italicized "that" refer to? The singular "misspelling" takes "makes"; the plural "sins" take "make." As we read aloud, we insert the supposed antecedent: "Misspelling is one of those sins that (misspelling) makes. . . ." Or we say, "Misspelling is one of those sins that (the sins) make. . . ." Now it's readily apparent that the verb must be singular.

Sometimes a sentence is so complicated that we need to write it out in separate phrases to determine the subject. "This book was written for the editor and the student who doesn't have a background in graphic arts." To determine what the clause "who doesn't have a background. . ." modifies, we break up the sentence:

This book was written
for the editor
and (for the)
student who *doesn't* have a background
in the graphic arts.

The other reading might be:

This book was written
for
the editor and the student
who *do not* have a background
in the graphic arts.

The difference in meaning that comes from the different verbs is obvious now. While this may seem like a lot of unnecessary work, we must remember that if action is required to assure absolute clarity, it can't be unnecessary.

Agreement between a noun and its pronoun must also be maintained. Errors come from failure to analyze the sentence. "His brother, *whom* he said had been a prisoner in Viet Nam, had been despondent for some time." Here the writer incorrectly assumed that "whom" was the object of the verb "said." Simple rearrangement of the sentence, "his brother—*who* had been a prisoner, he said—was despondent" would show that the pronoun was really the subject of the verb "was."

Some errors result from overcorrection. The mother who is so meticulous about proper usage influences her youngster to answer the phone with, "Whom is calling, please?" The all-too-frequent retirement platitude, "Thank you for all the kindness you've shown to my wife and I" is simply overcorrecting from the old "me-and-my-pal Barney syndrome."

The basic solution to the problem: Insist that any sentence that carries in it even the seeds of misunderstanding must be rewritten.

4. *Misplaced modifiers.*

It's mildly amazing that a misusage as obvious as dangling modifiers should occur so often. It gives credence to a popular belief that writers never read what they have written. While their major fault is holding the writer up to mild ridicule, dangling modifiers at best are sloppy usage that ought to be eliminated. Occasionally they can distort meaning or damage clarity.

Dangling modifiers may be adjectives, phrases, or clauses, though the most common is the participial phrase. All of them modify the wrong object because they're placed wrong in the sentence. A simple rule: The word immediately following a modifier is the one the modifier pertains to.

So when we write, "Coming out of journalism school, the language of picas and points was familar to me." As it's obvious that "the language" didn't come out of J-school, we must move the word that did come out of said school to follow the phrase. That word is "I," of course, so we rewrite the sentence, "Coming out of journalism school, I was familiar with. . . ." Dangling infinitives are almost as common as misplaced participles and are repaired in the same way: Move the associated word directly before or after the modifier.

Not quite a misplaced modifier is the illogical one, which is just as glaring and ridiculous. This is perpetrated by the writer who has accumulated a lot of facts, doesn't take time to organize them, and then looks for a little chink in a sentence where he can cram one or two. The result: "Having been born in Ireland, he decided to major in mathematics." This non sequitur may not convey inaccuracies; but it sure puts egg on the writer's face.

"Reading the final proofs, the embarrassing error was overlooked by the editor." The reader recognizes immediately—even if the writer doesn't—that the embarrassing error really didn't read the proofs.

Most of such errors occur when the writer is reluctant to use a period. Another phrase, another clause, another thought must be packed into this one sentence and by the time the end finally draws nigh, the writer has forgotten how the bloomin' sentence began. Simple and direct sentences eliminate danglers. Immediate rewriting of a convoluted sentence—which many writers are just too lazy to do—is a quick fix.

5. *Marks in pairs.*

Nonrestrictive clauses—and some others—are set off by *marks of apposition*: commas, dashes, quotation marks, parentheses, and brackets, and sometimes ellipses. We should think of these as two hands, holding that phrase or clause that can be lifted out without destroying the sentence. You have to have two hands to do that. So we need two marks of apposition. Whenever editors spot one of such marks, they should look for the second.

Perhaps the most annoying is the missing quote mark. All of us have had the irritating experience of reading a quotation and reading and reading. "Won't this character ever stop talking?" we finally ask in exasperation. Content finally tells us that the close quote has been lost. The reverse is just as distracting. We come to a close quote and wonder how long this has been going on. It's as disconcerting as to see a roadside sign, "Resume 35 miles per hour" when we hadn't noticed when we were supposed to go slower.

Marks of apposition will not always be in pairs; for the period can take the place of the second of such marks. "He hurried home, worried about his wife's safety." Here the period holds the far end of the phrase that the comma sets off at its beginning.

Of course, we also have instances where both the mark of apposition—a single or double quote—and the period are used. Now we must follow our stylebook in placement. Stylebooks like Roy Copperud's *American Usage and Style* and *The New York Times Manual of Style and Usage* agree: The comma and period should be placed inside the quotation marks; the colon and semicolon are placed outside. Question marks and exclamation points may come before or after the quotation, depending on the meaning of the sentence. Some examples:

John said, "The mail is late today."
Mary asked, "Has the mail arrived yet?"
The topics were "How to Design a Nameplate," "How to Conduct an Interview," and "How to Edit a Newsletter."
Have you read "Simple & Direct"?
The duchess said, "Take your hand off my knee!"

Some editors and writers alike fret at what they consider the illogic of these rules and there is a growing tendency these days to give to the comma and period the same flexibility of placement as that given to the other punctuation marks.

Notice the two examples above that end with a question mark. In the first instance—Mary's inquiry about these swift couriers—the quote comes outside the question mark. This is logical, of course. Her entire question, indicated by the ?, is a quotation and is so set off.

In the second example—where you're queried about your reading—it is only the title of the book that is quoted. Then the entire question is indicated. Again it's logical.

But the arbitrary and inflexible placement of the comma and period sometimes defies such logic. In the example about the topics of a workshop, there are three quoted titles. The first two are set off by quotes. But the third—about newsletters—really doesn't seem to be set off by the close quotes. For, coming outside the period that ends the sentence, the quote tends to be associated with the entire sentence instead of just one of its parts.

So many stylebooks call for the comma and period—just like the ? and the !—to follow the quoted word /single/ or phrase.

John insisted that the correct word was "tautology".

Here the quote is obviously associated with just one word, not the whole sentence.

That rationale becomes more apparent when there are two or more quoted words or phrases in one sentence: John insisted that the correct word was "tautology", not "redundancy". Now we quote one word, we mark off that part of the sentence with a comma, we quote the other word and, only then, do we end the whole sentence with the period.

The object of all punctuation is to make meaning clear and any publication's style should be based on this aim. But whatever style is adopted, it is necessary to follow it consistently.

6. *Filler words.*

Delete words or phrases that don't really say anything. "It is. . ." and "there are. . ." are the most common. Whenever you spot them, pause to determine whether they are necessary—as they are perhaps once in half a hundred instances.

Eliminate redundancies. There are no "rough estimates"; all estimates are "rough" so that adjective is redundant. "Accidentally stumbled" says not one thing more than just "stumbled." An object is "destroyed" or it isn't; there's no such state as "totally destroyed" or "partially destroyed."

Eliminate tautologies such as "a cold, wet rain" or "a widow woman." There is no dry rain; there is no widow who isn't a woman.

Strike out the current buzzword. During the interminable Watergate hearings, nothing ever happened then or now; it was always "at that point in time." Because these trendy phrases change with the phases of the moon, the editor must be aware of the chic clause of the moment and slice it off the moment it emerges.

Translate "officialese" into English. All bureaucrats, police officers, and denizens of the educational establishment are persuaded that their every word will be engraved on stone tablets. So the policeman would never report that a prowler ran out of the house. No! "The subject exited the occupancy."

All these are what Teddy Roosevelt called "weasel words," sucking life and meaning from a sentence.

7. *Agreement of introduction.*

Whenever the writer introduces enumeration, make sure that the introduction agrees with the actual list: "There are three major areas of concern: safety of the employee, security of equipment, safeguarding of industrial secrets, and maintenance of production schedules." In this case it's readily apparent that three concerns are introduced but four of them are actually listed. But often there are so many words in the so-called "list" that the actual items are not quite as obvious. In this case there may be a lengthy explanation of "safety of employees" before we get to "security of equipment," which is also followed by a long explanation. By the time we finally get to "maintenance of production schedules" everyone—including the writer—has forgotten just how many items were supposed to be in the list. Extra items occur when the writer gets an afterthought and doesn't go back to revise the introduction. Items may be forgotten when the editor sinks in the quicksand of too many words.

In this category, too, comes the need to add up all figures in a story. If we note that 73% of people polled are in favor of regulation of newspapers, 22% want absolutely no regulation, and 8% have no opinion, we have to explain why all this adds up to 103%. In this case there's an obvious error somewhere. But in some polls a person might give two acceptable answers and the total could legitimately be more than 100%. In that case the apparent discrepancy must be explained.

If the editor habitually adds up figures, most of the time everything turns out OK. But in those rare cases when things just "don't add up," the writer, the editor, and the publication are spared the embarrassment that otherwise they might deserve.

8. *Parallelism.*

Parallels are useful literary devices. As with music or painting, repetition of a theme is pleasing to the reader and delivers an accumulative effect that can be emphatic and even powerful. As in music, parallels can effect an intriguing tempo. Parallels also save words even as they give variety to sentence construction.

Parallel construction requires a consistent form or function. "She likes sewing, embroidering, and macrame." Here the form has changed: "Sewing" and "embroidering" are parallels, participles, but "macrame" is not and so is the black sheep in this little flock.

Parallels often have phrases or words that are understood rather than written out. "Jamie wanted to write a novel, convert it into a play, and act the leading role." In this case "wanted to" is understood with each of the parallel verbs.

With parts of phrases understood instead of written out, we can test true parallels by writing them in units:

He has bred, sold, rented for stud and ran dogs in New Mexico and Utah.

We can write this sentence as:

He has bred
 (has) sold
 (has) rented for stud and
 (has) ran dogs
in New Mexico and Utah.

Now we recognize that the parallels are phrases with the word "has" understood; so "ran" is obviously not parallel.

Proper handling of parallelism gives a certain elegance to writing, an oratorical and even poetic ring that is highly desirable. The copyeditor serves writer and reader well by making sure the technique is used correctly.

9. *Attribution.*

Facts that the writer has observed or can personally attest to are presented just like that: as facts. All other statements must be attributed to some source, preferably an authoritative one.

"The flood covered the first floor of the entire west wing of the Midvale Hospital." That is a fact that the writer saw and reports as such.

"Damage is at least $1 million, according to Dr. Robert Thorpe, administrator of the county facility." The reporter has no expertise to estimate damages; if he tries to, it will be dismissed as unauthoritative. So, properly, the estimate is sought from and attributed to someone whom the reader will accept as qualified.

It is most important to attribute quotations, especially direct ones. Usually quite long quotes, running for several paragraphs, may be carried by one attribution: Dr. Thorpe said, "The radiology lab is just wiped out." In a series of paragraphs, each a direct quotation, he enumerates other damage. But mischief sets in if his quotes are followed directly by those of another person. Dr. Thorpe's observations may wind up with ". . .Although insurance will cover only about 70% of the damage, we can draw from our own reserves to replace destroyed equipment." Then the next paragraph begins, "I anticipate that the federal government will give us substantial aid as we rebuild." This quotation continues for many lines before the reader finally learns, "'. . .,' said Marcilyn Grant, chairman of the hospital board of directors." Because the content of one quote blends so logically into the next, the reader may not be aware of the change of speakers. Attribution must be immediate and unmistakable.

Beware of anonymous attribution. Surveys show that readers are highly skeptical of unidentified sources. Indeed, there is often suspicion that the reporter has created this "source" as a cloak for a baseless report.

Organizational reporters who have to quote company officials should zealously seek to use the spokesman's name lest basic credibility be destroyed. Reporters for dailies may cover stories where anonymity must be preserved. If the storied "Deep Throat" of Watergate fame—or infamy—had to be identified, that scandal would probably still be unrevealed. Covering the Mafia, the reporter must protect an unidentified source. The victim of, or witness to, a crime may fear retaliation by the criminal and in such cases it's logical to withhold a name.

But organizational reporters rarely handle a story like that. Yet there is a current fad—to which periodicals become accomplices—to attribute statements to "a person who asked not to be identified." Rarely is this more than an affectation and we get such utter inanities as: "The office Christmas party will be December 23, according to a member of the committee who asked that her identity be withheld." That's inane—and so is the publication that plays along with such idiocy.

10. Repetition.

Especially in longer stories, the writer may repeat a whole section, often almost verbatim. Or some detail, used as a modifier in a sentence may echo, if not actually repeat, a previous statement.

Don't over-attribute. Organizational writers aren't as prone to this practice as police reporters and fire reporters for daily papers. A colleague swears that a recent story included "Thursday was Christmas Eve, according to police."

Words or phrases repeated too often may grate upon the reader, especially when they are unfamiliar or obtrusive. So synonyms should be used. But they must be logical and accurate and unobtrusive. At the same time we must avoid the "elongated yellow fruit syndrome." This refers to a writer who just couldn't use the same word twice in a story—a story that happened to be about bananas. Contrived "synonyms" must be avoided.

Some writers are reluctant to use "said" more than once. So their subjects bark, snarl, sneer, whisper, asseverate, state, declare, and do many other things rather than just say something. Those verbs can add color to a story and, when correct beyond misunderstanding, can convey both the obvious and implied substance of a statement. But all these synonyms allow the reader to infer far more than the writer may have intended and so there is a real danger of distortion of meaning. Good old "said" is always accurate; its repetition doesn't bother the reader.

11. Tense.

Be sure that the tense of verbs is not shifted abruptly within a sentence lest the relationship of time be distorted. And make sure that a continuing condition is described in the present tense no matter if other verbs are in the past.

"John Smith said he was afraid the plane would crash." Here both verbs are properly in the past tense: He was afraid yesterday and he said so this morning. But notice this usage: "John Smith said he is afraid that more accidents will occur at Hanover Airport." The action of saying was yesterday so he "said" it; but his fear continues today—and tomorrow—and so he still "is" afraid. Had it been phrased as so often it is—"John Smith said he was afraid. . .etc."—it would suggest that he had been in fear but that condition is now over.

Copyreaders should analyze sentences like this, for often they mean "John Smith *says* he is afraid that more accidents will occur." In this instance, "says" indicates a continuing state of mind. While he may have *said* so in the past, should his opinion be sought or volunteered at any time, he will *say* the same thing, he's afraid. Here the present tense of "says" is correct. So the editor must determine whether the "said" applies only to the statement made in the past or whether it describes a situation still in effect.

12. Sentence fragments.

While the purist would have us believe that we must always have a subject and a predicate, a complete sentence, that just isn't true. Just as we often talk in sentence fragments, so we may, for proper effect, occasionally use sentence fragments in writing. "That a 5-foot-2 girl just can't compete in basketball against a 6-foot-1 opponent is an accepted truism of the game. Not so! And Susie Trimble, she of those 5 feet (and 2 inches, of course) proves it every time she goes on the floor for the Amalgamated Widget team of the Women's Industrial League."

The only thing the editor must make sure of is that a fragment does not convey misinformation. Often fragments can put a pleasant change of pace into a narrative.

13. Confusing "explanations."

Frequently a writer, attempting to explain a complicated sequence, adds only further confusion. "The van, travelling toward Racket Lake on Route 22, began to make a turn to the north on Hoffer road." This tells the reader just about nothing. Not knowing in which direction the van was travelling "toward Racket Lake," we don't know whether a turn to the north was a right- or left-hand one.

Of course, if the editor himself is confused to start with, chances of not confusing the reader are quite slim. A map, even most rudimentary, can often clarify the situation for the copyreader; then subsequent action can be plotted on the sketch and articulated.

Mentally numbering the steps of an intricate sequence may help, too. "1. Ted Harper is awakened by a noise. 2. He sees light in neighbor's window. 3. His wife awakens and knocks over glass on bedside table. 4. Furniture crashes downstairs. 5. Harper realizes light he saw is reflection from his own house. 6. Etc., etc. By making a chronological chart like this, the editor understands the sequence of events. Understanding it, he can then check to see that the story relates the sequence properly in narrative form.

14. Dates.

Check every date on a calendar. Never assume that February 12 was Tuesday, just because the writer says so.

15. Second references.

It is easy to spell "Smythe" properly the first time it appears in the story—and just as easy to let it become "Smith" later in the story. Be sure that a second reference is just that, that the first reference has actually been made. Too often the reader is annoyed by learning, down in paragraph 12, that "Gatsby had been seen at the marina about an hour before the drowning." Gatsby who, Gatsby what? We don't know; this is the first time the name has ever come up. The writer had intended to bring the name into the third graf, thought better of it, and decided to introduce Mr. G. a little later on, then forgot and treated the first reference as a second one.

If an actual second reference is far down in a story, especially one where many names have been given, make sure the reader knows whom we're talking about at this point by adding a brief description: "At that time Gatsby, skipper of the second motorboat, . . .etc."

If two people have the same last name, be sure the distinction between them is made at every reference: "the elder Mr. Smith said. . . etc." or "Mr. Smith, the son, returned. . .etc." If we are talking about a man and woman with the same last name, it's almost imperative that we use a title of courtesy for her. This applies even when our style is to use only the last name for women. "While Smith used a hand extinguisher, Mrs. Smith ran next door."

One common usage that we must avoid is "the Smith woman"; to our typical reader this verges on the downright insulting.

16. Editorializing.

The copyreader must strip all "value words" from an objective story. We may refer to a person as "portly" but we can't say he's "fat." For there is no commonly accepted condition which is "fat." We may think a person is "fat"; he or his spouse may consider it "pleasingly plump." We can't say a man is "handsome" or a woman is "beautiful," for beauty is in the eye—and the evaluation—of the beholder.

We can of course, attribute evaluations to others. "Friends said the missing girl is a 'stunning blonde'. . .etc." Or we may say that "the audience applauded several times during the recital" while we can't say that the performer was "brilliant."

The editor must be very sensitive to the semantic differences of words. When does the "crowd" become a "mob"? When is a person "astute" and when is he "shrewd"? The copyeditor can sharpen sensitivity to shadings of meaning by frequently playing the he-you-I game. "He is a skinflint; you are frugal; I know the value of a dollar." "He's a coward; you're cautious; I am prudent."

An editor at an API seminar pointed out: "The 500 most commonly used words in the English language have more than 1,400 different meanings; people in different age groups and different parts of the country interpret meaning of the same word differently." The editor must know exactly which meaning the writer seeks to convey, then make sure that that's the meaning the reader of this specific publication will attribute to that word. Sometimes the word must actually be defined, sometimes it must be replaced by a less ambiguous one.

17. Cliches.

Avoid them like the plague! Occasionally a cliche makes a telling figure of speech. For that's how cliches began; the verbal pictures they drew were so colorful that other writers borrowed the phrase, admitting that no simile they could dream up would be as appropriate.

Often we use cliches to add a bit of humor to a piece, often by putting a new twist to it: "Drink is the curse of the working class" becomes "Work is the curse of the drinking class."

Or we may frankly admit we're using a cliche: "The rescue squad was as busy as the *proverbial* one-armed paper hanger." Here the comparison is descriptive and conjures up a vivid mental picture while that "proverbial" says to the reader, "You and I know that this is a hoary cliche, but doesn't it just fit here?"

18. Inadvertent sexism.

Beware of any reference to women that is not legitimate to the point. "Marion McClary, a 62-year-old grandmother, was elected president of the board of Mercy Hospital." Here neither her age nor her grandmotherhood has any bearing on the story.

But there are times when references to age and sex are highly legitimate. If a "62-year-old grandmother" decides to climb El Capitan in Yosemite with her 15-year-old grandson, both her age and her relationship to the boy contribute to the interest of the story. For women of that age don't habitually climb mountains. Still less frequently do they do it with a grandchild. Because the unusual is a factor in making news, these unusual attributes are legitimate.

There are still many occupations which are almost totally male. When a woman gets a job there, the unusual again makes news. If she's an average-sized woman on a job that we usually associate with strapping men, her height and weight may be pertinent. But her bust measurement, the color of her eyes, and the style of her hair are extraneous.

Such unnecessary descriptions of women are rarely demonstration of blatant sexual chauvinism. Usually accusations thereof are met with the most sincere disclaimers of sexism. But the unintended may still chafe the sensibilities of our readers and there is no need for gratuitous irritation that adds nothing to the legitimate story.

There are other, often unwitting, usages that may offend some of our readers. We don't have to point out that Gloria Gonzales, who has been in this country for only six months, has a Puerto Rican accent when we write about her promotion to section head in Production. But if she has earned an advanced degree in German and speaks it fluently, we might note that it is with an Hispanic accent.

Whether Jackson Delaney is black, white, or polka-dotted, has no bearing in a story that names him the company's outstanding salesman for the year. But if he's the first black man—or Chinese or Laotian—to do something significant in an area where minority members hadn't even been seen till recently, then color, nationality, or racial background is the very essence of the success story and not only may, but must, be used to tell the whole story.

Obviously even this lengthy checklist doesn't cover all the things the copyreader must look for in a story. Ultimately we come right back to where we started: The editor must taste the story and remove anything that's bitter or spoiled.

This is done in the final re-reading of the story. Here is where the editor looks for any unanswered questions which the reader might raise. "Why was there no one in the cafeteria when the microwave oven exploded? What was the lift operator wearing that saved her from severe floor burns when she was flung across the splintery warehouse floor? How did the policeman know there were three burglars when only two were captured?"

Every unanswered question gnaws a little at the total credibility of the publications. The answer must be given; if it isn't, there should be an explanation. "Police don't know yet how the small car squeezed under the tractor trailer because doctors would not allow Mr. Jamieson to be questioned today."

19. Legal implications.

By the nature of the stories they handle, organizational editors need not fear libelous material as much as their counterparts on commercial publications. But there are instances of libel in organizational publications; that these were committed unwittingly is no more excuse than is ignorance of any law.

Libel

While *libel* is defined by state law and so changes from one state to another, the Illinois definition is a commonly accepted one: "A malicious defamation, expressed either by printing or by signs, pictures or the like tending to blacken the memory of one who is dead or to impeach the honesty, integrity, virtue or reputation or publish the natural defects of one who is alive and thereby expose him to public hatred, contempt, ridicule or financial injury."

(Oral defamation is legally "slander" although words spoken on radio or television have, in some instances, been considered as libel instead of slander. Libel is the greater offense as it reaches more people than a slanderous remark and, of course, the printed defamation affects people far longer than the short-lived spoken word.)

In most cases a jury decides whether a statement has damaged a person and how much compensation must be paid to redress the wrong. As juries are more unpredictable than the weather in Michigan, it is often hard to arrive at basic simplification.

Although there are two kinds of libel, *criminal* and *civil*, most editors, certainly those of organizational publications, need concern themselves only with the latter. Criminal libel cases are virtually unheard of—and many lawyers consider such laws unconstitutional.

Some words are considered *libel per se*, defaming in themselves. When they are directed against a person, there is no need to prove that they are defamatory. Among such words are crook, swindler, hoodlum, racketeer, coward, kept woman, anti-Semite, and Communist. Some change over the years; during World War II it was libel per se to call a person a Nazi; today a jury might find it far less defamatory.

Libel per quod are words that while innocent in themselves, might in a certain context be defamatory. Now the jury must be convinced that such words did damage the plaintiff.

If libel has been found, the jury must determine how much damages to award. *Compensatory damage* seeks to redress proven loss by the victim. If a person lost a job, or a professional's business and income dropped because of the libel, those dollars may have to be made up by the defendant. A monetary poultice may also be ordered for mental suffering that the libel inflicted.

The jury may also levy *punitive damages* as punishment for the offense in addition to—or even in place of—compensation. If the President of the United States were libelled, the jury might decide that his standing was still so high that there was no demonstrated financial loss because of the libel. It might award a token compensation as little as a penny. But to teach the libeler a lesson and warn others against such language, the jury might assess heavy punitive damages. This makes libel the only offense for which a fine goes to the victim instead of into the public treasury. (Many a victim of assault or robbery might wish that fines levied in such cases came to them rather than go into governmental coffers.)

There are three major defenses against libel. *Truth, privilege*, and *fair comment*.

Truth, while a powerful defense, is not absolute in all states. Where it isn't, it must be shown that the defamation was published "for good motives and justifiable ends." It is for the public good, for instance, to uncover a bribery of a public official, defaming as that revelation may be. But a reporter cannot, just for the sake of sensationalism, report that a respected matron in the community had been a prostitute decades earlier. Here, although true, the publication has no justifiable purpose. Besides, it would be ethically repugnant to any responsible journalist.

Certain "privileged" information may be published without fear of libel even though it may ultimately be proven untrue in fact or in essence. A publication may print accounts of "any judicial, legislative, or other public and official proceeding" no matter how defamatory may be statements made there. If, in a trial, the prosecutor calls the defendant "a vicious animal"—certainly a defamation—a newspaper may print that statement even though the jury acquits. In most states, though, such reporting must be "fair and balanced." If only the prosecution's side of a case were reported, that could suggest bad motives which would negate the privilege.

Official documents, such as the register of who owns what property in a community, may be printed as privileged material. But even among public documents, some are secret: proceedings of a grand jury, most juvenile court proceedings, and some pleadings in open court before a case trial commences.

Fair comment gives a reviewer the right to evaluate the actions of a person in the public eye. This includes governmental officials, elective or appointed, and even candidates for office; administrators of justice including the judiciary and court officers; public and private institutions—universities, hospitals, churches, etc.—whose functions are matters of public concern and their officers and employees; and anyone in a pursuit that appeals to public acceptance—actors, athletes, artists, singers, etc.

It is fair comment as long as it pertains to the work of the person rather than to the person himself or herself. Comment must be honest, stated as an opinion, have a basis of fact, be free from impugning, corrupt, or sordid motives, and free of actual malice.

A reviewer then may say that "Brevanski played centerfield like the hunchback of Notre Dame" or "Cassandra's high notes would scare crows" but could not say "Brevanski is a cretin" or "Cassandra is a rotten mother."

The most intemperate language has been accepted as long as it is directed to the performance of the public figure. There is no demand for fairness, for impartiality, or for rebuttal. But it's a rare organizational publication that would run any unfavorable comment whatsoever, much less as caustic as this.

One of the most confusing aspects of libel is the presence of "malice." This is not the squint-eyed, snarling venom of a TV villain; legally "malice" is the deliberate publication of a known falsehood or a reckless disregard in ascertaining the accuracy of the account. Generally public officials (even though it's far from clear who falls into that category) must show such "actual malice." Other plaintiffs need show only "negligence"—the failure to act as a responsible editor would.

While this scratches only the tip of the libel iceberg, it is really all the organizational editor need worry about. As long as writer and editor are zealous in assuring accuracy and write with the common decency and good taste that is the norm for such periodicals, the danger of a libel charge is slight. Even if an untruth is printed, courts have held for the publication if it is shown that an honest attempt had been made to check for accuracy even if every last source had not been consulted. "Honest errors" are usually forgiven and if the publication runs a retraction of a false report, that mitigation is usually sufficient.

Laws against obscenity and treason are vague, both because of the permissiveness of contemporary society and also because of the difficulty of defining the offense, especially of obscenity. Here the conventions of the organizational world are so well-defined that there is extremely little danger of an organizational editor ever handling potentially dangerous material.

Copyright

Creative people have property rights in their creations. Just as a person must pay a fair fee to use someone else's land, buildings, or equipment, so must people who use someone else's writing, music, pictures, etc.

This is assured by *copyright* laws.

The editor who wants to use copyrighted material must obtain permission of the holder of the right. This may or may not entail a fee and that would vary, usually depending upon the nature of the reprinting publication and its circulation.

It is permitted to quote from a literary work in a book review, for instance. Although not strictly defined, "a reasonable amount" may be reprinted; obviously an editor could not print a whole chapter of a best-selling book. Quotations from historical and public documents may be used even though those full documents appear in copyrighted works.

News, as such, can't be copyrighted. When you see the copyright notice on a major news story, that merely covers the exact wording of the piece. But paraphrasing with intent to use the original article may be considered a violation. That's why you'll notice, that when a newspaper or wire service reports such a story, it will say "...according to a story copyrighted by *The Washington Post.*"

You can't copyright ideas, only the exact way in which they are presented, by verbal expression or illustration. Facts available to anyone can't be copyrighted. A reporter could not, for instance, copyright a list of names of slumlords that was uncovered by searching through court house files.

Few organizational publications are copyrighted, either in whole or piecemeal. For, while the fee is low, it is a waste of money and effort to copyright the typical organizational publication. Most editors would be happy to have their material reprinted: It broadens the audience that will read information favorable to the organization. Although no credit need be given for unprotected material, professional courtesy suggests that the editor should always acknowledge the authorship.

Often the original of a piece is unknown; we may not even know if it is copyrighted. (The copyright holder must mark such material either with the familiar *C* in a circle or by spelling it out.) If such designation is omitted in subsequent reprinting, though, its absence would not absolve an editor of violation. As usually it must be shown that reprinting protected material deprives the author of profit or credit, this would be a rare result of a reprint in an organizational publication.

Plagiarism

But *plagiarism* is mortal sin in journalism. This is the appropriation of another's writing and passing it off as the original work of a reporter or publication. This is stealing—whether the material be legally protected or not. The creator of material should always be credited.

To show that a publication was not attempting to usurp such credit, it was common to see it attributed to "Anonymous." The practice becomes rarer these days; usually we note the place where we found it—Reprinted from *New Corporation News*—even though we know that it did not originate there.

Editors may be victimized by their own staff's plagiarism. Those who print creative pieces are far more likely to encounter plagiarism, though, than those working with news stories. Whether it is an actual crime or not, running a plagiarized piece is embarrassing to the editor and deals a severe blow to the credibility of the publication. Immediate dismissal is too good for a writer who would so deceive the editor and the public.

The only sin worse than plagiarism—and this need not be illegal, either—is to pass off a work of fiction as a true report. The great 1981

> **MEMO:**
>
> **COPYRIGHTING AN ORGANIZATIONAL PUBLICATION is easy under the new federal law.** Although there are few instances when an organizational editor would need—or even want—such protection, when it is desirable, the procedure is simple.
>
> Place a copyright notice on page one of the publication and deposit two copies of the issue with the Copyright Office. The notice may be the letter C enclosed in a circle, the word "Copyright" or its abbreviation "Copr." Also to be included are the name of the copyright owner—the organization itself or an individual—and the year of publication.
>
> The copies must be deposited within three months after the date of publication—merely placing the Copyright Office on your subscription list will suffice. No form or special designation is needed.
>
> That is all that is needed to grant copyright protection.
>
> However, if you later desire to take legal action on the basis of the copyright, such as for copyright infringement, you must register it. To have maximum benefit, the registration must occur within three months of the publication date. Registration is accomplished by filling an application and paying a $10 fee for each issue.

Pulitzer Prize debacle made the public unusually skeptical of many publications. Again it was the editor who was the first victim. For the editor must trust the reporter and when that trust is violated, everyone involved winds up with egg-on-face and mud-on-professional-reputation.

The Editor as Collaborator

As important as these copyediting tasks are, the editor's job as a creative collaborator is even more important. At least it can be. But many editors fail to exploit this part of their job.

While the editor conceives many articles that the periodical runs, many are the brainchildren of the writer. This is especially so when the editor uses the services of freelancers.

When the idea first surfaces, the editor should discuss it with the writer, preferably in person, often by mail, sometimes by phone. If it's the writer's suggestion, the editor should become reasonably well acquainted with the subject to determine whether it is appropriate for the publication, from which angle to approach it, when it should run to complement the rest of the editorial mix. Sometimes the editor might see coverage as that of a main story and a sidebar or two or with strong photography and fewer words.

The editor must allow creative freedom to the writer, though. For many a time the writer, on the scene, sees the approach entirely differently than had been contemplated from a distance. Depending on the time allowed, the writer may talk, phone, or write to the editor suggesting a new angle, a new emphasis. The editor must always be willing to defer to the writer. For the person on the scene can much better evaluate a situation than one at some distant point. Editors of the old, defunct *Life* magazine were bitterly criticized by their own reporters as well as their peers in the competition because they decided, in New York City, how a story should be played and then had their photographers manipulate the event to make it fit into the preconceived pigeonhole.

Once the story has been written, the editor must always remember—though often that's hard to do—that it is the writer's piece, not the editor's. After the copyediting has been completed, it must still be the author's. While the editor may—and must—change some words or phrasing for the sake of accuracy and clarity, no changes should be made because the editor prefers to say it one way rather than another. The editor who changes "the paper races through the press at a mile a minute" to "the paper speeds through the press. . ." is tampering. "Speeds" is neither more accurate, more colorful, nor more clear than "races"; there is no justification in changing it.

The editor must be very careful not to change subtle meanings. Editors must be wary of qualifiers used by the writer. One editor changed "Almost all newspapers have a news editor" by deleting "almost." No sooner had the story appeared in print than the publisher of the writer's hometown newspaper berated him for inaccuracy. For that local paper was one of the few that do not have a news editor. The writer was well aware of the fact; that's why "almost" qualified the statement.

When the editor makes corrections in a manuscript, it should be in pencil that can easily be erased. As a matter of professional courtesy as well as a safeguard of accuracy, the editor should tell the writer what changes are contemplated. The writer can then take exceptions to those that would encroach upon the reporter's creative prerogatives or distort meaning.

Trade conventions, Newspaper Guild contracts, and a rare court case or two have recognized a writer's proprietory interest in a story. Even when the writer is on the payroll of a periodical and the work he or she produces belongs to the publication, it has been held that the writer can demand that his byline be removed from a story that has been substantially changed. Reporters are judged by bylined stories; one that turns out bad because of injudicious editing can detract from the writer's professional standing and credibility.

In case a story must be substantially rewritten, the original reporter should do that. This is accepted without the slightest doubt if the writer is a freelancer. But when the writer is on the staff, the editor may assume "Susan got paid for writing this so she has no kick coming if I give it to Joe for a rewrite." Even if this is unethical, as most writers would charge, the greater danger is to the morale of the staff. Not only will Susan's ego be devastated, Joe won't feel too good about it, knowing that the same thing could happen to him next time around.

If the editor avoids encroaching upon the writer's prerogatives, if the editor acts like a mentor, a guide, a backstop, and a collaborator, creative results can redound to the glory of writer and editor. The work that Maxwell Perkins did with Tom Wolfe's novels and Pascal Covici did as John Steinbeck's editor produced masterpieces. Both editors suggested and demonstrated many and massive changes. But when the manuscript was published, it was still the writer's alone.

(The first chapter of Thomas French's book *Steinbeck and Covici* has an excellent description of the ideal editor-writer relationship. Any editor, serious about his or her role as a collaborator, would do well to read it—in fact, the whole book.)

It is as a partner with the writer that the editor can be most creative. But it takes time and it takes diplomacy, two qualities that tend to come into short supply under the pressures of deadlines. Yet the discipline that must be self-applied by every creative person will persuade the editor to collaborate with the writer rather than taking the often attractive route of "it's easier to do it myself."

Chapter 6

The Editor

- [ ] as Executive
- [ ] as Communicator
- [ ] as Production Manager
- [ ] as Writer
- [ ] as Copyreader
- [✓] as Typographer
- [ ] as Art Director
- [ ] as Newspaper Designer
- [ ] as Magazine Designer
- [ ] as Newsletter Producer
- [ ] as Circulation Manager
- [ ] as Contractor

Glossary
Index

A publication has four components: *body type, headlines, art,* and *constants*. No matter what kind of publication, principles of using these components are identical.

Body Type

Body type must be easy to read. It is the main channel to carry communication. It must be chosen with care and used with skill.

Body type refers to use, not to size. It is used for large masses such as the regular type in a newspaper; *display type* is used for headlines of various kinds. Body type may be as small as 4½-point for classified ads or phone books or as large as 18- or even 24-point in "coffee-table" books. Display may be as small as 12-point, with no top limit.

Body type should be *Roman*, a face with thick and thin strokes, modulated curves, and serifs. Roman is the only type race with adequate *readability*. It's easy to read even large masses of type in a Roman face. Readability is a measurable quality and the editor should insist on using demonstrable criteria rather than let anyone substitute personal taste for the measuring rod.

Body type should be *big on the slug*. The primary letters—a, e, m, x, etc.— should be high in relation to the *ascenders* such as b, d, h, l, etc. and to the *descenders* such as g, p, q, etc. The printer refers to this as a big *x-height* and x-height varies greatly among type families. The designation of type size by "points" is the common—but imprecise—method. An 8-point face, for instance, is 8 points from the top of the *h* to the bottom of the *p*; but the actual, operative size is that of the primary letters which can vary greatly within one point size.

(Printers measure by the *point*, one-seventy-second of an inch, and *pica*, 12 points. Points are used for small vertical measurements; picas for horizontal ones such as the length of a line and large vertical ones as the depth of a column.)

Body type should have round *bowls*, the circular part of the letter. The *o*, for instance, is all bowl; the *c* and *e* also have bowls. So do a, b, g, etc. The bowl that is closest to a circle instead of an oval has the highest readability.

This roundness is reflected in the *lowercase alphabet length*, the *lca*. This is the length of a line consisting of the 26 small letters, measured in points. Most printers' type specimen books will indicate this size. A good 8-point body type will have an lca of about 118 points. This reduces to 2.85 characters per pica, *cpp*. The greater the lca, the rounder the letterforms and the smaller the cpp.

Leading

Body type must be *leaded* adequately. Leading—pronounced *ledding*—is adding extra space between lines of type. Like the difference between single space and double space on a typewriter, leading is a major factor in readability. Leading is done in ½-point increments.

For periodical body type, 1-point leading is usually adequate. For 8-point type, this leading is designated as *8-on-9*—an 8-point letter on 9 points of space—or *8/9*. Use your own body type and have three samples—about 1 column by 5 inches—set with ½-, 1-, and 1½-point leading. Trust your own eye—still the editor's most useful instrument—to single out the best one.

Avoid small type. Readers not only find it uncomfortable to read, they are suspicious of it. "The fine print" is viewed as an attempt to meet some legality of printing information that the reader isn't supposed to be aware of and when he or she does, becomes a Catch 22.

Body type should never be smaller than 8-point and often it should be larger. In newspapers, 8- or 9-point—with the proper x-height and lca—will usually be proper. Magazines will often need 9- or 10-point. Newsletters, often with a typewriter "setting type," have only two choices: *Elite* type with 12 characters in a horizontal inch, or *pica*, with 10 characters per inch. The larger face is the desirable.

Once a body has been chosen, the editor must live with it for a considerable length of time. So the choice should be deliberate.

Line Length

Another long-range decision—although subject to temporary variation—is the line length. The basic length is set by the format chosen, in tabloid a 4- or 5-column page; in a magazine or newsletter, 2- or 3-column. But in any format, a new line length may be used as a change of pace.

Each size of a typeface has its own *optimum line length*, that which is easiest to read in terms of ease, comfort, speed, and comprehension. It

1

LEADING—extra interlineal spacing—has a major effect on the readability of body type. If leading is inadequate, the reader gets a feeling of constriction and reading is not at all pleasurable. On the other hand, excessive leading gives the effect of the type block "unravelling" and is also unpleasant. Interesting enough, either error in leading actually makes it more difficult—physically—to read because the eye often will pick up the wrong line to read after the "empty sweep" it has made from the previously read one. Body type with unusually short descenders will require more leading than faces with normal or long descenders. That's because the reader sees the space "between lines" as that between the primary letters and so the area occupied by descenders and ascenders is to the reader, "interlineal space."

2

LEADING—extra interlineal spacing—has a major effect on the readability of body type. If leading is inadequate, the reader gets a feeling of constriction and reading is not at all pleasurable. On the other hand, excessive leading gives the effect of the type block "unravelling" and is also unpleasant. Interesting enough, either error in leading actually makes it more difficult—physically—to read because the eye often will pick up the wrong line to read after the "empty sweep" it has made from the previously read one. Body type with unusually short descenders will require more leading than faces with normal or long descenders. That's because the reader sees the space "between lines" as that between the primary letters and so the area occupied by descenders

EFFECT OF LEADING is demonstrated by these four copy blocks set in 10-point California. First example is "set solid," 10-on-10. Second specimen is set 10-on-10½, "leaded a half point." Third example is most pleasant as well as physically easier to read; it's 10-on-11. Final specimen is set 10-on-13 and demonstrates how over-leading causes type "to fall apart."

3

LEADING—extra interlineal spacing—has a major effect on the readability of body type. If leading is inadequate, the reader gets a feeling of constriction and reading is not at all pleasurable. On the other hand, excessive leading gives the effect of the type block "unravelling" and is also unpleasant. Interesting enough, either error in leading actually makes it more difficult—physically—to read because the eye often will pick up the wrong line to read after the "empty sweep" it has made from the previously read one. Body type with

4

LEADING—extra interlineal spacing—has a major effect on the readability of body type. If leading is inadequate, the reader gets a feeling of constriction and reading is not at all pleasurable. On the other hand, excessive leading gives the effect of the type block "unravelling" and is also unpleasant. Interesting enough, either error in leading actually makes it more difficult—physically—to read because the eye often will pick up also has a *readability range*, a minimum and maximum length beyond which it's just too difficult or unpleasant to read in any sizable quantity. Type set too narrow looks choppy and makes the eye bounce back and forth like riding a pogo stick on a cobblestone alley. Type set too wide makes it difficult for the eye to find its way back to the start of the next line.

These three measurements are all based on the *lowercase alphabet length (lca)* of the particular font of type. That's a single line containing all the small letters of the alphabet in that face and measured in points. That gives us, then, this formula:

$$O = lca \times 1\frac{1}{2}$$
$$Mn = O - 25\%$$
$$Mx = Mn \times 2$$

O is the optimum length; *Mn* and *Mx* are minimum and maximum lengths, respectively. We should always stay within the readability range and as close as possible to the optimum.

As each type font has its own lca, the editor should make out this chart for each face used for body purposes. Until that is possible, you can use a rougher chart:

$$O = 42\ characters$$
$$Mn = 32\ characters$$
$$Mx = 64\ characters$$

On a typewriter we always set the line length by characters and so this second chart is OK for newsletters. But with regular type, line length is specified in picas. The chart based on the lca shows lengths in picas (or points converted to picas); the second chart, based on character-count, must be translated into picas.

To do that, take a block of the typeface involved. In each of 15 lines, count out 42 characters. Measure each and find the average. Once you have the average for the optimum line, the other two are found by simple arithmetic.

A 4-column tabloid is called *op format* because its line length is at, or close to, the optimum.

When a narrow column—10 picas or shorter—is used consistently, whether on a broadsheet or a tab, it's referred to as an *N-format*, N for "narrow." All elements used in this format are designated as *N-matter*.

Justification

Another variable is *justification*. A justified column has straight margins, left and right, effected by slight changes in the space between words. All type, to be effective, must be set flush left. This is based on the instinctive action of the reader who, when one line has been read, automatically comes back to the start of that line—the *axis of orientation, A/O*—to start each successive line. When the reader does come back, the type should start right there to avoid a break in reading rhythm as the eye looks for the beginning of the next line.

Some editors choose *ragged-right setting* for their body type. Spacing between words remains constant; but the line may end at a hyphen or, if no hyphenation at all is used, at the end of a word. So the degree of raggedness can vary markedly.

There is a lively debate about the value of ragged-right type. Proponents like it because it's "new." They claim that a constant spacing between words facilitates reading and point to the horrendous *rivers of white* that erode some columns of type when excessive spacing is required to justify the line.

Opponents insist that lines of the same length allow an even, pendulum-like eye movement from line to line and stress that highly repetitive actions are most comfortable and effective when they are done in identical, rhythmic patterns. They also point out that at op line length, there are few rivers and that variations in word-spacing are undiscernible to the naked eye.

Most typographers agree that justified type is easiest to read in large masses and that ragged-right should be used in small quantities as an accent—and as any accent should be used.

There is absolutely no saving of time or money in ragged-right setting with typesetting machines. A typewriter customarily produces ragged-right; to justify requires an extra typing. But it is usually well worth the investment of time and effort; the straight right margin makes the typewriting look more like type and gives an extra air of authority.

Let's note that the Ten Commandments, the Koran, the Laws of Hammurabi, and like documents say nothing at all about setting type. The recommendations just given are just that: guidelines, not dicta. If

READABILITY CHART is drawn on actual body type used by publication. Optimum line length (Op) should always be objective of editor. Lines should never be narrower than Mn or longer than Mx. Such chart should be prepared for every face used in body size.

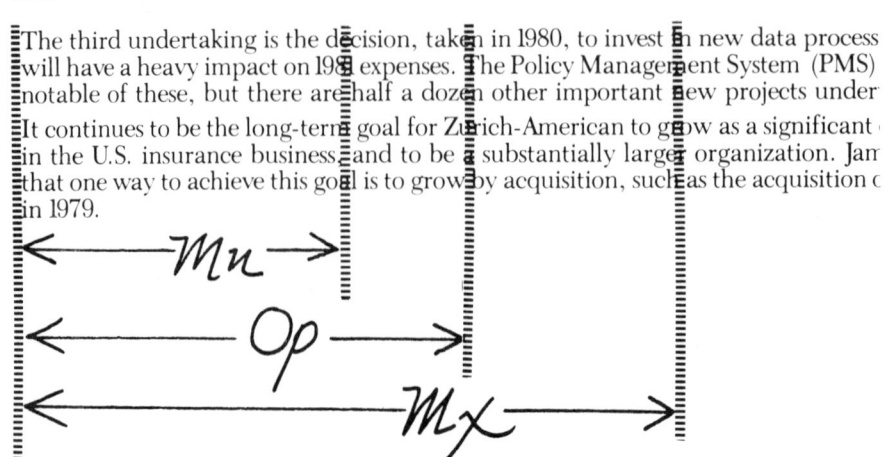

for any reason it isn't possible to set justified type within a budget of time or money, go ahead and set ragged-right; no editor will be hanged for that. Editors must be pragmatists if nothing else.

Body type should not be set in Italics or boldface if the material is more than, say, 300 words. The great departure on tonal value from that of normal type often scares away the potential reader, especially when boldface or Italics start a story. And avoid the use of boldface paragraphs to break up masses of body type. Neither a full graf nor starting random paragraphs with a line of boldface is adequate for breaking masses, research shows.

Body type should never be set in decorative shapes. It may be tempting to create a Christmas tree or a candle or bell with the president's Yuletime message. But it's hard to set—harder yet if it is set in readable form—and costly in time and money.

The most functional use of Italics is for *bio blocks*, a few lines of type that tell something about the writer of an article. These are most common in magazines although newspapers use them, too. Usually they run at the end of the piece and the lightness of the block makes it desirably unobtrusive.

There is a running debate whether names of people within a mass of type should be set in boldface, a fairly common practice. Pro: It emphasizes names and names make news as *Time* magazine has so often reminded us. Con: It encourages scanning as the reader searches for familiar names and reads only about them. Many editors fear that skimming may lead readers away from stories they'd find interesting if only they sampled a little bit. Bold names in the middle of a sentence break the smooth reading flow and make the page look like it's breaking out with measles.

Reverse and Tint Blocks

Body type should not be printed as a *reverse*, where type appears as white on a black or color background. Reverses are always hard to read, they are even harder in any type less than 10-point and especially in Roman where the thin strokes and serifs tend to fill in during printing.

Almost as bad as reverses are *tint blocks*, areas of gray or color upon which block type is *surprinted*. As the contrast between type and background is reduced, so is the *visibility*—and hence the readability—of the body type.

Should the tint block be in color, only yellow can be used at its full intensity if type is to be surprinted. All other colors must be lightened up by sprinkling the area with tiny white dots via the *Ben Day process*.

Avoid *runarounds*, where type is narrowed for several to many lines, then resumes full width. A small picture or display type may then be placed in the resulting opening. Varying column-width breaks reading rhythm; the shorter line is usually under the readability range.

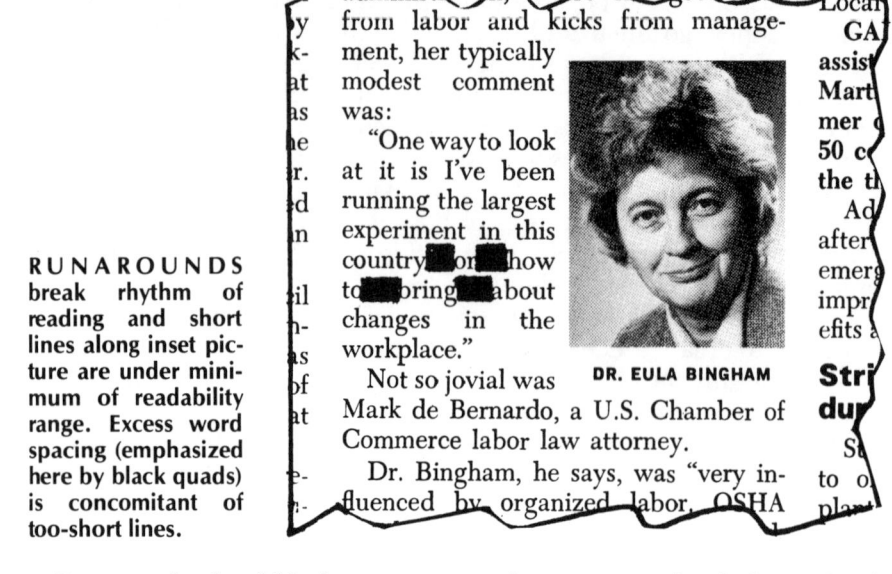

RUNAROUNDS break rhythm of reading and short lines along inset picture are under minimum of readability range. Excess word spacing (emphasized here by black quads) is concomitant of too-short lines.

> from labor and kicks from management, her typically modest comment was:
> "One way to look at it is I've been running the largest experiment in this country on how to bring about changes in the workplace."
> Not so jovial was Mark de Bernardo, a U.S. Chamber of Commerce labor law attorney.
> Dr. Bingham, he says, was "very influenced by organized labor, OSHA

DR. EULA BINGHAM

Paragraphs should be kept at a normal maximum of eight lines. Grafs will often run longer, just as they'll often be shorter. But eight lines is the largest "mouthful" that the reader can comfortably "chew" and too many long paragraphs will discourage and slow reading.

Eight lines is the minimum, however, for a leg of type. Shorter ones look as if they're just tucked into the page as an afterthought.

Don't worry about *widows*, lines less than completely full. Experts argue even about definition. Is a widow less than half a line? Three-quarters? A third? Solve the problem by ignoring it. Widows can be erased only by resetting the line—or several lines. This is worth the cost only if the widow is horribly awkward. If the last line of a whole column consists of only "ed," rewrite the line above to tuck in that minuscule syllable. Or if the eye must move all the way from the bottom of one leg of type to the head of the next to read a line consisting of "ly," some unwidowing is indicated.

Some editors are especially sensitive to widows in captions and write such matter to square off exactly. This usually results in stilted writing that is worse than the widow.

Indent all paragraphs. The custom of showing a new graf by starting its first line flush left but with a blank line above it is trendy. The reader has learned to recognize the white area of a normal paragraph indent as a signal. Absence of the signal can be confusing, especially when in the pasteup process the blank line is swiped so that the final line of the story can be squeezed into the column.

Indenting of grafs is not needed, though, when we use *paragraph starters*. Also called *pepper*, these are *bullets* (large periods); *squares*, solid or outline; *check marks*, numbers, or large Q's and A's. These are used for *itemization* as we list a series of individual items in a long list: people who were promoted, projects planned for the coming year, budget details, etc.

Numbers may be used as itemizers but only if such items are listed in order of priority.

Tabulation

If material is presented in tabular form, make sure the columns are not too far apart. That space should never be wider than 12 to 15 characters. A setting like this can confuse the reading eye:

January 8%
February 11%
March 18%

We might move the columns together, about 10 characters apart:

January 8%
February 11%
March 18%

Or we may use *leaders*, rows of dots or dashes (also spelled and pronounced "leeders"):

January 8%
February.................... 11%
or
March ---------------------------- 18%
April ---------------------------- 7%

If you narrow the space between columns, make sure that there is room for the longest word in the first column, the *stub*. It doesn't work to have something like

Red   27%
Blue   22%
Heliotrope. . . . . .ooops!

Initials

Decorative initials can break large masses of body type. These are most commonly used—and accepted by the reader—in magazines and booklets. *Sunken* or *inset* initials are tucked into the top-left corner of a column of type, when the first two or more lines are indented. Inset initials should align at the top with ascenders of the adjacent line and at the bottom with the baseline of the lower line. This is difficult to do as the peculiar arithmetic of type sizing rarely makes an automatic accommodation. So we usually use *rising* or *stickup* initials. These align only with the baseline of the first line of body type. This is easy to do, of course, and the white space alongside the initial also helps relieve the mass of gray.

Initials may be a larger size of the body type or of the headletter or

His style of dress is preppie. The subtle, brown and red plaid shirt, dark blue tie and khaki-colored pants perhaps are a reflection of his undergraduate days at Washington and Lee University. But Professor Gill's style of dress is not the only influence of his W&L experience because there, influenced by several "outstanding professors" he developed the philosophy which is the very basis for Radford's honors program—"never expect less than a person's very best."

and juices not only keeps me
"Sports activity keeps me al
needs at work, home and ever

Ken Skrzesz, of Glen Burr Director and a participating da semble. Glen founded the gro

Arriving on a Fri aware that it wo dozen Radford s ately into work ronment of St. T our respective portico and I to their own until Sunday at ƒ assignments for the course

Kansas City: *Bob B* spoke at a data pro ing conference on ing's impact on security spo sored by the University of ′

this is a matter of some concern. Like co that give us the funds we need to permit creased opportunities for all our people

Jamieson pointed out several reasons v satisfactory. *"For one thing," he noted, "a perienced the second worst underwritin; poor results are due, in part, to the diffici*

INITIALS are effective in breaking large masses of body type. Capital J in lower right is "rising initial"; others are "inset." Capital H and A are from "Radford" of Radford College, Virginia; K (in Kansas City) is from "Life" of Touche Ross, New York; and K in lower left is from "Money Tree" of Avco Financial Services, Newport Beach, California.

from an entirely different font. They are designated by their height as compared to that of the body type they're used with. A 36-point initial used with 9-point body type would be a "4-line initial."

The word that begins with the initial and, often, two or three more, are set in capitals. Ideally, about 10 caps should be used but this depends on the opening words, of course. We prefer not to break a closely-linked phrase—John H. Brown or West Berlin—even if they are longer than 10 letters.

Some editors like to begin a story in a newspaper or magazine with a larger-than-usual body type. This can be pleasant but it can also be a nuisance in setting. Often those opening grafs will also be set in 2-column line length. At least eight lines should be set in the larger face and/or wider style lines. Ten or 12 lines would be even better. Ideally the change from larger type and from wider lines should not come at the same time. You might, for instance, set eight lines in 10-point at 25 picas, four or five lines in 8-point at 25 picas, and then break down to the 12-pica column.

In large masses body type is gray and unappetizing. If such type occupies an area larger than that of a dollar bill, some kind of "typographic raisin" must be added to the gray "gruel" to make it palatable. To do this, typographers have tried a number of devices to lighten large masses of body type.

We have tried *subheads,* two or three words set in bold caps of the body type and centered. Then we tried to start random paragraphs with a line in boldface, sometimes capping the first words. Then we set complete grafs in boldface, always seeking to break that overwhelming mass of gray type. None of these techniques worked.

The only effective method we know now—though someone may devise a more efficient technique at any time—is the *breaker head.* This is the same copy as that of the subhead, set in 12-point of the headline type and flush left. This method works for newspapers and magazines. Usually the editor sets specifications something like this: "Any story that runs longer than 10 column inches (you put in your own numbers) will take breakers at intervals of 4½ to 6 inches."

Pulled Quotes

Another device used by both formats is the *pulled quote.* An interesting sentence—usually but not necessarily a quotation—is extracted from the story and set in 12- or 14-point or even larger. It is enclosed by

INSET INITIALS give pleasant typographic color to page of "Research in Action" of Virginia Commonwealth University in Richmond. Note how left arm of T hangs into margin, and lower serif aligns with left margin. Moving letter 1 pica to the left would properly align its stem on margin.

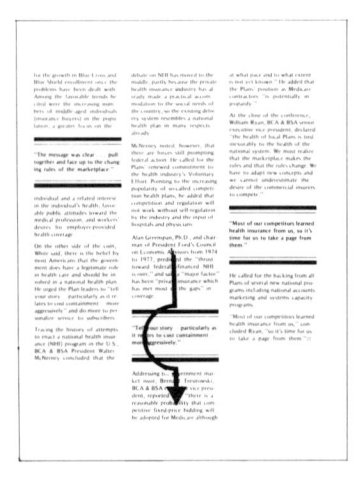

PULLED QUOTES effectively break up masses of gray body type. Unfortunately, they create jumpovers (such as indicated by arrow) which readers find inconvenient. When material below jumpover is very small, as in center column, danger of it being overlooked and unread is increased.

a decorative rule at the top and bottom, then dropped, again at random, into the body type where some relief is required. This technique is more popular in magazines and seems to work better there; in newspapers its value is dubious.

In newspapers pulled quotes act as a billiard cushion which caroms the reading eye upward and into the next column. There and in magazines, pulled quotes break the train of thought of the body content. Often they encourage skimming as the reader looks for the quote as it appears in body type. Many editors think the dangers of such usage are greater than the hoped-for benefit; others use them only with great caution.

Pulled quotes should be dropped into a paragraph, never between grafs.

A more useful style is to set an interesting sentence in larger type just as it occurs in the text. IF YOU CAN IMAGINE THESE CAPITALS TO BE IN 14-POINT REGULAR LETTER (NOT CAPS) YOU CAN SEE HOW THIS CHANGE IN SIZE WOULD ADD A SPOT OF TYPOGRAPHIC COLOR. And the eye would read right through this graf with no change in the narrative flow.

Sandwiches add color to a block of body type although that is not their primary function. They are usually used as *reefers*—to refer the reader to an associated story on another page. There might be a page-one story on the organization's annual meeting. The reefer, MORE ABOUT THE MEETING, would be set in bold caps of the body type, regular size, and sandwiched between two decorative rules. The reefer is dropped into the middle of the third paragraph of the story or at about 20 lines, whichever comes first. Reefers may also run at the top of the second column under a multi-column head.

Sandwiches are kept shallow, never more than three lines of type. There's no space between that type and the rules but 6 points of space run above and below the sandwich to separate it from the story.

Boxes

Sideless boxes are good devices to add color to a page. Conventionally, the same decorative rule as that used for sandwiches makes the box. This might be a *Ben Day rule* that looks like a strip of gray; a *coinedge* that looks like the milling around a half-dollar; a *wave rule*; or one of many such borders.

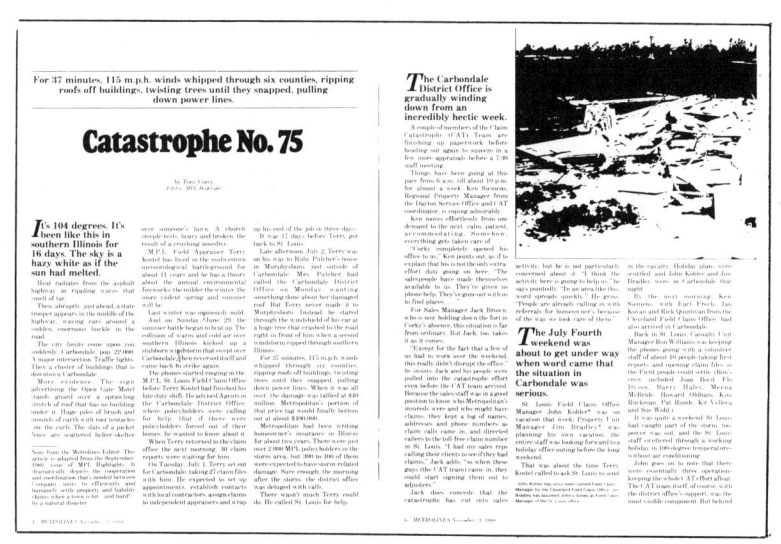

up, we couldn't check coverage...."

And that's where the third and possibly most vital element comes in—the Scranton Computer Center.

*T*he center houses Metropolitan's master file of policyholder information for all the Company's electronically issued policies.

Any claim that comes in is checked against the master file to verify that the claimant does have coverage and that the paid

EFFECT OF PULLED QUOTES is achieved without jarring reading rhythm by simply enlarging part of body copy itself. Same size example, left, shows how displayed sentence reads into body type with no break in thought.

The Need for Adolescent Health Care

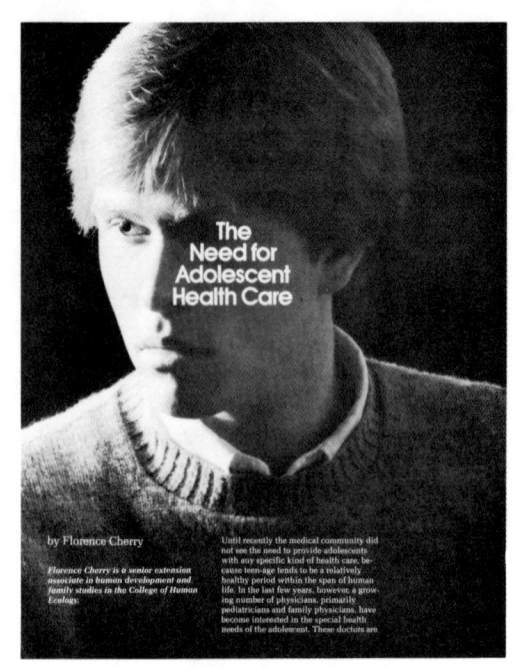

by Florence Cherry

Florence Cherry is a senior extension associate in human development and family studies in the College of Human Ecology.

Until recently the medical community did not see the need to provide adolescents with any specific kind of health care, because teen-age tends to be a relatively healthy period within the span of human life. In the last few years, however, a growing number of physicians, primarily pediatricians and family physicians, have become interested in the special health needs of the adolescent. These doctors are

REVERSING HEADLINE onto opening picture is very dramatic. Apparent "disfiguration" of human face may disturb some readers however.

Body type within such boxes is boldface, to add to the color, and sometimes it is indented a pica at the left. In such case the headline is flush left. Or body type may be set at regular column widths with the head centered.

Sideless boxes should be not much deeper than 3½ inches.

Full boxes are popular at the moment. They are most effective with a simple 4-point rule. Care should be taken that the corners meet precisely. This is done by extending each side of the box—made with acetate tape—a pica beyond the corner, cutting through both layers of tape at a diagonal, and peeling away the unwanted border. The result is a mitered corner.

Rounded-corner boxes require more care in the making. They're done with acetate material, eight pieces for a box. The corners, quadrants in varying sizes, are joined by straight pieces of tape. The process is simplified by making the horizontal element—two corner pieces and the straight rule—to the proper widths for a specific publication and duplicating them by Photostat. When the page is made up, only the vertical sides need be placed. Care must be taken so that the curves and straight lines match perfectly. Even a slight mismatching creates a slovenly effect that discomforts the reader.

There must be adequate space between the box and the enclosed type, just like the margin on a page.

A full box is most effective when no larger than 6x4 inches, horizontally or vertically. It is highly doubtful that a box that encloses a whole page is worth the time and material of making it.

Boxes are weak functional substitutes for a picture. A box with rules lighter than 4-point simply fails to add adequate color. And a box around a picture is redundant. A box can be effective, though, if it encloses a story and one or more pictures to define the entire group.

Either full or sideless boxes may be used to hold *bright type*, a body type contrasting to the one regularly used. For instance, with a normal Caledonia body type, we might use Optima as a bright. And frequently the accenting face is set ragged right. This technique is most effective with short articles and can be used in both newspapers and magazines.

Even typewritten newsletters can use bright type as the conventional Square Serifs typewriter face can be contrasted by a Sans.

When body type is arranged in horizontal rectangles, its mass doesn't seem to be as great as when it is in vertical areas. Because the reader is always more willing to embark upon a shorter story, *horizontal layout* will encourage readership.

1-Up

Another interesting technique is *1-up* or *flat-out*. This can be done on a 4-column newspaper page or a 6-column magazine center spread. In the 4-column space are placed three columns of regular-measure type. The extra fourth column is used to expand the *alleys* between columns of type. This particular placement is called "3-across-4." On a 6-column spread, we'd use only five legs of type, thus: "5-across-6."

REVERSED TYPE makes pleasant cover design for "Pulse" of Zurich-American Insurance Companies, Schaumburg, Illinois. Major industrial clients of company are listed on front and back covers. Specimen at right shows actual size. Using type solely for ornamental purposes is frowned upon; but in this case it conveys information properly as well as creating pleasing pattern.

HEADLINE is made integral part of art. Although head is lower than start of story, in second column, it is properly placed because reading eye will instinctively go from bottom of left column to top of next one. This specimen is from "Human Ecology" of New York State College of Human Ecology at Cornell.

Note that the type is set in regular line length, not at some odd lengths that the printer inelegantly calls *bastard measure*.

Flat-out is used at the top or bottom of a page. At the bottom, it is often enclosed in a wide sideless box to avoid a sawtoothed effect. At the top of the page, the headline gives the straight margin many editors prefer.

Headlines

With headlines the difference between newspapers, magazines, and newsletters usage is far greater than with body type.

The primary need in a headletter is *legibility*, the characteristic that makes a few words pop off a page and into the mind of the reader. Sans Serifs have the highest legibility of the type races but Romans are high enough to be perfectly acceptable.

Because of their size, the construction of headletters is apparent even to the untrained eye and idiosyncratic faces should be avoided. Be particularly wary about *splayed* letters, those like M and W made with bowed strokes rather than straight ones. If you look at a headline set in any given face and any letter or letters stand out as glaringly different from the common form of that character, it's usually a sign of basically weak type design and you're probably better off seeking a different face.

In newspapers, it's most efficient to use just a single family of type for heads. The best face will have an Italic form which we then use in an approximate ratio of four Roman heads to one Italic or vice versa. It is far more efficient to get contrast between the vertical and oblique letterforms than between a normal and heavier weight of the vertical alone.

Some editors choose condensed headletters because they can thereby get an extra unit or two in a 1-column head. This is false convenience, though; by making it a trifle easier for the headwriter, we make it much more difficult for the reader. In headletters we seek the same round bowls we do in body type.

An *accent face* adds sparkle to a page. This may be the very heavy version of the regular headletter—Ultra Bodoni to accent regular Bodoni Bold, for instance—or it may be from a different race—a heavy Square Serifs for a Sans Serifs headletter, for instance.

For a magazine, the editor has two equally good choices. Some editors will use a single family just as the newspaper editor does. Others will seek a connotative face that by its design reinforces the verbal content of the headline. A story about orchids, for instance, might have a head in a graceful Old Style Italics or a Script; a prediction about the future might use a face that looks like a computer readout or the magnetic letters on a check.

Often the magazine editor will use flavorful type for feature articles and use a single family for regular features, especially the pages that carry straight news.

One-family heads are set on a machine; connotative faces are usually done in acetate type.

Acetate Material

Acetate material—not only type but ornaments and textured screens—comes in two versions. Both are printed—in black or white—on thin, clear acetate sheets that contain several complete sets of one font. *Stick-on* letters are cut out of the sheet, placed into position

ORNAMENTED LETTERS OF Victorian era make pleasant designs but legibility is too low for headline use.

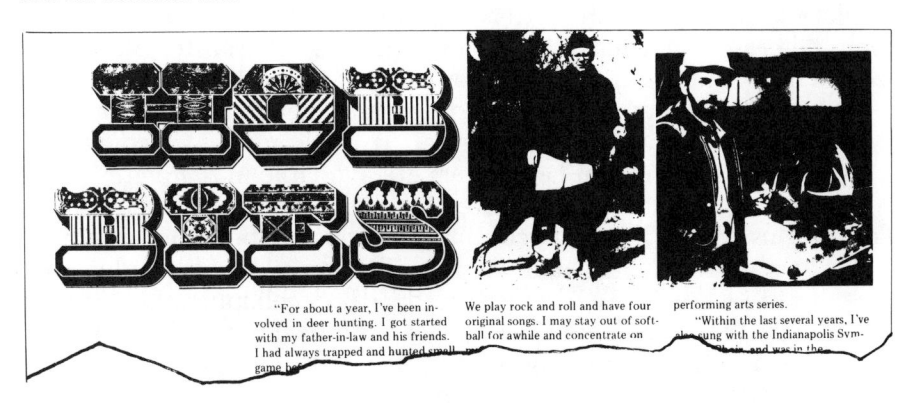

TYPE SURPRINTED on halftone must be placed so background is continuous and contrasting. This effective use is from "Hot Tap" of Transco Companies, Houston, Texas.

on the pasteup and then *burnished*, smoothed down so tightly that they become almost a part of the pasteup, affixed by a clear wax backing on the sheet. *Transfer* letters, or *rub-off*, are placed in position over the pasteup paper and rubbed with a flat tool. The letter leaves the original sheet and adheres so tightly to the pasteup that it looks as if it were printed there.

A guideline is printed below each stick-on letter so you can line them up. Draw a guideline about 1/16 of an inch from the edge of a piece of work paper. Now cut each letter out and position it along the edge of your worksheet, with the guideline on your pencilled line and the letter flapping free off the edge. When you have the entire word or phrase hanging from your worksheet, carefully position the whole collection onto your pasteup sheet. Burnish down the letters, and finally cut away the guideline portions and take them away on your work paper.

If stick-ons are improperly placed, they can readily be lifted and replaced, but if a transfer letter goes down in the wrong place, it can only be erased, not moved. The utter finality of transfer placement scares many editors and they prefer to work with stick-on.

If a newsletter is produced by photographic means, acetate heads can be affixed to the typewritten original. If the letter is Mimeographed several styles and sizes of headletters are available in *template* forms, shapes cut into a plastic plate through which a stylus can trace and cut letterforms. When heads are cut into a stencil, it is best done on a light table to make the images highly visible. The stencil should be placed on a semi-resilient surface and a piece of thin silk or cellophane placed over the stencil. This prevents tearing. Both the backing and the silk are available at office-supply stores.

Head Specifications

For newspaper heads, a simple set of specs will assure maximum efficiency:

Headlines should be set flush left.

Headlines are most legible in downstyle.

One-column heads should rarely be deeper than three lines. A 4-liner will work only if the words are few, short, and familiar.

Multicolumn heads should be no deeper than two lines.

Any single line of a head should have no more than about 32 characters. The total characters in a multiline head should not exceed 45. (We give or take a character or two here, especially with familiar, short words.) If the head goes much beyond these limits, it will become plodding and lack immediacy and excitement.

Each line of a head should extend into the last leg of body type.

In multiline heads, it doesn't matter which line is the longer.

Ragged-right margins on heads are good; they look informal and inviting.

Spacing between words should be 1 en. (An *en* is a horizontal space half the height of the type. Thus, when we're setting a 36-point head, its en is 18 points. An en is often called a *nut quad*—a quad being a blank space. This distinguishes it from an *em* or *mutton quad* which is twice as wide as the en or is the height of the type.)

Word spacing should never be changed, especially reduced to make a poorly written head fit in the given space. Such a *busted head* should be rewritten to fit.

No leading should be used with headletters; the normal space between lines, created by an invisible *shoulder*, is the proper interlineal spacing.

There are three styles of heads. ALL-CAP SETTING IS THE LEAST LEGIBLE. THIS IS BECAUSE WE RECOGNIZE WORDS BY THEIR SILHOUETTE, ESPECIALLY THE UPPER ONE AND, IN THE CASE OF CAPS, THE FORM IS A NONDISTINCTIVE RECTANGLE.

An Improvement Is Upper-And-Lower As In This Sample. It Is Much Better Than All-Caps But Is A Bit Harder to Read. Each Capital Is Like The Hook On A Barbed Wire Fence That Snags The Reading Eye.

Downstyle heads are capped just as body type is: The first word of a sentence or headline is capped and so are proper nouns; all other words are in lowercase. As this is the style we read most frequently—in thousands of lines of body type—it is easier for the reader. It's also easier to write and a trifle easier to set.

Downstyle, sometimes abused by the total elimination of capitals, is a sophomoric affectation; worse, it's misspelling. To write "january" is

MEMO:

Albertus
abcdefghijklmn
ABCDEFGHIJK

Aster
abcdefghij
ABCDEFG

Americana
abcdefghij
ABCDEFG

Baskerville
abcdefghijkl
ABCDEFG

Antikva
Margaret
abcdefghijk
ABCDEFGH

Benguiat
abcdefghijkl
AA ABCDEFG
AA ÆB ÆÆ ÆH ÆK

Arrow
abcdefghijklm
ABCDEFGHIJ

Beton Bold
abcdefghijkl
ABCDEFGHIJ

LITTLE KNOWN HEADLETTERS that have excellent typographic color, sound design, and good character count are shown here by courtesy of Visual Graphics Corporation. All faces are 24-point and designated by manufacturer's titles, which often vary for same face. Note "alternate characters" in Benguiat and Lubalin Graph.

THE EDITOR AS TYPOGRAPHER 139

MEMO:

Caledonia
abcdefghijkl
ABCDEFGH

**Columbia Bold
abcdefghijklm
ABCDEFGH**

**Craw
Clarendon
abcdefghij
ABCDEFG**

Delta Medium
abcdefghijkl
ABCDEFGHIJ

Eurostile
Extended
abcdefgh
ABCDEF

Friz Quadrata
abcdefghijk
ABCDEFGHI

Lubalin
Graph
abcdeefgh
A A A B C D E F
U V V V W W

**Meridien
abcdefghijk
ABCDEFGH**

Solitaire Bold
abcdefghijkk
ABCDEFGHIJ

**Zapf Demi
abcdefghi
ABCDEFG**

abcdefgh

meanline, stem, ascender, x-height, baseline, bowl, serif, descender

TERMINOLOGY OF TYPE. Readability of body type depends on tall x-height and roundness of bowls. Note ratio of ascenders and descenders to height of the primary letters on this specimen.

as glaring—and embarrassing—an error as to make it "Yanuary." This misuse is frequent in bylines, probably by people who fancy themselves the poor man's e.e.cummings. But he was a certifiable eccentric. Most educated and cultured persons consider this a gaucherie.

Headlines should be simple in form and large in size. The more important the story, the larger the headline; this is the way the editor grades the significance of a story.

One line of 48-point has more impact than two lines of 24 and this simplification is desirable. Simplification has generally eliminated second and third "decks" on newspaper headlines. (A deck is a unit of a head set in a face and size different from those of other units.) When a second deck is used, it should be at least two lines deep for a 1- or 2-line main head. A 3-line main head requires a 3-line deck.

A category of heads called *bimos* (pronounced "buy-moes" and short for *bimodular*) is useful for both newspapers and magazines. The simplest and most popular is the *kicker*. This is a small and short head, generally underscored, that rides above and slightly to the left of the main head of one or, preferably, two lines.

The kicker should be half the point-size of the main head. It should be written short, ideally no wider than one-third the overall head width. The main head is indented: 1 pica per column in N-format, 1½ picas per column in op format. This indent pushes the larger main head away from immediate competition with the weaker kicker. It also builds in definite areas of white space, called *fresh air* by the typographer, and thus lightens the page.

The *reverse kicker* gets its name by reversing the ratio. Now the kicker is twice the point-size of the main head. It is underscored to make it consistent with the regular kicker although it certainly doesn't need the added optical weight that the kicker does to keep it from floating off into the wild blue yonder. The reverse kicker is written no more than half the length of the whole head and the main head is indented 2 picas per column for N-format, 3 picas per column for op format.

The reverse kicker has so much impact that it is appropriately called a *hammer*.

A *wicket* consists of two short lines of small type followed by one line of twice-as-large type. A *tripod* reverses this ratio: A word or two set in large type is followed by a 2-line element of type just half that point size.

In both the wicket and the tripod, the first part of the headline is written ½- or 1½-column width. This is to prevent the 1-pica separation between the two modules of the head from aligning or coming close to the alley which separates columns of body type. Should that happen, the bimo would look like two separate heads running side by side.

The main head, the second element, should be at least twice as long as the first in a wicket or tripod head.

The final bimo is useful on magazine pages or, in a newspaper, on feature or picture pages; it doesn't work in a regular newspaper page. It's the *slash head*. Two short lines of small type run in the upper-left area of the head. One pica lower and to the right of the head area are two lines of type twice as large. The two modules are separated by a heavy rule—at least 4- or, better, 6-point—running at a 45-degree angle, northeast to southwest. The strong diagonal adds dynamic tension to the page.

When counting characters to determine whether the head is too wordy, you do not count the bimo, the subordinate head.

In content, magazine and news heads vary more than in form. There are two kinds of heads: The *definitive* or *summary* head capsulates the content of the story: KIDNAPPER RELEASES HOSTAGE. The *connotative* or *teaser* head seeks to pique the curiosity of the reader without giving much, if any, specific indication of the content: FREEDOM AT LAST.

(Note that throughout this book, headlines are set in all-caps. This is merely to distinguish them in body-type form and doesn't mean that actual heads should be set that way.)

Newspapers tend to use summary heads; magazines have a fondness for teasers.

Summary heads have grammatical rules—somewhat different from English—that must be followed lest the reader be disturbed. Articles are eliminated. A comma takes the place of "and." Periods are never used; if the head has two thoughts (a quite undesirable situation) a semi-colon separates the phrases. Forms of "to be" are eliminated in the passive voice. We don't say SMITH IS PROMOTED; it's just SMITH PROMOTED.

The past tense in a head is shown by a verb in the historic present. FIRE RAZES PLANT means that it happened yesterday.

Future tense is shown by the infinitive: NEW PLANT TO OPEN means "will open tomorrow"—or in the future.

Past tense is used only for the pluperfect, to show that one action took place before another one in the past:

**HOSPITAL HAD SURPLUS
IN '74, AUDITOR SAYS**

meaning that an accountant yesterday revealed a condition farther back in the past.

Single quotes are used instead of the conventional double ones:

**'SUPERB PERFORMANCE'
JONES TELLS EMPLOYEES**

Note that the customary comma after the quote is eliminated.

A colon often designates the person being quoted, directly or indirectly, or identifies a topic or a place:

**BROWN: 'EXPORTS TO RISE
NEXT YEAR'
MEXICO: NEW OIL FIELDS
GROWTH FORESEEN**

A dash following a quote also identifies the speaker:

HEALTH CARE BEST EVER — SMITH

The reader is unaware of the niceties of headlines grammar. But when its rules are violated, the reader is uncomfortable without knowing why.

A simple headline code will make it easier and quicker to instruct the typesetter. The *3-digit code* is probably best for organizational publications. The first number indicates the column width, the second tells the number of lines, the third, the size and face. Thus, "2-2-36 BB" means "2 columns, 2 lines of 36-point Bodoni Bold." The editor abbreviates the name of the type as much as possible: "C" is Century; "T" is Tempo, etc. Adding "X" indicates Italics and "B," Bold. So "48 TBX" is 48-point Tempo Bold Italics.

The editor should prepare a *headline schedule*, a chart showing the actual heads used in the publication. Some editors simply show the typeface, 24-point Century, let's say, and let the headwriter decide how wide to make a head and how many lines to give it. The result is often a head that far exceeds the maximum number of characters previously noted and/or is inconsistent in form with the other heads in use. A good schedule, the *head sked*, will show a 1-line, 1-column, 24-pointer, a 1-column 2-liner, a 2-column 1-liner, etc., all the other uses of that face. All the Italic forms will be shown separately as will the bimos using that face. Preparation of the schedule will weed out the nonfunctional heads and will show the editor exactly what head will result from any given instruction.

The connotative heads used in a magazine, of course, are not shown in a schedule for each is a one-of-a-kind. A typewritten newsletter really doesn't need a schedule if it uses only the typewriter for heads. But a single chart does offer a modicum of convenience. If acetate letters are used a conventional schedule is desirable.

The schedule shows, in addition to the actual head and its code, the

FAMILY TREE OF ROMAN LATIN ALPHABET shows development of our major tool for communication. From roots of Semitic and Greek alphabets, Roman developed both alphabet and letterform. First offshoot was Text or Black Letter. Then came Monotonal with two branches, Gothic and Sans Serifs. Square Serifs, too, split into Egyptian and American ethnics and Written also has two, Script and Cursive. Ornamented faces develop from all the other ethnic groups and have three divisions: Shadowed, Shaded, and Novelty. Notice strong similarity among all letterforms that enable instant recognition of letter itself and then variations that give both typographic and semantic coloration.

unit count of the head. This shows the headwriter the maximum count for any given column-width. For newspapers, where heads must fit into prescribed widths, unit counting is essential. For magazines there is usually considerably more flexibility although somewhere, of course, there is a maximum.

In *counting a head* we note that a W is much wider than an *i* and that we can't simply count the number of characters in a head. We assign:

1 unit for all normal lowercase letters such as *a*, *b*, *c*, etc., and cap *I*.

½ unit for *l*, *i*, spaces, and punctuation. (In some fonts, *f*, *t*, and *j* are also skinny characters; look at your own headletters and see if this is true.)

1½ units for *m* and *w*, and most capitals.

2 units for *M* and *W*.

Some editors make sure they have enough room by counting all lowercase letters as 1, all caps as 2, *M* and *W* as 3, and spaces as 1.

Take a long headline and mark off one column; count the units in it. Average this for 10 such samples. That gives you the maximum (to write on the head schedule) that will fit into a single column. Do the same for two columns, etc. Or you can simply take a 1-column unit count and multiply by 2, 3, and 4. The width of the alley will rarely add even a single unit to the count of multicolumn heads.

Newsletter Headlines

The editor of a newsletter that uses acetate headlines can operate just like the newspaper or magazine editor. If, however, all heads must be set on a typewriter, the choice of styles is quite limited.

The *inset head* is placed into a rectangle left blank at the top-left corner of a column of body type. A *hanging indent* head starts at the left margin of the column. The story starts immediately after the head, in the top line, and all succeeding lines are indented a pica or two at the left. The hanging indent may be one or two lines deep. The *read-in* head is actually the first word or two of the story, set in all-caps. A typewritten version of regular typeset heads is also used, the head running above the story.

All typewritten heads are in all-caps. We sacrifice some legibility because we need the extra bulk of the capitals. Do not, however, seek to get extra optical weight by underscoring heads; this decreases legibility far too much.

Jump heads are those that identify that portion of a story that has been *turned*, continued from another page, usually the first. While jumps are not a good device and hence jump heads should be used only most sparingly, they are needed on occasion and then should be signalled as different from regular heads. This is best done by putting some visual device—a star, bullet, square, or whatever—at the left of the line, then a pica of space and then the head. If the head has two lines, the second aligns at the left with the first type, not the signal.

Jump heads should be as large as they'd be if the body type under them were an independent story. The key word or phrase of the page-one head should be repeated. One- or two-word *label* heads should be avoided.

Headlines may be playful on occasion and even puns are forgiven if used in moderation.

In magazines, connotative headletters often create visual puns. The

MEMO:

Bookman Demi w/Swash

abcdefghijklmnopqrstuv

ABCDEFGHIJKLMNOPQ

bdeffiKlm n o pqr tuvwy

AABBCDEFGHIJK STUVVWWWXYZThfi

(&&&.,:;!?""''--·*$¢%/£)

LMNOPRR

Avant Garde Gothic Medium

abcdefghijklmnopqrstuvwxyz

cefffiflffiffltvvwy

ABCDEFGHIJKLMNOPQRSTUV

AACACEAFAFRGAHTKALALAL MNTRRA SSSTSTTHUTVVW

LETTERFORM MODIFICATIONS can add interest to headletters. Bookman Demi demonstrates "Swash" letters, those with elongated, decorative strokes. Those swashing to the left are used at start of words, those with extensions to right are finial letters. Swashes should not be used within words.

Avant Garde uses "alternative characters" which may appear within a word. Many of them are "ligatures," two letters actually joined such as CA. Note combinations such as TH and UT which are not connected.

146   EDITING THE ORGANIZATIONAL PUBLICATION

MEMO:

Arpad Outline
abcdefghijklm
ABCDEFGHIJ

ELEKTRIK
ABCDEFG

Broadway
aabbcddee
rsstuuvw
PQRSSTU

Fraktur
abcdefghijklmn
ABCDEFGH

Caslon Antique
abcdefghijklmn
ABCDEFGHIJ

HADRIANO
ABCDEFGH

NEULAND
ABCDEFGHIJ

COMPUTER
ABCDEFGHIJKL
1234567890

Charme Bold
abcdefghijklmn
ABCDEF

SAPPHIRE
ABCDEFGH

CONNOTATIVE LETTERFORMS, many of them Ornamented —can reinforce flavor of magazine article. Many of these faces, shown by courtesy of Visual Graphics Corporation, have only capitals. Known as "titling fonts," they were used originally for book titles. Notice Fraktur, original form of Text used in Germany, and Sapphire, designed by Gudrun Zapf, first woman type designer.

word SINKING, for instance, sliced at an angle, looks as if it is settling into water or quicksand.

Headlines contribute much to the personality of a publication just as clothes often indicate the personality of people. Sans heads are business-like and contemporary; Modern Romans are more easy-going.

Proper selection of headletters and of headline forms and crisp writing are major tools for communicating and every editor must master the art.

TYPE STRIPPED ONTO HALFTONES—be it reverse as here or positive—may easily become illegible because of variegated background. Such type should always go onto single, solid, contrasting background.

Chapter 7
The Editor

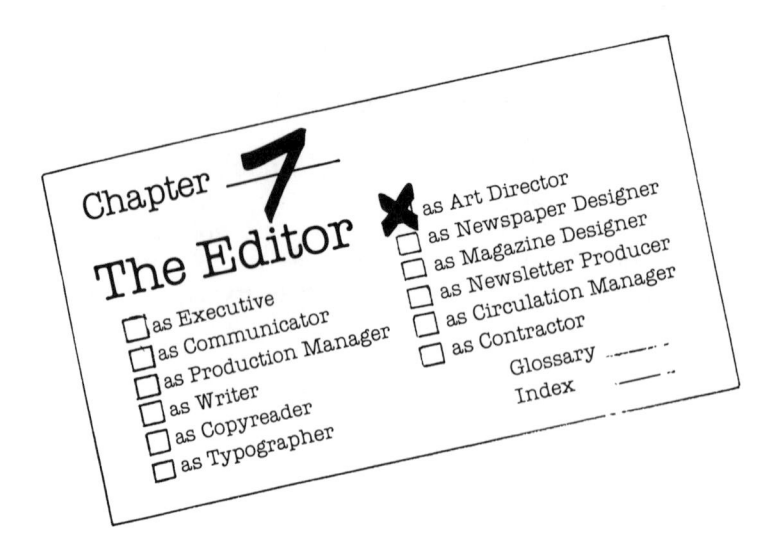

- [ ] as Executive
- [ ] as Communicator
- [ ] as Production Manager
- [ ] as Writer
- [ ] as Copyreader
- [ ] as Typographer
- [x] as Art Director
- [ ] as Newspaper Designer
- [ ] as Magazine Designer
- [ ] as Newsletter Producer
- [ ] as Circulation Manager
- [ ] as Contractor

Glossary
Index

Ever since early humans scratched drawings into the walls of their caves, pictures have been an important tool for communication. That is just as true today as ever before.

Pictures have three major uses: They can set a tone or mood for an article; they can lead the eye through a printed page and into essential type blocks; and, most important, they can communicate, either by themselves or by reinforcing words.

Pictures should always be used for one or more of these purposes, never just to fill up space or because they are available.

There are two kinds of pictures: *photographs* and *hand art*, that made by human hand rather than the camera. Pictures are also classified as *line* and *halftone*. Line art consists of simple lines and areas of black; comic strips and cartoons are typical line work. (Type is also line matter.) Photographs are produced as halftones. The photo, also called *continuous-tone* art, consists of blacks, white, and varying values of gray. In order for the printer to reproduce these grays while using only black ink, the continuous tone is broken down into a pattern of tiny dots. Where the dots are large, with little white paper showing between them, the eye is fooled into "seeing" a dark gray. Where dots are small and much white space surrounds them, the effect is of a lighter gray.

This screening is done in two ways. The photo may be converted to a screened negative, with those tiny dots, which is then stripped into the negative of the rest of a page of a newspaper or magazine, a line plate. Or a *Velox* may be produced. This is a photoprint made of those halftone dots rather than actually varied gray tones. The Velox is placed in the pasteup with type and other line material and stripping is eliminated. Such screened prints are also called *PMTs, photo mechanical transfers*.

Pictorial Cliches

Before an editor orders a picture to be taken—by the editor or someone else—the purpose of the photograph should be written out, actually written out. "I want a picture to show that Ann Southfield has been with the organization for 25 years." If nothing else, this technique will minimize the pictorial cliches that are the bane of the organizational editor.

A list of such cliches should be compiled by every editor with the vow, "I'll never use one of these unless I absolutely have to." That list is long, headed by the Grip-and-Grin shot. Close by comes the Paper Passer, said paper being a check, the first Christmas seal, or other transcendental document. The Plaque Presenter, the Pointer, Three-People-with-a-Piece-of-Paper. . .ah! ad infinitum.

Each of these shots uses a vague, imprecise symbol. The handshake that we might be tempted to use with Ann, can mean goodbye, congratulations, welcome, I don't know what else to do with my hands. If we want to say "25 years with this company" we might pose Ann with 25 years worth of ledgers (if she's an accountant), with or on the product the company was making a quarter-century ago, or in front of the old office building where she first worked.

Photo Specifications

Decide where to take the picture; the background can often add much to the narrative. Will you use props? Are they easy to obtain or do you need to mount a search for them? How far in advance will your subjects need to be notified? What happens if a snafu occurs; can you make an alternative picture or must you reschedule?

When you notify your subjects be sure to give your phone number so they can reach you if plans go awry. Stress that they must be on time, that you'll wait only x minutes. And obey that deadline rigidly! More time is wasted waiting for tardy idiots than it took to build the pyramids. But word gets around amazingly swiftly that you won't stand for lallygagging, that the person who comes late just doesn't get in the picture. This policy will get you plenty of flak as you institute it; but the long-range benefits are well worth the momentary hassle.

Three people ought to be the maximum number in a photo; five is the absolute maximum. If a group is larger than this, you might break it into logical subdivisions: This is the infield, the outfield, and the battery of your baseball team. Obviously there are times when the group just can't be divided; in that case, grit your teeth and proceed.

Subjects must be grouped tightly. Space between heads is always wasted; minimize it by pushing heads close together. This requires that subjects be moved close, much closer than they'd normally place themselves.

If subjects cannot be moved, the photographer almost always can. If we shoot three people head-on, the wasted space between heads will be as great—or even greater—than the usable area occupied by the heads and faces. But if the photographer moves over to shoot at about a 30-degree angle, the heads will be close together, often even overlapping, and wasted space is eliminated.

Often the organizational publication must show umpteen people getting some kind of award. If the cameraman stays in one spot, we'll wind up with one picture. . .repeated umpteen times. The photog should grab a couple shots from the side that shows the presenter's face well. Then move around to the opposite side for a couple more. Then come around and shoot over the shoulder of the presenter. Moving the camera takes away a trifle of the deadly dullness of repetitive poses. But it's best to avoid the *record shot*—one that shows the actual dull event— if an alternative is possible.

It is better to ask the people involved to meet you in an adjacent room or area after the actual ceremonies. This offers many advantages. You can vary poses, the angle of the camera, perhaps even the lighting. You can take time to pose properly and adjust your camera to its maximum efficiency. And often you save the subjects embarrassment; many of us aren't used to posing before a large audience.

The background should be selected carefully for these—or any— pictures. Public rooms, where so often we have to shoot, frequently will have quite gaudy wallpaper. In life, our eye tends to shut off this background by concentrating on the subjects. But in the photograph, leaves may swirl out of a subject's head like Medusa's serpentine tresses. Just as bad are the light fixtures that emerge like elk horns from the skulls of our subjects.

Backgrounds should be as simple as possible. Try to get light ones for subjects with dark hair or clothes and vice versa for blondes and those in light clothing.

Make sure that there is adequate light; often it can be augmented by the simple expedience of an assistant holding an outspread newspaper or cloth to reflect extra light upon the subject. This device is especially useful when we must photograph white and black people in the same group. Dark complexions always require considerable light; but when we shoot a group, we might get so much light on the darker people that we wash out the paler faces. In this case, pose dark people to one side and reflect light on them alone leaving only ordinary illumination on the light-complexioned.

Avoid flash pictures. They create dark, menacing shadows behind your subjects and sometimes put hoods on eyes to give a sinister appearance to an utterly innocent subject. Be sure that any light you're using doesn't accentuate 5 o'clock shadows, multiple chins, overhanging eyebrows, or bags under eyes. If flash must be used, try to lift it from the camera and hold it as far out as you can stretch your arm or the extension cord.

Move close to the subject. Backgrounds and foregrounds are almost always a total waste. You want the "picture," the important element, to be as large as possible on both the negative and the photoprint.

Photo Taboos

Organizational publications have far more photo taboos than general-circulation periodicals do. Avoid showing people holding cigarettes or beverages; even in this permissive age, many of your readers will be uncomfortable to see themselves or their colleagues demonstrating such dissolute vices. Never show a subject in an awkward or unflattering pose. A simple gesture of pushing back forehead hair can make a person look like a baboon tracking down head lice. Your readers may accept—and enjoy—Raquel Welch's cleavage, but they want the necklines on their co-workers' dresses to be discreetly high.

Never show even a trace of lingerie. Avoid bare skin on male legs between sock tops and trouser cuffs. Don't ever show a woman in a crouching position.

Don't show dirty dishes on a dining table; they look like the shards of

PEOPLE PICTURES are used large for dramatic effect in "Ingalls Today" of Ingalls Memorial Hospital, Harvey, Illinois. Silhouetted pictures are done in mezzotint screen. Note how body type on right-hand page is set around profile. Page: 8½x11, in black and white.

a Roman orgy. Don't show the legs of people sitting at a table for a panel discussion. Often they are awkwardly twisted and more times than not, when five people are seated at the table, 11 feet will show.

Be sure to read the instructions for use of a camera and each brand of film you use. It's best to stick to one brand of photographic materials. Not only does that minimize the instructions you have to read, you'll soon grow familiar with the capabilities of your film, chemicals, and photo paper—and, if you do your own darkroom work, with one set of procedures for developing and printing.

Now the picture has been taken and the print lies on your editorial desk. The first thing is to attempt to correct the deficiencies of the photographer.

If the cameraman has failed to group the subjects tightly enough, often they can be moved together by cutting the photo and moving the parts closer together. Cutting should be on straight lines, never around a silhouette especially of a human head or face. The edge of the overlapping portion is rubbed with a grease pencil or felt-tip pen before it's pasted into its new position. This technique is relatively easy; you needn't be an artist or technician to do it well. But it does require some practice. Your investment in this practice can pay high dividends.

Retouching

For a more common flaw, the blending of subject into background, a simple retouching technique can often save the day. Professional retouching is done either on the negative (a difficult and costly procedure) or by airbrush on the glossy, neither technique which is available to the typical organizational editor. So we use a gray *tempera* paint which comes in tubes or in watercolor cakes that range from 20 to 80 percent gray. Or you can buy a small jar of gray poster paint and lighten or darken it by adding white paint or black India ink. (Always add the darker color to the lighter paint.) A small saucer or piece of glass is a good place to mix paint. A fine-pointed paintbrush, called a "bright" and available at any art supply store, is used. Put just a tiny bit of paint on the brush.

Always work with gray, never pure white or black. Good retouching should be most unobtrusive.

If the subject had dark hair and/or clothing and is posed against a dark background—the most common error—outline the dark parts with a fine line of gray paint. Then, while the paint is still wet, with your thumb feather the paint down into the head or shoulders. The effect will be of a soft backlight and will define the subject nicely.

If a light subject blends into a light background, again outline the subject with gray paint. This time, though, feather the wet paint into the background. Now the effect will be of a soft shadow and the necessary separation between subject and background.

Tempera, called "poster paint," is washable. If you make a mistake, a tissue and a spot of spit will remove the error so you can start all over again.

If unwanted herbiage grows from a subject's head, it can be painted out with tempera. The paint dries flat so no brush marks show, another asset. The paint should be applied to create a rectangle, or at least that portion of one against which the subject's head is placed. Rooms are made up of rectangles and if we add a new, gray one, the eye won't even be conscious of it.

If the background is a busy and confusing one, it may be painted out in its entirety. But the effect is not too happy; the subjects seem to be in a vacuum. *Ghosting* the background is more effective. Acetate material (like stick-on letters) has a spattering of white dots. When this is applied to the background, it is toned down so it no longer distracts the reader yet it still suggests the actual conditions under which the picture was taken.

Now the editor is ready to "find the picture in the photo." The "photo" is the entire print; the "picture" is that portion which communicates. All extraneous pictorial matter must be removed, just as blue-pencilling eliminates superfluous words in written copy.

A useful aid in finding that picture is a pair of *cropper's Ls*, store-bought or homemade. L-shaped pieces of plastic or cardboard, about 1½ inches wide with arms from 12 to 18 inches long, are laid on a photo to define rectangles and help the editor find the most useful one. Remember that the rectangle need not be oriented the same way the whole photo is; it can be at a slant, if that creates a more effective picture.

Crop Marks

Although cropping is the equivalent of cutting, we don't actually cut the photo. If we did that, we couldn't change our mind. Also, we couldn't file the entire photo for future use, perhaps to be cropped to create an entirely new picture.

Crop marks produce the same effect as cutting, yet leave the photo intact. These marks are made in the margin of the photo with a grease pencil, which can easily be wiped away with a tissue should we change our mind or before the photo is filed. If the "picture" you're cropping out of the photo has edges parallel to those of the photo, you can just mark the chosen width by two marks in the bottom margin of the print, and the depth by two marks on one side. But if you're getting fancy and the "picture" is tilted compared to the print, you need to put crop marks in all four margins so the platemaker knows exactly what to extract from the original. If there are no crop marks, the platemaker goes to the

CROPPERS Ls are useful tools for "finding picture in photo." Some Ls show inch increments as here, but plain ones cut from cardboard are just as effective.

margin of the print.

Between the crop marks that show the width of the picture, we write the size that the plate should be. This may be given in picas or by the percentage of reduction (which we shall soon discuss). Size instructions may also be written on a projecting paper tab.

Be sure to write the size of the desired plate, not that of the actual cropped rectangle—as is too frequently done. If the plate should be the same size as the original photo, we write *S/S* for *same size*.

Pictures should generally be *shot down*, the plate made smaller than the original photo. This reduces the size of any flaws in the original. Only on the rarest of occasions do we *blow up*, make a plate larger than a photo. This is usually done when we need a picture of an individual

100-line screen

← 22 picas →

CROP MARKS show area of photograph to be used by platemaker. Note that size indicated in lower margin is that of plate and not of original photograph.

and all that's available is one of those little coin-in-the-slot photos. This is most often necessary in case of unexpected death when we can't shoot a new portrait.

Rarely are the plate and picture the same size. So the editor must have a quick and easy way of determining the size of the plate before it is made. For the making of the plate and the dummying of a page are often done simultaneously.

INSTRUCTION TAB is affixed to photograph, then folded over. It may be narrow, as here, when only percentage reduction is given, or it may be full width of photograph with crop marks and new size in picas written on tab.

Reduce to 63%
COM NEWS PAGE 5   85 screen

Scaling

Finding the size of the plate is done by *scaling* and we have three methods of doing that. The first is plain arithmetic. The formula is:
  W:H = w:h
The width is in the same proportion to the height no matter how the photo is blown up or reduced.

Usually we know the width of the plate, one or more columns of a newspaper or magazine; we must find out the height. Assume we have a photo, the cropped portion of which is 6x9 inches. (Note that we always give the horizontal measurement first. So this picture is a vertical rectangle.) We want to make it two columns wide, 4 inches. Now the formula is:
  W:H = w:h
  6:9 = 4:h
Reduce the equation by multiplying outside numbers which will then equal the product of the inside figures. So now:
  6h = 36
  h = 6
Because we started out with dimensions in inches, the 6 here is in inches, of course. We can use picas just as well.

This procedure can be done with a simple tool, a "circular slide rule," called a *scaling wheel*, or, a *proportional scale*. This has two disks, one slightly larger than the other, movable and mounted on the same axis. To find the dimensions of a plate, align the width of the photo on the inner wheel with the new, desired width on the outer wheel. Then find the height of the photo on the inner wheel; the number facing it on the outer wheel will be the height of the plate. Note that both dimensions of the photo are on the inner ring; dimensions of the plate are on the outer one. When the dimension of the photo, say its width, aligns with that dimension of the plate, a little window shows the percentage ratio. In our example, when the 6-inch width of the photo aligns with the 4-inch width of the plate, the plate will be 66.5 percent of the original size. We may indicate this on the photo or the tab as instructions to the plate-maker rather than write the desired new dimension. Usually the percentages don't come out as neatly—and obviously—as here.

Many editors prefer the *common-diagonal* method. It works this way: Lay a piece of tracing paper (or a plastic gridded sheet) across the cropped area of the photo, the "picture in the photo." Draw a diagonal from lower left to top right. Mark the desired new width. From that point raise a perpendicular to touch the diagonal. This is the height the plate will have to be. If we complete the rectangle, we have outlined the area of the plate.

If we know the height, we measure it, and a perpendicular line

> **MEMO:**
>
> PICTURE SCALING using the common-diagonal method.
>
> To find the height of a picture, ABCD, after reduction: Draw the diagonal AC. Measure the desired width of the plate, AE. At E raise the perpendicular, EF, until it meets the diagonal. From F draw a line parallel to the base, FG. The height of the plate will be AG.
>
> To find the width of a picture, HIJK, when it is reduced to a specified height: Draw the diagonal, HJ. Measure the desired height of the plate, HL. From L draw the perpendicular, LM, until it meets the diagonal. Draw MN parallel to the sides. The width of the plate is HN.
>
> When, infrequently, we have to enlarge a photo, OPQR: Draw the diagonal, OQ, and extend it, at least to S. Measure the desired width of the plate, OT. Raise the perpendicular, TU, and draw the parallel, UV. The height of the plate is OV.

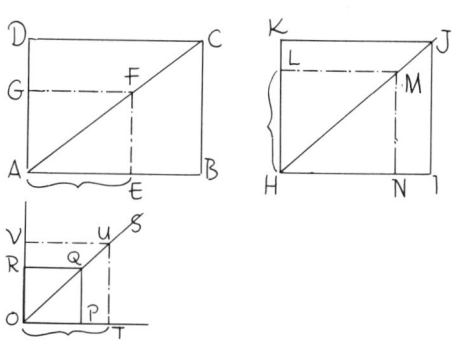

drawn to the diagonal will be the desired width.

The method is simple; it is accurate; it eliminates weird fractions that may result from arithmetic; you just measure the line and you know the new dimension. It is also easier to visualize how each element in the original will look when reduced when we can see its actual dimensions.

Cropping Specifications

Always leave room for a moving object to move into. If we crop too close to the front of that object, it seems to be bumping into the side of the picture.

This lebensraum can greatly affect the mood of a picture. If a person in a picture has plenty of space to look into, the effect is one of freedom and optimism. If the person's nose is right against the edge of the picture, the feeling is one of confinement and pessimism.

"Never amputate." Don't crop a picture at a joint, fingers, elbow, shoulder, knee, etc. This has a disturbing effect on the reader.

Don't cut tentatively into the human head. If you want to come into

AMPUTATION EFFECT is unpleasant to reader when human figure is cropped at any place indicated here. Cropping at head, from top, should be just above eyebrows.

the top of a head, cut between the eyebrow and hairline, never just take off a small slice of the skull-pan. For a tight profile, crop just in front of the ear. Sometimes a dramatic effect can be obtained by cropping between the lower lip and the bottom of the chin but never make like a guillotine at Adam's-apple level. If any of the neck is shown, there should also be enough of the shoulders to make a pedestal for the head.

Make sure that cropping eliminates only nonessentials. Some editors are so indoctrinated to tight cropping that they sometimes make a vice out of the usual virtue. In some instances what first appears to be wasted area really adds to the interest of the picture. A vast sky can express freedom and happy expansion; a large area of water around a boat can emphasize the vastness of the sea and the fragility of the small craft. Sometimes it's necessary to leave a large area of inconsequential space between two figures just to show their isolation from each other.

One form of cropping is the *mortise*, whose most common form is the *notch*, where one corner of a picture is cut away. Into this blank rectangle is inset caption matter. This device is useful only when there is a great waste area at a corner and must be used with unusual discretion.

The *bay* is a rectangular notch cut into a side of the picture. An *internal mortise* is completely surrounded by the picture.

Care must be taken that no mortise cuts into an essential element in the photo. *Interlocking mortises* have two pictures notched so the corners fit into each other. This should be zealously avoided.

Most rare is an irregular mortise where one or more small rectangles project out of the main area of the halftone.

Silhouetted halftones, *silhos*, especially useful in magazines, have the entire background cut away, giving the subject great prominence and emphasizing detail. This is a useful device when detail is important but might otherwise be overshadowed by less important elements. Silhouettes also build large areas of white space into a page, always a desirable situation.

MORTISES can eliminate dead areas in photos. Captions are often run in resultant space. Top left is "bay mortise"; top right is "notch" and lower photo has "internal mortise."

In a *modified silhouette*, the basic picture is a rectangle from which projects a small silhouetted element. The modified silho has at least one—and usually two or three—straight edges. This treatment is similar to the irregular mortise.

The larger a picture, the greater its impact. So a good picture, we are told, "should always be one column wider than we first think." This can't be accepted literally and 100 percent of the time; there just isn't enough space in a typical organizational publication. But this axiom should encourage the editor to use one large picture rather than two or more small ones.

INTERLOCKING MORTISES are fussy and contrived. Worse, in many instances pictures are distorted and reader is confused.

SILHOUETTE HALFTONE makes strong display for this page from "Georgia Alert" of the Georgia Department of Education. As general rule, however, it is best not to silhouette human profiles lest likeness be distorted.

A popular but lamentable practice also involves cutting photographs—to create a *collage*, a term so often misused we must define it. A collage (the word comes from the French for paste) is created by pasting together many small bits of photographs into a single unit, somewhat like a photographic mosaic. It is often confused with *montage*, a single photograph made from two or more negatives. Collages are confusing and impossible to identify. They should be outlawed. . . even if that means editors must find a new way to record The Company Picnic or The Annual Office Party.

Picture Identification

Every picture must be identified!
This applies to the cover of a magazine as well as to the tiniest shot in a collage and everything in between.

Editors seek "localness" of photographs. A school board publication doesn't want pictures of "just kids," cute as they may be and excellent as the photography may be. They want pictures of "our kids." Yet, if these pictures aren't identified by name as "our kids," that tremendous value of localness is thrown away.

It is impossible to identify people in a collage, another grave deficit against its use.

There are three styles of identification. We usually call *idents* in magazines *captions*; in newspapers, *cutlines* or just *lines*. All are collectively called "caption matter."

All publications use *i&e-lines.* the i-line (*identification line*) is the name of the subject. Usually it's set in all-caps of the caption type and

Stitching

Setting the stitch length for a new job run on the Sheridan folder/stitcher/trimmer is journey operator Robert R. Mason, a Columbus Local 147B member at Xerox.

JAMES R. McCLINTICK
. . . optimism amidst turbulence

CATCHLINE set flush left with cutlines indented are used by "Union Tabloid" of Graphic Arts Union.

I&E LINES used by "Union Tabloid."

centered. The e-line (*exposition line*) tells something about the subject. Usually it's in downstyle, centered, and begins with an ellipsis. So the i&e-lines look like this:

SARAH H. WHITSON
. . .named vice-president

In some publications, more often magazines, i&e-lines are set flush left.

The i-line is often used by itself, without the e-line.

Mostly used in newspapers are *catchlines-and-cutlines*. The catchline is set in a headletter in sizes from 14- to 24-point, following the capping style of headlines. The catchline may be centered (the most usual form) or flush left directly under the picture. The cutlines are set in regular caption type and run under the catchline. They must stay in the readability range, so 3-column pictures carry cutlines set in 1½-column measure and 4-column pictures carry two legs of 2-column measure.

A pleasant variation is to set the catchline flush left and then indent the cutlines generously at the left, be they in a single or double column.

How It's Done
THE PROCESS OF distilling alcohol from grain was explained to Rep. Bob Whittaker of Kansas on a recent visit to Farmland's alcohol plant at the research and demonstration farm. Dr. Don Graham explains it as Farmland executives and aides to Whittaker look on. Whittaker serves on the House Energy and Commerce committee. — (Photo by Frank Whitsitt).

CATCHLINE STYLES below show conventional centered element (left) and one set flush left. Examples at top left shows sideline treatment.

¡Viva AA en Mexico!
AA Photo by Bob Takis
The Mexican Government Tourism Office recently asked for several photographs of AA Mexico promotional materials for use in a presentation to travel agents, wholesalers and others at the Tourism Office's big "Tianguis Touristico" travel show in Acapulco this June. Yolanda Trevino Schausten, administrator of system boards in employee relations at HDQ, shows off a panoramic Mexico destination display which will illustrate for Touristico participants what AA is doing to help promote Mexico travel.

Special gift for special friend
Employees of the Abilene, Texas, store surprised Jerry Franks, Westgate Mall news stand operator, with a new wheelchair during ribbon-cutting ceremonies commemorating the store's recent reformatting. The chair replaces one employees gave Franks several years ago. □
— Palma Johnson, correspondent.

The *sideline* is display type, in one or two lines, running in an area under the left portion of the photo and the cutlines running to the right.

In all instances, the display line acts as an easy transition from picture to type and its use increases readership of the caption and materials below that, as much as 25 percent.

In magazines, cutlines (or captions) usually run without catchlines. Often the first word or two are capped as a read-in. While acceptable in magazines, this technique has proven useless in newspapers.

When long cutlines are not required—when, for instance, we have several pictures illustrating a single news event—we use a *singleton*, a single line of type, usually in 12-point. Magazines may use regular caption type. Singletons often run far longer than our formula allows; that's why it's necessary to have only one line lest the reader become lost in returning for the second line.

Sans Serifs are excellent caption letters, especially in magazines where it's essential that caption type be distinctly different from regular body type. In newspapers, boldface captions are customary, editors explaining that the color of boldface approximates that of a halftone and thus tends to tie pictures and type into the single integral unit they're supposed to be. Magazines usually do not use boldface captions on feature-article pages but often do so on news pages.

When there are many people in a picture, especially when they are posed in a random fashion, a "keyline drawing" is often the only effective way to identify people. A simple outline of each person in the picture is drawn on tracing paper and a number given to each form. In the cutlines, then, we need merely say, "3. Myrtle Bostner, 4. Jane Dowe, 5. etc. . . ."

Caption Specifications

Pictures are read like type is: top to bottom, left to right. Most editors accept the latter and almost always captions will remind the reader that identification is "left to right," "from left," "l-to-r," or in similar notations. But too frequently, people in the front row are identified first. Actually, identification should begin at the left of the top row. Because of the confusion, we should call them "Top row, center row, front row." (If there are more than three rows. . .forget it! No one, not even people in the picture, will bother reading the picture, much less the caption!)

Captions should begin by describing the action in the picture (and there darn well better be some!) and the "news peg," the reason the picture is being run. Then people are identified.

Organizational publications have to use many long and unwieldy titles. Lest they complicate identification, these should not be used for first reference. Write the regular caption, then, in a separate

THE EDITOR AS ART DIRECTOR   163

Paw power team, without camera shy Thunder

1. Tinker
2. Tia
3. Cochise
4. Apache
5. Tabee

KEYLINE DRAWING is useful for identification when subjects are not in neat rows. Technique works just as well with animals as with humans.

paragraph, bestow the titles. (Yes, captions can be—and should be—broken into 8-line grafs just as any body type is.)

In standard newspaper usage cutlines are written in the historical present. The famous photo of the Hindenberg burning in New Jersey was taken over half a century ago. But in the picture the dirigible is ablaze at this very moment.

However, there is another school of thought which holds that this "standard" newspaper form makes for stilted and artificial captions. So many editors—even some newspapers—write captions in the past tense: "The dirigible Hindenburg burned over New Jersey on May 6, 1937."

A typical caption might read something like this:

> Pulling the switch to start the new dynamo is John H. Gregg (wearing white hardhat) while Janet McDowell and Keith Connoly join the applause of hundreds of Consolidated employees crowded onto catwalks above.
>
> Mr. Gregg is vice-president for operations for Consolidated's Western Division; Miss McDowell is president of Local 799 of Amalgamated Energy Workers and Mr. Connoly is coordinator of the State Board for Alternate Energy.

Notice that the leading actor is identified first by some obvious device, the action performed, detail of costume (or here, the hat) or position. In this case, with a man and woman also to identify, we need give only the name. But if this distinction isn't possible, we'd have to say something like "Janet McDowell (left) and Bethany Reccardo."

When people must be identified by rows, a popular style goes like this:

> Also receiving certificates were:
> Top row (from left): John Cleary, Ann Anthony, etc., etc., Robert Means;
> Middle row: Anthony Bedell, etc., etc., May Browning;
> Front row: Betty Princeps, etc., etc.

Note that the introductory phrase leads into the names with a colon, the left-to-right is in parentheses and that each row starts with a new graf.

Hand Art

Hand art has its best use in setting mood. And sometimes it replaces photography that would be difficult to obtain; if you're doing a piece on alcoholism and its effect on your organization, you'll have a hard time

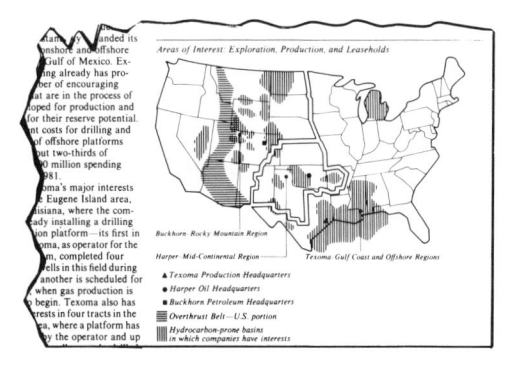

MAPS are pictorially pleasing while packing much information into small area. This, in four colors, is from annual report of Peoples Energy Company, Chicago.

finding someone to pose as the village drunk. Hand art is also useful in conveying abstract concepts.

Expository art is an especially useful category of hand art. It consists of maps, charts, graphs, and diagrams. The value of maps to explain international news has long been known. Now we find that it's equally high for local news. Indeed, the map can be something as localized as the floor plan of your building.

Graphs are particularly valuable in handling "number stories." All organizational publications are having to carry more and more stories involving numbers: budgets, annual performance reports, projections for the coming year, etc. Almost always, these numbers are significant only in relation to other sets of numbers, this year's performance compared to last year's, profits compared to gross volume, etc. A few simple lines on a bar graph can pack a lot of information into a small space and

REVERSE ART can give a new twist to a conventional subject and add typographic color to a page. Example at left is of soft-pencil technique; that at right, conventional pen-and-ink sketch.

166   EDITING THE ORGANIZATIONAL PUBLICATION

convey it quickly and accurately and understandably. Often graphs can be ornamented for greater eye-appeal.

Hand art provides pleasant textural contrasts to photography. When the editor doesn't have an artist's services available, photos can be converted to what appears to be hand art by manipulation of the platemaker. The simplest is *line conversion* or *linear definition*. Using special photo paper, the continuous grays of a photo are converted to simple black and white; the effect is that of a bold crayon drawing or poster. Editors can also have photos copied by Photostat to determine if the effect is one they want and also to retouch the conversion if essential detail has been lost.

Special screens create the halftone effect by using dots of irregular shapes. *Mezzotint*, which looks like crayon on a toothy drawing paper,

PHOTO MANIPULATION. Illustration above is line conversion, that at right above is horizontal-line halftone. At right is fine mezzotint, which comes in several degrees of boldness.

is a favorite. So are *parallel lines, concentric circles,* and literally dozens of others. All these techniques are simple to execute and there should be little, if any, extra cost.

Special screens are inexpensive and if your printer doesn't have any, it is not unconscionable to demand that at least one or two be made available to you.

Most pictures are close to a 3x5 ratio because most photographic materials come in this proportion. This is a pleasant shape, close to the "Golden Rectangle" of the ancient Greeks. But when we can contrast such typical photos with a long, tall, skinny picture or a wide, shallow one, we add "dynamic thrust" to a page. The photographer should always be urged to look for ways of obtaining such accent. A group of people may be posed on a stairway, for instance, to get a high vertical photo. And the editor should look for ways of cropping a conventional photo to obtain dynamic shapes.

We must be careful, however, not to attempt to force an inherently horizontal picture into a vertical rectangle. This usually comes about when the editor arbitrarily leaves room in a dummy before actually knowing what the picture will be, then squashing the photo into the available space rather than letting it assume its own logical shape.

A *dominant photo* is essential for good page design, acting as the nucleus for a strong pattern. Layouts without such a strong core, look accumulated rather than planned. The designer calls this the *hen-and-chicks* principle. The dominant photo—which should be at least 50 percent larger and, preferably, twice as large as the next-sized picture—becomes the hen around which cluster the smaller chicks. The subordinate photos should vary as much as possible in size and shape and tone.

Even when pictures are independent of each other, we need a dominant one on each page. In a picture *combo*, a grouping of photos on the same subject, the "hen" is essential.

Never use two or more pictures of exactly the same size and shape if you can possibly avoid it; the result is static and unexciting. But there are times when pictures must be exactly the same size: for instance, portraits of people who have received promotions or service awards. Here the danger is the *checkerboard effect*, caused by even rows and rows of photos all of the same shape and size and usually of tone as well.

The checkerboard is best broken by arranging the pictures so they create an irregular silhouette rather than a neat rectangle. This uses a bit more space, of course, but it isn't wasted space, it's insurance against reader disinterest.

If the rectangle must be used, there are ways of altering the checkerboard at least a little bit. Customarily, i&e-lines run under the portrait; if in one instance the ident is placed above the picture, the deadly monotony is relieved at least a little. Only once in any line should this

168 EDITING THE ORGANIZATIONAL PUBLICATION

DOMINANT PHOTO, top center, is strong nucleus for attractive page pattern from "Colonial Williamsburg News" in Virginia.

technique be used and, in the whole layout, not more than once in 20 pictures.

Another accent is to silhouette a picture instead of keeping it in the customary *square halftone* form. (A square halftone is a rectangular one, rarely, and never necessarily, a true square.) Another technique is to replace a portrait with some device in line, the trademark or monogram of the organization, the year in a distinctive typeface, or some appropriate ornament.

CHECKERBOARD EFFECT is broken by irregular, rather than rectangular, grouping. Note, in third row, third portrait has caption above it to break up regularity of row. This is from "PG&E Life" of Pacific Gas & Electric Company, Seattle.

While it would not be politic to single out an individual in a group like this to be the dominant portrait, we can use the hen-and-chick technique by using a nonportrait photo as the nucleus. We might, for instance, have an overall shot of retirement ceremonies as the hen around which the portraits cluster. Sometimes a piece of symbolic hand art can be the dominant element.

"Don't use the same picture twice!" This sound advice is often misunderstood. An editor waxed indignant when it was suggested that this had occurred in her magazine. She pointed out that different people—and so identified in captions—were in each photo. But in each instance, the photo showed two people in white laboratory coats peering through a microscope; this was "the same picture."

A frequent abuse of this advice is to use several shots of an individual, usually to run with a long interview. If the subject is photogenic and the photos show a good variety of expressions, this can be a good device. Unfortunately, most of the time such a series shows the subject running the gamut of emotions from A to B and "the same picture" not only gets monotonous, it appears that the editor is trying to stroke someone's ego, especially if the repetitive portrait is of one of the top brass.

An interesting technique, especially for magazines, is to silhouette a person by cutting the figure out of a photograph, pasting it onto a piece of blank paper and drawing in a background. This might be used, for instance, to show what plans Mike Malloy has for his upcoming retirement. We would, of course, be careful that this technique did not place the subject in any embarrassing—if imaginary—situation.

Marker Art

A form of expo art is the "marker," a combination of photography and some kind of hand-produced element such as the "X-marks-the-spot" or a dotted line showing where an addition to a building will be erected or the path of a new driveway to the parking lot. Such art, ideally, should be produced by a *combination plate*, made by using two

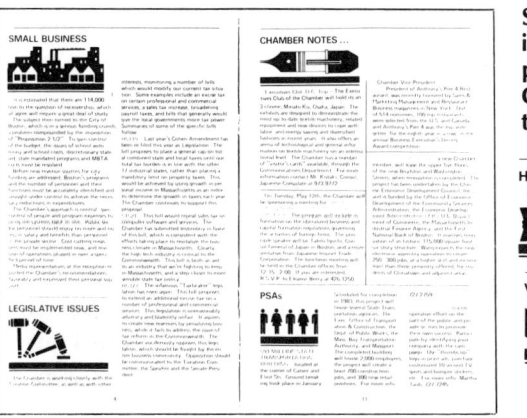

STRIKING IDEOGRAMS add interest to otherwise staid pages of "Boston," of Boston Chamber of Commerce. Section names are in color.

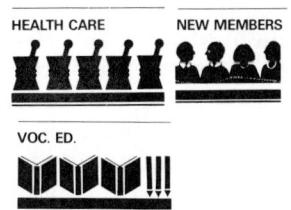

negatives, line and halftone. If the marker art is applied directly to the photograph, in reproduction it will not be in pure white or total black because all areas of a halftone have some kind of screen. A combination plate, though, keeps the markers in pure line against the grays of the halftone. The art is drawn on a transparent plastic *overlay* which is placed on the photograph to show its proper position. The platemaker then combines the two kinds of art.

Sources of Art

Many sources of art are available for organizational publications. The editor can personally shoot photos. Many organizations have photo departments whose services can be enlisted on an official or volunteer basis. Other photography comes in from correspondents, staffers at outlying points, or freelancers. These sources provide not only art but a lot of headaches. Too often absolutely execrable snapshots come from them and the political pressure to use them is great.

The editor must establish levels of photographic quality, instruct the sources about them, and then enforce the rules by not running poor photos. While it is painful—and often impossible—to throw out a poor photo that yet has high interest for at least some readers, in the long run the editor will be better off if quality control is rigidly exercised.

Colored Polaroids should be absolutely verboten. Even the best of these reproduce like a printer's nightmare. . .and rarely does the editor get the best of these.

The best reinforcer of quality control is to require the photographer to shoot the picture the second time. Ah, how quickly the lesson is learned and quality rises.

Photographs may be bought from photo agencies. They will give you catalogs of *stock photos*, or you can ask for a photo, say, of a crowded parking lot. The agency will send you several dozen so you can make a choice. Prices depend on the use you intend for it. News magazines will pay many hundreds of dollars for the use of a great action photo; a magazine with small circulation may pay only a couple bucks. You may buy a photo for limited one-time use, like the cover of a magazine, or you may obtain indefinite use; the price will vary. But the cost is always low and the quality is superb.

Excellent photography is available for free from many sources. Tourist bureaus of foreign countries, states, provinces, and even cities are delighted to supply you with glamorous shots of their homelands. Manufacturers are pleased to send pictures of their products in use in interesting settings; there is always opportunity to link your organization with others that you do business with.

Trade associations and interest groups from United Way to Save the Whales have a good supply of art free for the asking and the United States and Canadian governments are veritable treasure houses of photography.

Clip Art

For hand art, the best source—other than your own artist—is a *clip book*. Pictures—in every medium from oils to pen-and-ink—are printed, in booklet form, on slick paper, ready for pasteup. Books are inexpensive and provide pictures grouped by subject matter: Christmas, sports, kids, animals, cooking, etc., etc., etc.

Collections of last-century line art, now in the public domain, are sold in trade-book form. Anyone who buys such a book can use the art any way desired. This bothers some editors who fear their art may show up simultaneously in the publication of some organization in the same block. That fear is statistically unfounded. Realistically, we know that the reader of Heavenly Hospital's magazine will rarely, if ever, see Amalgamated Widget Corporation's tabloid.

To dispel even the slightest worry, though, clip art can readily be modified to make it uniquely your own. If a little girl is wearing a white dress, convert it into black or gray. Add or subtract backgrounds. Crop innovatively. Combine two or more pieces of art into a single collage.

The editor of a Mimeographed newsletter has the most difficult problem with art. The simplest method is to draw or trace line work into the stencil. The picture must be kept simple and cutting should be done through silk or plastic as suggested for headlines. Shading can be added by simply placing a textured sheet of plastic under the stencil and rubbing with a smooth instrument.

Many national organizations—notably church and charitable groups—offer pre-cut stencils. You type onto the regular stencil, then cut a hole, and paste in the insert.

Electronic stencil cutters reproduce pasteups; then art can simply be drawn or clipped and pasted into position. Halftones can be reproduced by such stencils but the results are usually less than totally satisfactory. Line art comes through very well.

The best way to learn the techniques of stencil art is from the sales office of the company that makes the machine you use. They're usually most anxious to have their customers demonstrate the versatility of their duplicator and will spend much time showing you the best way to expand the use of your own machine.

Editors often wonder if there is any use for ornaments or decorations in a publication. They fear there isn't because the movement toward *functionalism*—which demands that every element on a printed page do a useful, necessary job—has generally stripped pages down to the bare essentials. But any device that will capture the attention of potential readers and lure them into actually reading is functional.

Ornamentation and decoration ought to be used for definite purposes. They should be appropriate to the verbal copy and definitely subordinate to it. Ornaments are a typographic cherry on the whipped cream; a little goes a long way. The editor's main concern should be not to overdo these devices.

CLIP-ART MANIPULATION can eliminate any chance of same illustration in two publications. Original clip art is figure of girl at top left.

Top center shows addition of three other pieces of art: two girls and tree in background; steps are drawn. Top right changes tonal value of hair, sweater, skirt and socks. Lower left adds background; lower right combines with other hand art to make headline. Lower center, acetate shading sheets make Ben Day patterns for blouse and skirt; legs are cropped and background rectangle is drawn by hand.

Constants

A cross between art and type are those elements of a publication that we call the constants: nameplate, masthead, folio lines, headings, and logos.

The *nameplate* (also called the *flag* but never, correctly, the *masthead*) is the name of the publication in display form at the top of page one of a newspaper or magazine cover. A good flag should be legible, distinctive, appropriate, and handsome. The editor should examine the flag with an unprejudiced but merciless intensity. If it fails to meet these standards, it should be redone.

Many nameplates are legible and fairly attractive, but often fail to be distinctive. If just ordinary type is used, the effect is that of signing your name with a typewriter; it is not a signature. But it is easy to make even the most humdrum nameplate become unique. Letters may be overlapped or joined. The dot on an *i* or *j* can be replaced with the organizational emblem. A short word may be inset into the bowl of any letter.

An uncommon alphabet may be used without manipulation, or handlettering may be used. But, because lettering is a very specialized art form that even great artists have rarely mastered, this assignment should not be given to an amateur.

MASTHEAD IS PERSONALIZED for "Lord Facts" by running picture of different employee, chosen at random, each month as "illustration." This guarantees readership of element that otherwise is usually ignored. Lord Corporation is in Erie, Pennsylvania.

Saint Louis Public Schools

School & Home

National award-winning publication Vol. 18, No. 6 March, 1981

C☉MPASS

Vol. XI No. 4 April 1981
Northwestern Financial Corporation

C✚RING

Southeast Alabama Medical Center/Dothan, Alabama February/1981

ORNAMENTED NAMEPLATES are very popular with organizational editors.

"School & Home" of St. Louis Public Schools uses ampersand to add bit of flavor to its Oldstyle Roman flag.

"Compass" of Northwestern Financial Corporation in North Wilkesboro, North Carolina, replaced the O in Oldstyle nameplate with company insignium.

"Caring" of Southwest Alabama Medical Center of Dothan uses familiar Red Cross of healing arts to give distinction and appeal to its flag.

There can be a happy exception even to this admonition. The editor of a magazine for a Canadian metals company chooses an employee to write the nameplate each issue in his or her own handwriting. This is reader involvement at the best level.

The masthead carries the name of the publication—in identical form to that on page one or the cover—of the editor and staff, and of the publishing organization, the mailing address and perhaps the phone number, and other pertinent information. Laws in many states require the names of certain officials in the sponsoring organization.

Listing the names of all reporters and correspondents is an excellent morale builder. The masthead also can be the wall where we hang plaques (awards won by the publication) and certificates (of membership in such groups as the International Association of Business Communicators).

The masthead should be condensed to occupy minimum space. Most readers ignore it; those who need the information will seek it out. The

"The Children's Hour" of Milwaukee Children's Hospital decorates its nameplate with stylized human forms. Bars and small type at top left are in black; name and symbols, in bright green.

"Phoenix Quarterly" of Institute of Scrap Iron and Steel in Washington leans heavily on symbolism. Just as legendary phoenix—shown in handsome stylization in Q—rose from ashes, so does reclaimed metal.

"Eagle" of Anheuser-Busch in St. Louis is appropriately decorated with bird it is named for. In realistic form, eagle echoes more stylized version which is company trademark and is reproduced in top-right area of flag.

masthead often runs with the table of contents in a magazine and on the opinion page of a newspaper. Sometimes it is incorporated with the *mailing indicia*. This is the area left blank to paste on the address label and next to it is any information required by the Postal Service regarding the mailing status of the periodical.

Folio lines should appear on every page. On a newspaper, these carry, in one or two lines, the name of the publication, perhaps the city of publication, perhaps the organization name, the date, and (the original meaning of "folio") the page number. On a magazine, its name appears on the even-numbered pages, the date on the facing pages. In both instances, the page number (minus the actual word "page") should appear in the outside corner. Newspaper folios usually run at the top of the page; on magazines, they can run either at the top or bottom. It is malfunctional to run page numbers in the outside margin, halfway up the page. This trendy placement inevitably hides the numbers under the reader's thumb.

176   EDITING THE ORGANIZATIONAL PUBLICATION

Pages from organizational periodicals are often torn out to send to relatives and friends if they carry the picture or news about an employee, to officials to demand information or action on a public issue, etc. These *tearsheets* are useful only if fully identified.

Headings are the unchanging labels that appear on regular features such as retirements, promotions, etc. All should bear a strong family resemblance to each other as well as to the nameplate. Type should be distinctly different from the headletter. Often they are ornamented with art but the pictorial element should be discreet and unobtrusive. A distinctive panel or frame can provide visual unity.

Headings should be used sparingly; too often they are lifeless and give no clue to the transient reader such as a headline might.

Many editors, instead of using *art headings*, give the name of the feature in a bimo (thus attracting regular readers) above a news head (which we hope may attract the transient.)

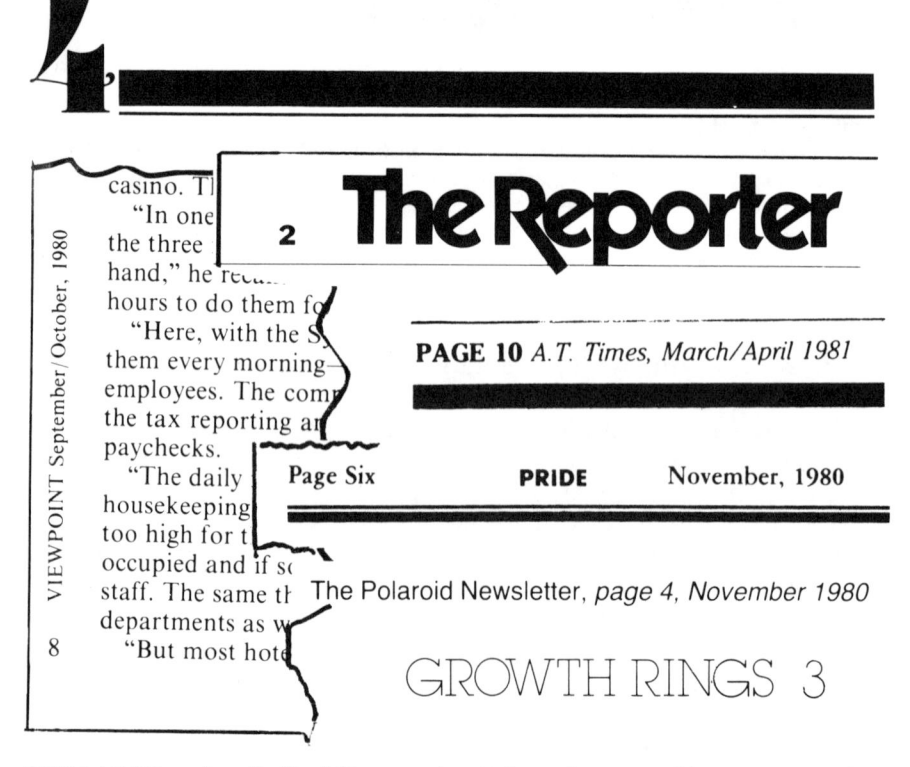

FOLIO LINES are handled in different styles. "Viewpoint" runs sideways on page but note that page number is properly oriented. At top, page number becomes strong ornamental device and heavy bar adds typographic color. "The Reporter" duplicates its nameplate in folios. "A.T. Times" places folio with 9-point rule and "Pride" uses Oxford rule. "Polaroid Newsletter" is in quiet and conventional style, and "Growth Rings" is large in size but light in weight.

THE EDITOR AS ART DIRECTOR 177

NAMEPLATES in organizational publications tend to be more distinctive than those of general-circulation newspapers and magazines. Although examples here are all type without much decoration, each has touches that make it unique.

"Tablet" for University of Chicago Hospitals and Clinics has classical Roman letterform, manipulated just a trifle. Foot serifs of T and A join, as do top bars of E and T. Note how bottom serif of L bends around bowl of B. Large area left blank for mailing label focuses attention on name itself. Very small reproduction of University seal is unobtrusive in folio lines.

"WVU Report" of Western Virginia University in Morgantown uses interesting Modern Roman, enhanced with discreet but handsome monogram which subtly repeats WVU forms.

"Bulletin" of Portland State University in Oregon uses Novelty Ornamented face.

"Off The Cuff" of Harleysville (Pennsylvania) Insurance Companies starts with plain Sans and overlaps letters to make highly distinctive design.

"Talk Time" of Mother Church of Christian Scientists, Boston, Mass., manipulates Shadowed Ornamented face. Note how lowercase *a* and *i* tuck under arm of capital Ts.

TABLE OF CONTENTS pages vary markedly in style. "Elizabethtown Magazine" of Elizabethtown (Pennsylvania) College repeats front and back cover designs with their captions in left-hand column; in the right-hand column miniatures of inside art add interest.

"Profile" of IBM, Canada Ltd., Don Mills, Ontario, repeats its cover shot with caption; masthead is carried in shallow strip at bottom of page. "Panhandle Magazine" of Panhandle Eastern Pipeline Co. in Houston runs its table of contents and masthead on last page with full color miniatures of inside-page art.

Color

As ancient, widespread, and effective as the use of art is the use of color. The first book printed by movable type was lavishly decorated with color and the printer ever since then has recognized its value in communication.

There are two kinds of color. The simplest—and therefore the least expensive—is *spot* or *flat color*. This is the use of a color, alone or in combination with another hue or black, to print type, art, rules, and ornaments. *Process color* reproduces the full spectrum of nature.

The artwork for process color—a full-color photograph or transparency—is placed before the platemaker's camera. An orange filter blocks out all the red and yellow components of the picture and allows only the blue elements to create a negative which at the same time is screened in a halftone dot pattern.

A green filter allows only red elements to form a screened negative; a purple filter blocks red and blue, creating a screened image of the yellow components. Each of these is a *color separation*. The process is long, complicated, and costly.

From each of the three color separations—and from a black-and-white rendering of the original colored art—is made a halftone printing plate. Each plate is printed in its own color. (We might note that the color we refer to as "red" is actually *magenta*, a more purple hue; the

COLOR is used in two major areas and in one minor one for "Entre Nous" of l'Association des enseignants franco-ontariens of Ottawa, Ontario. Headline and nameplate are in bright red as is box that surrounds nameplate area. Page, 8½x11, carries four 11-pica columns.

"blue" plate is printed in *cyan*; and the "yellow" is actually a *lemon* color.) A sophisticated optical illusion is now created. When tiny yellow and blue dots are printed side by side, for instance, the reader's eye mixes the two colors optically just as a painter might mix yellow and blue paint to create green pigment. Varying the relative size of the dots produces different hues of green, from that of grass to that of jade. The more white of the paper that's visible between the dots, the lighter the *tint* of the green.

Adjacent red and yellow dots produce varying hues of orange; red and blue make purples. Black dots make a deeper *shade* of the colors.

Many of the tens of thousands of hues discernible by the human eye combine all the primary colors. Human skin tones of all races, for instance, have the red we might expect but combine yellow and—surprisingly to most of us—also blue.

Each of the four colors requires a trip through the press. One color may be printed, the press washed up and the second color produced. Big "color presses" actually are four separate presses, built into the same complex, with paper going automatically and directly from one to the next.

Spot color is produced from *mechanical separations*. The artist makes a separate drawing for each color to be printed. This eliminates the need for costly optical separations and even more costly color correction.

An interesting yet inexpensive way to use spot color is by a "duotone." Original art is a black-and-white photo. From it are made two plates; one is printed in a color, the other in black. The result is a new, third color. When black and orange, for instance, are combined in a duotone, the picture appears in sepia; the two original colors are no longer distinguishable. The effect is pleasant and its cost—the same as any spot color—pays a handsome dividend.

Some editors believe that all pictures on a page or spread must be either in process color or in black-and-white. Not so! A good b&w photo can enhance a full-color one. And vice versa. A picture should never run in full color just because such art is available. Many a picture is stronger in black-and-white than in color. Decision to use color should always be based on its effectiveness in a specific situation.

Just as b&w and process color can be compatible on a single page, so can line and halftone art.

When spot color is used, it should be in bold, simple masses. No more than three areas of color should appear on any page or double spread. The areas may be large but if there are more than three, they start competing with each other and their effect diminishes.

Color is most effective when used for nonverbal elements: boxes, rules, and ornaments. Color should never be used to print body type and only cautiously in printing headlines. Nameplates may be printed

THE EDITOR AS ART DIRECTOR 181

in color because these really are not read, they are recognized as ideograms. Standing headings, too, are recognized rather than read and may be printed in color.

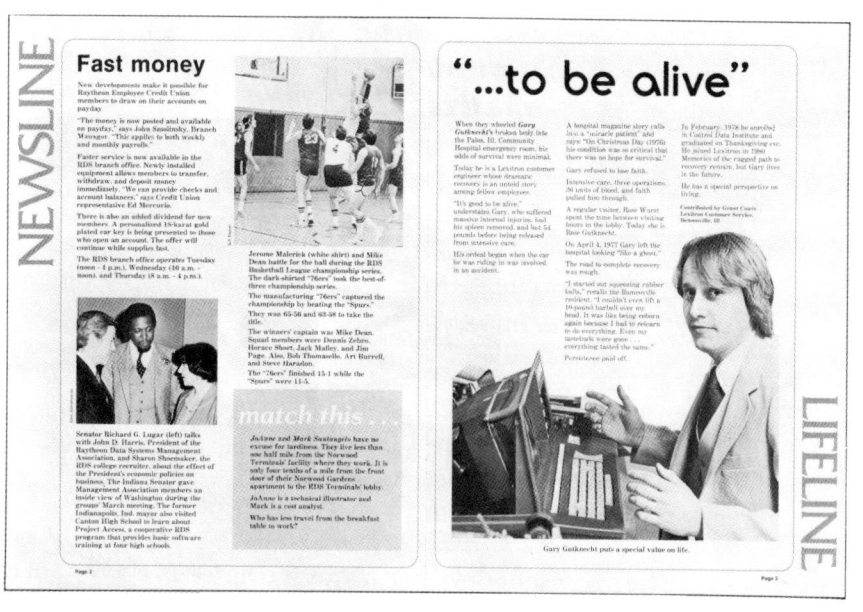

THREE AREAS OF COLOR—maximum for effectiveness—are used well on spreads from "Comline" of Raytheon Data Systems, Somerset, Mass. Strong section logos which run sideways and tint block at bottom of left-hand page are in grass green. Same color is used for nameplate on front page and will vary from month to month. Page: 9x12.

182   EDITING THE ORGANIZATIONAL PUBLICATION

LIFESIZE PHOTO adds great impact to page of "Ingalls Today" of Ingalls Memorial Hospital, Harvey, Illinois. Notice inset initial in POA, necessary to direct reader because headline is so small.

Tint blocks can be a pleasant device. An area is printed in a *screen* of a color, a plate peppered with tiny white dots which lighten the tone of the color. Red, screened down far enough, becomes pink, for instance. Over this tint block is surprinted matter in black: headline, body type, and line art. Halftones should never be printed over a tint block, the image becomes muddy. (Nor should halftones be printed in color; details wash out.) Line work may be surprinted on a tint block.

Another good way to use spot color is through *internal silhouettes*. In this technique, the color, either full-strength or screened, is laid down in a background rectangle or free-form mass. But a shape is "cut out" of the colored area, and into that white area is printed a black halftone or line art.

Yellow is the only color that can be used full strength as a tint block. All others must be screened down. If the background color is too deep, the visibility—and hence the legibility—of surprinted type is reduced, often fatally. We must always maintain, if not the maximum, at least a marked difference in tonal value between type and its background. This is also true when gray is used as a tint block. Such a screen should be no darker than 20 percent, lest the type become lost in the murky background.

The editor must always check a tint block, gray or color, to make sure that the pressman hasn't allowed it to "plug up," to become blotched and muddy.

If the editor has only one spot color available, it's best to avoid the primary or secondary hues. Rather than red, use burnt orange; use olive rather than Kelly green. Be sure the color is strong enough to be visible; a headline printed in yellow, for instance, is wasted; no one can see it, much less read it.

Research shows blue as the favorite color of all people. Women prefer red as a pure color and violet as a tint, a color to which white has been added. Men choose blue, in full color, tints and shades. Brown is the most versatile of colors, appealing to men and women alike and with enough "guts" to carry headlines.

We must be careful to avoid misuse of colors lest a bad psychological effect be created. *Cool colors*—blue, green, some yellows—are not very appealing in the middle of a January blizzard. And *warm colors*—red, orange, brown—may make the reader more uncomfortable during an August heat wave. A picture of a steak printed in green may disquiet the appetite and a human face in blue conjures fears of anemia or debilitating disease.

Color is an excellent editorial tool. But it is costly and we must always ponder whether the added expense will pay off in readership. If you can't afford color, don't wail. All layouts must be strong in black-and-white to start with. A good b&w page can be enhanced by color but it is attractive enough to stand on its own. (A poor b&w page will rarely be strengthened—and often weakened—by the addition of color.)

Because of its added cost, color usually tempts the editor to overuse it, to get full value for the price paid. Just the opposite, though, is the secret of good color: Use it sparingly. Color is a typographic spice that is most effective when, like culinary spice, its effect is subtle and controlled.

The many uses of art and color—to communicate, to attract, to lead the reader through the page, to set a mood, and to establish a character—should be mastered by the editor. Inept usage tends to make the publication look busy and amateurish.

PROJECTING ELEMENTS from one area to another tie them neatly together. Notice how little *p* in nameplate breaks through folio rules into page itself. So does tassel on mortar board in top right of nameplate area. Two halftones project upward into area above them in "People" of American International Group of New York.

Chapter 8: The Editor

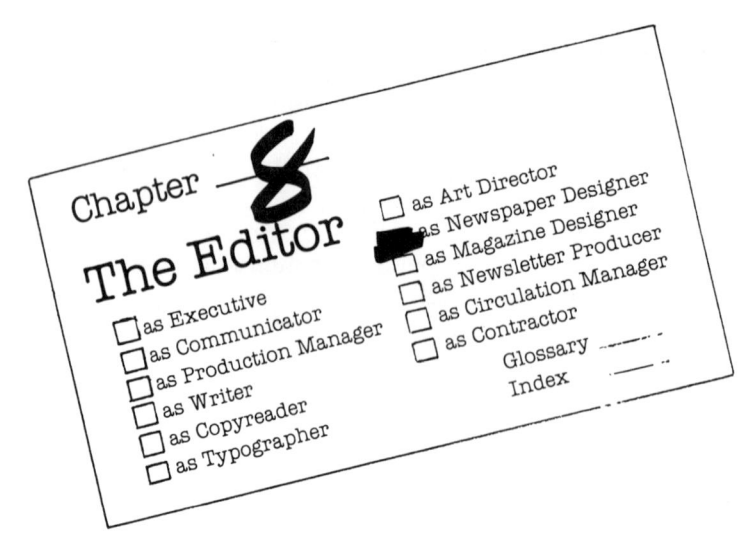

- [ ] as Executive
- [ ] as Communicator
- [ ] as Production Manager
- [ ] as Writer
- [ ] as Copyreader
- [ ] as Typographer
- [ ] as Art Director
- [ ] as Newspaper Designer
- [x] as Magazine Designer
- [ ] as Newsletter Producer
- [ ] as Circulation Manager
- [ ] as Contractor
- Glossary
- Index

A cornflakes box is much different from a perfume bottle or a sardine can or a garment bag. For the content dictates the package. As newspaper layout is the packaging of the news, the news *budget*—all the material available for a specific issue—will determine what the front page, and all other pages, will look like.

The budget of an organizational newspaper won't be as kaleidoscopic as that of a daily newspaper where one day a President abdicates and the next day a routine fire alarm is the biggest event to report. But there will still be marked differences in the contents of an organizational publication from issue to issue and the editor must be prepared to present whatever that content may be in a way that is most attractive, easy, convenient, pleasurable, and rewarding for the reader.

10:30 Formula

Any layout formula must then ignore specifics and be broad enough to handle any combination of stories and pictures. Such is the *10:30 formula*. Envision a clock face superimposed on a newspaper page. Page design starts in the upper-left corner, approximately 10:30 on the clock dial, and continues in a clockwise progression.

Page layout begins in the top-left because there the reader begins the task of consuming a newspaper—or any other—page. This is the *primary optical area (POA)* where, since the earliest days of childhood, the user of the Latin alphabet has been acclimatized to start looking at, and then reading, a printed page.

That same indoctrination tells us that when we reach the lower-right corner, we have finished the page. We turn or flip the page of a book, magazine or newspaper, or, if it's a 1-page piece, a letter for

> **MEMO:**
>
> POA
>
> TA
>
> GUTENBERG DIAGRAM shows action of reading eye. It enters page at top left, the primary optical area, POA. Arrow shows reading gravity, pulling eye down to lower right corner, the terminal area, TA. Crosses show fallow corners where extra optical magnets are required to guide the eye into those areas.
>
> Just as humans dislike going against gravity by climbing stairs, hills, or ladders, so the eye resists going against reading gravity, upward, to the left, or anywhere in that quadrant as shown by the wavy lines.

instance, we throw it in the out basket or wastebasket or dispose of it some way. This is the *TA*, the *terminal area*. And the *reading diagonal*, from POA to TA is the basic path of the reading eye.

The eye doesn't scoot straight down this simple path, of course. When it is actually reading, the eye swings from line to line somewhat like a pendulum. Visually attractive elements can lure the eye into other areas of the page. Indeed, we place these *optical magnets* throughout the page to lure readers through the whole page. Such lures are especially needed, and used, in the *fallow corners*, top right and lower left, where the eye is least apt to wander on its own.

The reading diagonal is also called *reading gravity* because of its strong and constant pull on the reading eye. It is a descriptive term because it describes the effect on the reading eye so accurately. Just as you and I prefer not to move against gravity, up a ladder or a hill or a flight of stairs, so the eye resists any attempt to make it move against reading gravity, upwards, to the left, and anywhere in between.

We must constantly be aware of the pull of reading gravity and arrange elements on a page so the eye is never forced to go "backwards."

The Nameplate

The first element that is placed in page one is the nameplate. The conventional style is to run the nameplate across the top of the page. We may place a headline, a story, or a picture—or any combination thereof—above the flag, in the *skyline* position. Or we may use a nameplate narrower than full-page width, move it around on the page and make it a *floating flag*.

For this discussion, let's assume a 5-column *tabloid*. Very few organizational newspapers are broadsheets, with pages of about 15x21 inches; most are on pages half that size, tabloid size. If optimum line lengths are used for body type, the tab page will have four columns. Some editors will stay with the conventional 5-column page and a few, especially in Europe and some parts of Canada, may even place six too-narrow columns on a tab page.

For a 4- or 5-column page, the editor would be wise to have two or even three variations of the nameplate. One size could be centered on four or five columns. Another size could be used in 3-column measure. Depending on the style of the flag, it might be possible to arrange its elements in a 2-column area with the nameplate set in two or three lines instead of the customary one. In its narrowest form, it may be reversed—white on black—or be in black on gray in order to give adequate weight to a small area. The nameplate is a strong visual unit and by having it available in more than one size, the editor can use it as an integral part of the page design.

Once the flag has been placed, we start on the 10:30 formula. We place a strong *attention compellor* in the POA, 10:30 on our imaginary clock face. As the reading eye comes into this page, it must be grabbed at once.

The strongest attention-compellor at our disposal is a halftone. But we must be wary of running a picture in the POA of every front page lest we create a visual cliche that cannot attract a reader.

If for any reason we can't use a photo up there—we had one there in the last issue, we don't have a good picture, or the lines of force move in the wrong direction—we can use any strong optical magnet. In approximate descending value, such elements are:

A strong headline;
A piece of hand art, especially expo art;
A strong head with a small portrait;
A box.

Color, in any form, is a strong magnet and will enhance the lure of any of these elements.

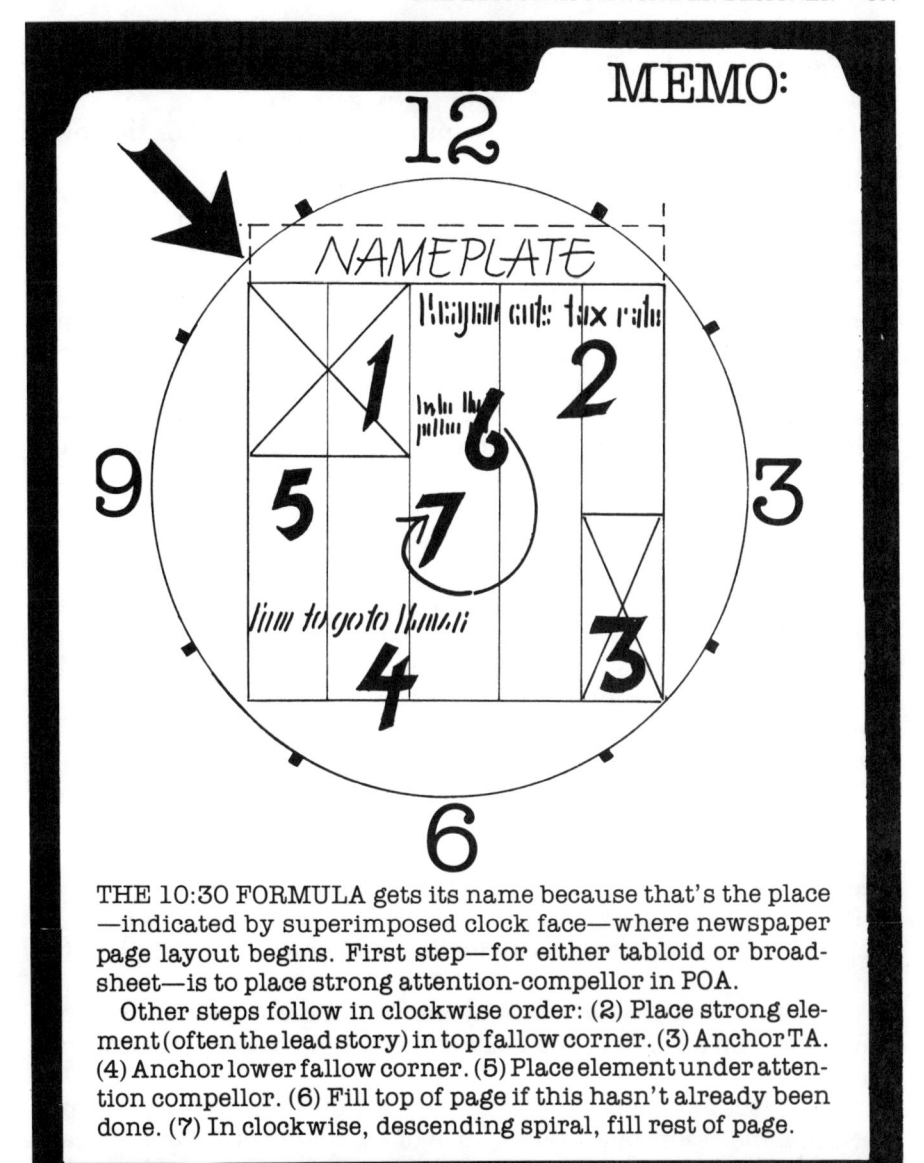

THE EDITOR AS NEWSPAPER DESIGNER 187

MEMO:

THE 10:30 FORMULA gets its name because that's the place —indicated by superimposed clock face—where newspaper page layout begins. First step—for either tabloid or broadsheet—is to place strong attention-compellor in POA.

Other steps follow in clockwise order: (2) Place strong element (often the lead story) in top fallow corner. (3) Anchor TA. (4) Anchor lower fallow corner. (5) Place element under attention compellor. (6) Fill top of page if this hasn't already been done. (7) In clockwise, descending spiral, fill rest of page.

Once the POA has been secured, we move clockwise into the top fallow corner, 1:30. This is the place where broadsheet dailies customarily display their lead story. Although the tab editor doesn't feel tied down to this position, more often than not this is where the main story of the issue is placed. As we indicate this on our sketch dummy, we merely place the head, leaving until later the disposition of the story.

The next step is to *anchor the corner* at the lower right, the TA. This can be done with any strong element although pictures and boxes are the favorite. If a headline is used as an anchor, it should be no higher than 2½ inches from the bottom of the page.

Our next stop on our clockwise progression is to anchor the lower fallow corner.

Then we go back up to the element in the POA. If that was a photo, and if a story runs with it, we will run the story directly under the picture.

"Picture above type" is one of the axioms of typography. And it's based on sound principles. The eye is caught by the attractive picture, then, instinctively and surely, it moves directly downward into the caption, from there into the headline, and then into the story.

Unrelated photos should be as widely isolated as possible from each other. There should be at least one picture on every page and there should be some art in the basement of each page.

Sometimes we paint ourselves into a corner and have to place a picture alongside the accompanying headline. A passable—but not an ideal—technique is the *tuck-in*. The headline runs in the first or first two columns; the picture (it's usually a 1-column mugshot that's used this way) runs in the next column to the right. Body type runs in all three legs and squares off at the bottom. The head can be any width needed; most usually it will be 1- or 2-column. Most usually the photo will be one-column to break a tombstone at the top of a page. The picture may be wider, however.

A *semi-tuck* is a pleasant variation and provides a bit easier empty sweep. Now the legs of body type are squared off top and bottom. The picture runs at the top right of this area leaving a 1- or 2-column area as deep as the picture. Into this space the headline is centered.

If there is an opening at the top of the page, we fill that as the next step. Then, in a clockwise, descending spiral, we fill the rest of the page.

(Note that a single element may perform more than one function. Should we run a *banner head* clear across the top of the page, it would anchor both top corners.)

As we place any element on the page, there are several things we must keep in mind. Most important is to avoid *jamming* or *bumping* headlines. Two or more heads side by side horizontally are *tombstones*; when a narrow head rides directly under a wider one, we have an *armpit*. Either kind of jamming is undesirable because the heads compete against each other.

A tombstone can be broken only by separating the heads with at least a column of body type or a picture. A *hood*, a 3-sided box around a head, is inadequate to break the stone. At least eight lines of body type must separate heads in the same column to avoid an armpit. This means that a story under a multi-column head must run in each column, directly under the headline. Or a picture can run right under one side of the head with the story in the remaining columns. This is a *canopy* and is the only practical device, other than a box, to link pictures and words horizontally.

If the paper is folded—tabs may or may not be—there must be attractive display below the fold. For the reader may see only the bottom half, the *basement*, at first glance and it must be appealing enough to lure the reader into picking up the paper. Ideally the basement ought to have an attractive piece of art and at least one multicolumn head.

Stories should be arranged so that when a dollar bill is laid horizontally anywhere on the page it will touch at least one display element. A concentration of body type materially greater than the area of a bill will look forbiddingly cold and gray and will scare off many a potential reader.

Arranging type in a horizontal layout is an effective way of avoiding this massing of unrelieved body type. An added advantage is that a horizontal story appears considerably shorter than if it were run vertically. As the reader will always jump into a short story sooner than into a long one, this illusion gains us at least a little added readership.

There is one notable exception to the horizontal layout; that is the *tower* or *chimney*. Two columns are filled entirely with stories under 2-column heads and/or with 2-column pictures. This built-up unit gives a strong vertical thrust in contrast to the basically horizontal elements that make up the rest of the page.

Similar to a chimney is a roundup. Here a group of small items is gathered into a larger unit that may or may not be a full column deep. An inclusive headline titles the roundup and each item carries a smaller head, all of identical size. Roundups are a popular device. The reader likes them because the items are short; the editor likes them because they bunch up a lot of little items that are messy to dummy into a single element that can carry a headline large enough to be an effective part of a page pattern. Promotions, for instance, can be handled neatly in a roundup. The major head might be in 36-point:

**SMITH'S MOVE TO VICE-PRESIDENT
LEADS PROMOTIONS IN ACCOUNTING**

The item about Smith would run under this head. Then would come a series of about 14-pointers, MATTHEWS MOVED TO TOLEDO, CARRUTHERS NAMED SUPERVISOR, THREE ADVANCE IN MIAMI TERRITORY, etc. These may alternate between Roman and Italic or be in just one form.

A vexatious problem is trying to compromise between two pressing needs: to have an adequate *story count*, the number of pieces on page one, and to avoid *jumps*, continuing stories on inside pages.

The front page of a newspaper should be a showcase of that issue's contents. While there is no magic number of heads that should run on a page, it is obvious that only one or two will usually be inadequate. If the reader is interested in those two topics, everything is fine. But if they fail to grab attention, it's nice to have a couple others ready to do the job. A generation ago, daily editors often placed as many as 20 heads on page one. They just ran the opening paragraph or two and then continued the story to an inside page. Today's reader actively resents jumps and the editor who uses them must do so with trepidation. How then do we reconcile this obviously conflicting need? When a story is just plain too long to run on page one, it can often be divided into a main story (which runs on the front page) and one or more *sidebars* (which can run on an inside page). By using a reefer which says something like, "More about HOLIDAYS on page 5" instead of the peremptory "Turn to Page 5," we build actual readership.

The narrow line between too few stories on page one and too many jumps is a difficult one to define. The editor must do it more by visceral reaction than by formula and must reevaluate decisions on the basis of the news budget.

All the while these decisions are being made and elements are being placed on a page, the editor must strive for pleasant balance. A device many editors find useful is to visualize the page as a sheet of plywood, hanging freely on a pivot at the *optical center* of the page, 10 percent higher than the mathematical center. Each element that's dummied

HORIZONTAL FORMAT is stressed by "Publishers' Auxiliary" of National Newspaper Association, Washington, D.C. Index and inside page teasers are in an unusual position immediately under the flag. Note sidehead at foot of page.

THE EDITOR AS NEWSPAPER DESIGNER 191

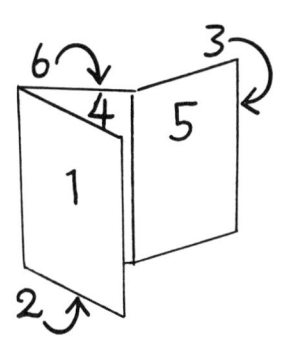

SIX-PAGE FORMAT is used by "Tempo" of St. Joseph Hospital and Medical Center, Phoenix, Arizona. Pages 8x12 are all on one sheet with conventional letter-fold. Diagram shows page numbering.

onto a page is thought of as a piece of wood—its thickness varying with its optical weight—that is nailed onto the plywood.

As the first element is placed—unless it's a 5-column one—the page will be out of balance. With the next element we try to bring it back into balance. We will never succeed entirely—and that's good. For a perfectly symmetrical page would hang absolutely straight. Such a static arrangement is not particularly interesting and a perfectly balanced page should not even be sought, even if it were possible to achieve.

In the process of eliminating nonfunctional elements, we have thrown out vertical *column rules* and horizontal *cutoff rules*. None of them is functional except with *wild pictures*. When a picture runs by itself, with no accompanying story, it's wild or *self-standing*. Such a picture, as well as one under a canopy head, must be separated by a cutoff rule from the unrelated story immediately under it. Reading gravity is so strong and the pix-above-type convention is so strong that the reader will almost automatically move directly from art to words. If the two are unrelated, the reader feels cheated and put-upon—and if there's anything an editor doesn't need it's a disgruntled reader.

We do use horizontal rules today but only for cosmetic purposes. It is difficult to make a persuasive case for column rules except on a rare page that we want to look drastically different from all others. There is neither need nor justification to use such rules as dividers between stories: The conventional 1-pica alley is adequate and that white space helps lighten the printed page.

Horizontal rules may be fashionable at any given moment and that is an acceptable reason to use typographic devices. We must assure our readers that our publication is contemporary. For we can never forget that our publication must compete for the reader's time in a highly competitive marketplace and that fashionability is a major sales factor for everything from women's clothes to bathroom cleaners to periodicals. But we must use cosmetics functionally, never overdoing them to the point where they become counterproductive.

Some editors just put in heavy horizontal rules at random. Others use them as cutoff rules under pictures and where body type wraps to the next column. Perhaps the most consistent and controllable device is the *30-bar*. This is a heavy rule—6- or 9-point—that runs below a squared-off block of body type. If, for instance, a story is squared under a 3-column head, the 30-bar would run across the bottom of that block for three columns. If, however, the first or third column ran longer than

THIRTY-BARS are used within page but not at its foot in "Veritas" of University of Miami, Florida. Hairline rules run at side and foot of this tabloid page. Concentrations of body type would be relieved by breaker heads.

THE EDITOR AS NEWSPAPER DESIGNER 193

THIRTY-BARS run across bottom of each story in this spread from "Sarnia Division News," Dow Chemical of Canada, Sarnia, Ontario. At bottom of spread, 12-point rules give effect of sideless boxes.

the other two, as a *dogleg*, the 30-bar would run under only the two equal columns. If all three columns were of odd depth, there would be no bars at all. Thirty-bars run only under their own story. The bar would run three columns wide under one story; there would be a break for the alley and then a 2-column bar. The bar would not run unbroken clear across the page.

Boxes

It is possible to get typographic color by the use of boxes. This useful color device comes in two varieties: full and sideless.

A *full box* has four sides. The rule may be a plain, solid rule or it can be textured. Ben Day rules, which give the effect of a gray band; coinedge rules, made of small parallel lines like the milling around the side of a coin; *wave rules* of various wavelengths; and *Oxford rules*, a combination of a heavy and a light parallel rule, are among the choices an editor can wisely make. The rule must be heavy enough to add adequate color to the page for that is its primary purpose. A plain rule must be at least 3 points thick and a 4-pointer—or even wider—is usually more effective. For decorative rules the editor's eye must be the gauge of effectiveness.

A pleasant effect is obtained by using a 2- or 3-point plain rule for the sides and a rule twice as thick at the top and bottom. On occasion it can be pleasant to use the heavy rule at one side and the bottom of the box, giving a shadow effect. The heavy vertical rule should be at the outside of the page but the emphasis should always be on the same side. This means that a box can be used only at one side or the center of the page or we lose much of its flexibility.

A box should not be wider than four columns nor deeper than about 9 inches. If it gets much bigger, it encompasses an area larger than the eye can see in reading position and the effect of the box is lost. For the same reason, boxes are less effective when they run across the fold of the page. One-column boxes are best when no deeper than about 5 inches; 2-column boxes should be no deeper than 7 inches and are most useful when only about 3 inches deep.

Sideless boxes are best when they are shallow, 3 or 4 inches for a 1- or 2-columner, and no deeper than 6 inches for any width. Wider sideless boxes are generally used for 1-up material (discussed in Chapter 8) or to tie together picture and story horizontally.

A full box should be handled like a tiny page. Just as the regular page requires adequate margins, so there must be a margin within a box, usually 1 or 1½ picas. And the foot margin should never be skimped.

(Page margins are generally determined by the width of the *paper page* in relation to that of the *type page* after the basic format has been decided upon. A good margin for a tabloid newspaper is 3 picas at the top, 4 at the bottom, 4 at the outside, and 3 at the gutter (inside) margin. Although we must adjust the specifics to our own situation, we must remember that skimpy margins distress the reader although not as severely with newspapers as with magazines.)

Prepacks

The ultimate use of the box is for a *prepack*. An arbitrarily chosen area is enclosed in a full box, often with a simpler rule than is used for

PREPACK at top of page is bordered in cyan in "Mobil World," international publication of Mobil Oil Corporation, New York.

ordinary boxes. This space is laid out like a little magazine page, the *free page* discussed in the next chapter. Lots of white space is used, pictures are treated far more informally than the regular square halftones used on newspaper pages, and body type is set at measures other than increments of regular columns. Headlines need not be from the regular headline schedule but may use connotative type.

This element is "prepacked" before regular page layout begins. The objective is to make it up during times when the pressure of deadlines has been removed, so both editor and printer have a little more time to come up with unusual treatments. Then, as regular page layout is begun, the prepack is called for on the dummy and placed on the pasteup grid as a single unit, just as an intricate ad might be placed in a commercial newspaper.

The tiniest boxes of all are *sandwiches*, used to enclose referrals. They are sideless and made of the same rules as sideless boxes are. Sandwiches are dropped into a paragraph about 3 inches from the start of a story.

Dominant Head

Inside pages are made up by the same principles used on page one, with extra care paid to one need, a *dominant head*. This head is the heaviest, optically, on a page and so acts as the nucleus for a good page pattern. When such a dominant head is missing, the page will look accumulated rather than patterned.

To dominate, a head must (a) be at least one column wider than the next heavier head; (b) be at least one step in point size larger than the next head; and (c) have at least as many lines as the No. 2 head. If all three of these requirements cannot be met, the one or two that can must be increased by two or three steps rather than one. The essential need—no matter how it is achieved—is that the dominant head be obviously the heaviest on the page. It is the weight, not the position, of a head that makes it dominate and so it need not run at the top of the page. But, as the customary practice is to run heavy heads high on the page, the dominator will usually rise to, or near, the top.

Page one also needs a dominant head. But our lead story almost always carries a head heavy enough to dominate and so the editor need not take special steps to assure its presence.

Each inside page needs a folio line, customarily at the top of the page.

Some editors, cramped for space, will run an extra column of body type across the gutter of the inside spread. This makes reading difficult as the type runs on two different planes. Not quite as bad but still undesirable is running a headline across the gutter on both facing pages.

DOMINANT HEAD in columns 1-2 make nucleus for strong page pattern in "Banknotes" of Toronto Dominion Bank, Toronto, Ontario. Page: 11½x15½ on very light cream paper.

Mag-Tab Layout

Apart from the cover, a magtab is laid out just as a newspaper is. But an interesting technique developed by *Tie Lines*, published by Michigan Bell, is worth looking at. Column 1 of each page is set at 16½ picas and enclosed in an 18½-pica box. This is the *panel* and carries short stories as a roundup. The rest of the page, called the "editorial well," is made of three 13½-pica columns. It may carry major news stories or, most frequently, magazine-type articles which are displayed in the freer style of such media. This combination of free and formal pages gives flexibility in presenting material of various kinds and seems appropriate to the basic idea of a magtab.

In laying out a page, the editor must make sure that the path of the reading eye is as simple and direct as possible. The reader should never be forced to say, "OK, I've read this far. Where do I go from here?"

The young reporter is always admonished by the gruff but lovable city editor, "Don't back into a story; jump into it!" And we want the reader, too, to jump into the story. Any delay in travelling from headline to story increases the chances that the reader will wander off elsewhere.

This results from several common but nonfunctional techniques. One is placing some element, usually a 1-column picture, between the end of the headline and the start of a story. Not as bad a barrier but still less than desirable is the *editor's note*. Editor's notes are too often redundant and innocuous. Any pertinent information in such notes can readily be woven into the story itself. If it is necessary to tell something about the writer, it can be carried as a bio block at the end of the story.

Dutch wraps, where a story moves into an adjacent column that is not covered by the head, may also confuse the reader. We note that this need not be confusion with a capital C, which it isn't, but that any confusion, no matter how trifling, annoys the reader and ultimately an accumulation of little irritations may finally bring reading to a halt.

The most annoying of misdirections is the *jumpover*. We place a 1-column picture in a column of type, expecting the eye to jump over the photo to continue reading type below it. Unfortunately, the reader will almost always bounce upward and to the right to continue in the second column. Pulled quotes, the names of columns, similar labels, and even sandwiches deeper than three lines—all form similar, undesirable barriers.

The empty sweep is the path of the eye when it is not actually reading type, the return from the end of a line to the start of the next, or the path from one column to the next. This sweep should be as short and direct as possible. If we have a 3-column head with a 1-column picture in the

FOUR-AND-A-HALF FORMAT is used by "Tielines" of Michigan Bell Telephone, Detroit. Column-and-a-half panel at outside of page carries straight news; three conventional columns usually carry softer news. Notice how figure in right page overlaps panel to tie two areas together.

second leg and type in the two outer ones, the eye will have to jump across the photo, from column 1 to 3. This is too long a sweep and we'd prefer to place the picture in one of the outside columns.

To test the simplicity of the reading path, a simple technique can be used. Place your finger on the page or the dummy. On that path where the eye is reading, keep the finger touching the paper; on empty sweeps, lift the finger, in an exaggerated motion, off the paper and into the new reading position. If any sweep is too long or too complicated, it will become apparent more forcefully than when we simply run our eyes along that path.

Each tabloid page is designed separately with no consideration to the facing page, for the reader sees only a single page at a time.

An essential factor in readership is adequate and consistent spacing. The editor should prepare a chart, either verbal or pictorial, which shows proper spacing. And then these specifications must be enforced rigidly. Spacing may be increased to justify a column, make it come out exactly the depth of the type-page, but should never be decreased to squeeze in an extra line or two. A typical spec sheet:

1. Use 1 pica of space:
   a. Under the nameplate (and above it, if it floats);
   b. At the end of a story, replacing the 30-dash;
   c. Above and below a sideless or full box;
   d. Above and/or below rules used at the top and bottom of 1-up material;
   e. Above a picture within the page;
   f. Between catchline and cutlines;
   g. Between cutlines and related headline;
   h. Above breaker heads.
2. Use 6 points of space:
   a. Between picture and catchline;
   b. Between headline and story;
   c. Between headline and byline;
   d. Between cutlines and cutoff rule;
   e. Immediately inside the rules of a box, a sandwich, or the rules enclosing 1-up material;
   f. Under a picture using i&e lines or just i-line;
   g. Under a breaker head.

Some editors, instead of using pica increments will use *Bls*, body lines. Two BLs are dropped in instead of 1 pica and one BL is used instead of 6 points. This method increases normal spacing by some 50 percent, 2 BLs usually equalling 16 or 18 points. The result is a lighter page and this technique is most useful when the headletter may be a trifle heavier than ideal.

The editor must keep in mind the function of page layout: to turn the looker into a reader and to keep a reader consuming body type until it's all gone or—more realistically—as long as possible.

Chapter 9

The Editor

☐ as Executive
☐ as Communicator
☐ as Production Manager
☐ as Writer
☐ as Copyreader
☐ as Typographer
☐ as Art Director
☐ as Newspaper Designer
☒ as Magazine Designer
☐ as Newsletter Producer
☐ as Circulation Manager
☐ as Contractor
Glossary
Index

The layout style that most people would call "magazinish" uses free pages with large areas of white as distinct display elements. By contrast, a typical newspaper page is a *formal page*, a rectangle filled with typographic elements; any white space is incidental and almost accidental.

Good layout, like all good art, demands discipline. In formal pages that discipline is maintained by the quite rigid column divisions on the

DOUBLE SPREAD gives great impact to opening of 3-page story in "Alcoa News" of Aluminum Company of America, Pittsburgh. Both photographs are in full color. Note the effective use of expository art in the top-right corner. Page: 8½x11.

199

MEMO: Diagonal Arithmetic

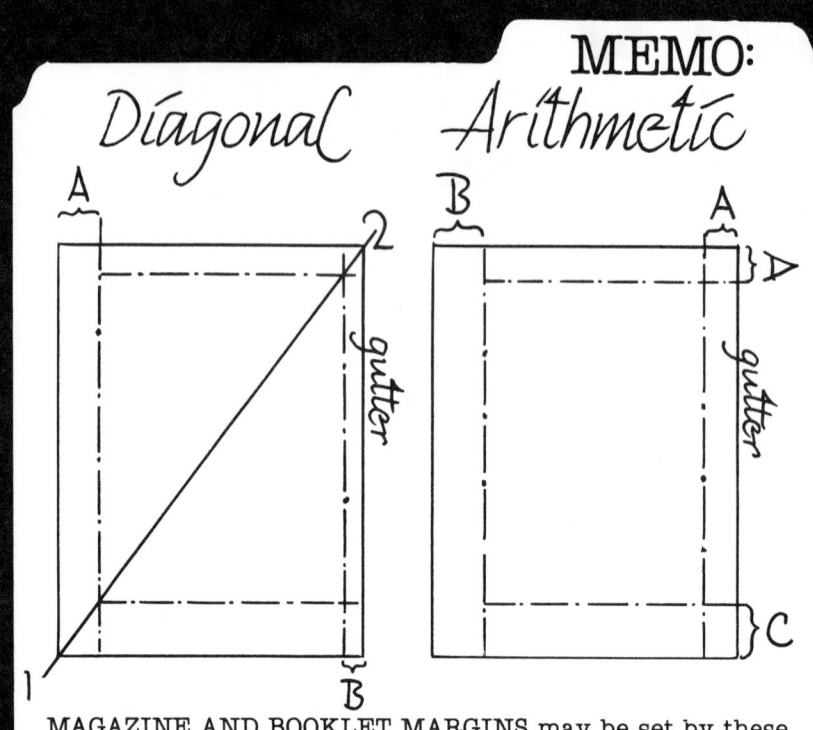

MAGAZINE AND BOOKLET MARGINS may be set by these simple methods.

By the diagonal method: Draw the diagonal, 1-2. Arbitrarily determine the outside margin, A. Where that margin hits the diagonal marks the foot margin. The gutter margin, B, is half of A. Where it intersects with the diagonal indicates the head margin.

By arithmetic: The gutter, A, is one-eighth the width of the page. The head margin is the same as A. The outside margin, B, equals A plus one-sixth of A. The foot margin, C, equals B plus 2 picas.

page and by the need to fill the page rectangle neatly and completely. On free pages, with large areas of white space and typographic elements not necessarily confined into rigid columns, discipline must be imposed by the editor.

Freedom too often becomes license and that applies to page layout as much as to any creative effort. The editor then must define "rules" of layout. Some will be articulated, many will be just felt. This book will suggest several criteria. If the editor follows them, the result will be a good, workmanlike layout. To achieve the incandescence of genius, though, the editor must break some of the rules. But the rules which are based on demonstrable principles and success must be understood

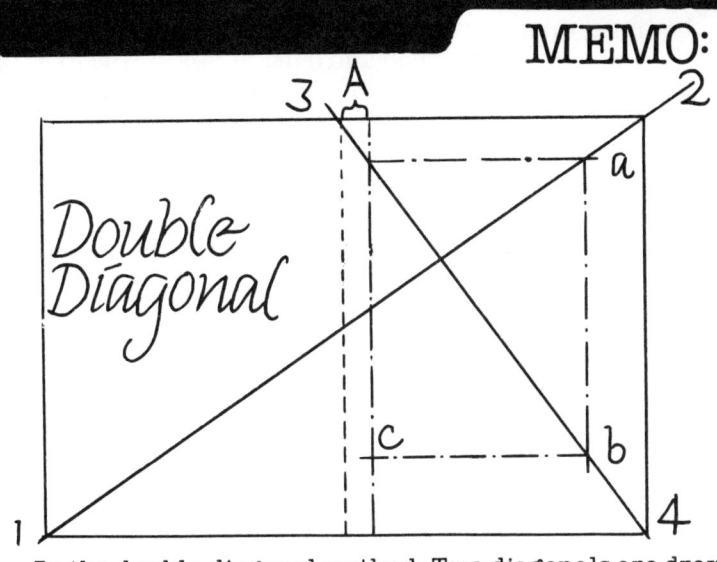

> **MEMO:**
>
> **Double Diagonal**
>
> In the double-diagonal method: Two diagonals are drawn, 1-2 across the 2-page spread and 3-4 across a single page. Draw the gutter margin, which is arbitrarily determined. From where that margin hits the 3-4 diagonal, draw the line marking the top margin till it hits the 1-2 diagonal at a. From there draw a line parallel to the edge of the page until it hits the 3-4 diagonal at b. This defines the side margin. The line from b to c shows the foot.
>
> For the simplest—and often the best—method, the editor simply uses the finest of all instruments, the human eye.

before they can be effectively ignored to meet unique demands. The admonition that all admonitions must be taken with a grain of salt is still valid.

The first admonition: Every *spread* (we always design a magazine in a series of two facing pages) must look organized—planned, not accumulated. There must be a consistency throughout the book which begins with the basic format of the magazine.

Margins

The editor must first determine page margins. The margins for your magazine may be quite different from those of another's, but they must be consistent throughout yours. They may be arbitrarily determined or they may be set by formula.

For an 8½x11-inch page, a common margination is 4 picas at the head, 5 at the foot, 4 at the outside, and 3 at the gutter. There's nothing magic about these numbers and you may want to come up with a set of your own. But these are nicely proportioned and any variation will probably be based upon these dimensions.

Another formula makes the head and outside 5 picas; the foot, 6; and the gutter, 4. (The size and position of the folios is a slight factor in deciding on margins.)

You must remember that skimpy margins, which have cyclical popularity, are not pleasing to the reader. Just the opposite, the currently popular deep head margins, often as much as 18 picas or even more, are annoyingly out of proportion and often look just like what they are: a waste of expensive printing paper.

While we will not rigidly tie our layout to them, columns must be defined. Again using a typical 8½x11 page, we usually divide it into three columns of 13 picas or two of 20 picas. The narrow columns are divided by 1-pica alleys, the wider columns by a 2-pica strip of white. These specifications are modified to fit the type-page that results when margins are determined.

A basic formula says that a good layout should be *functional*, *organic*, and *invisible*. In a functional layout, every element does a necessary job, contributing to communication. While this does not mean that there can be no ornamentation on a page, it does make us consider twice any trendy device that is used just to follow the fad. An ornament, for instance, may be part of the functional bait that lures the reader into an article; but doodads that merely clutter up the page should be eliminated.

Functional Layout

Functionalism demands that elements that do perform a necessary job do so in the most efficient manner. We need headlines, obviously, and so these are functional elements. But they may become nonfunctional if we don't use them properly. Typically nonfunctional headlines are those set at an angle across the page, those running vertically or sideways, set in wavy or jumpy lines, or *stacked*, when one line sits right atop another with no spacing between.

Other misuses include breaking a word into two or three lines without hyphens, setting Script or Black Letter in all-caps, running a headline across two or more different backgrounds such as starting the head on plain paper and continuing it on a halftone or tint block.

Nonfunctional elements should be purged from the page. At best, such an element is a waste of material and handling time, and it's a rare editor whose budget allows any waste, even if measured only in pennies. Even worse, though, the nonfunctional too often becomes malfunctional; if it doesn't do a good job, it usually does a bad one. If it doesn't attract readers, it distracts them; if it doesn't convey information clearly and quickly, it fuzzes up the message.

Organic Layout

An *organic layout* is one that grows, like a flower or a tree, from the "seed," the message we must convey. The kind of article and its mass in type, as well as the supporting pictorial matter, determine the final layout. Often their influence is so great that the editor says, "This spread just laid itself out." The arrangement of the pieces was so obviously logical that there was neither need nor opportunity to look for any alternatives.

This is why the editor should always wait till all the pieces are at hand before beginning the process of fitting the jigsaw puzzle together. To plan a page pattern ahead of time and then force the elements to fit will invariably result in a stilted layout that, while not necessarily bad, is not as good as we want all our pages to be.

Invisible Layout

An *invisible layout* seems at first, to be a contradiction of terms. Elements must be visible or they can't be read. But we don't want the arrangement of them to be too apparent. We don't want the reader to say, "Hey! Isn't this a good-looking page!" or "Look how neatly these pictures line up." All we want is "Gee! I must read this piece!"

That means, in the words of at least one prizewinning editor, "Don't be cutesy!" While it's hard to define cutesiness, most editors know it when they see it.

Codfish Formula

Another useful guideline—that the editor must feel free to ignore when the situation demands—is the *codfish formula*, COD. Concentrate, orient, dominate.

D stands for "dominate." Each spread must have a dominant element, the "hen" of the hen-and-chick formula we've already discussed. This is usually a piece of art although a headline may do the same job. Whatever the element, it must be obviously the heaviest on the spread, the nucleus around which the pattern is built.

O stands for "orient." Also called the "buddy system" or the "no-orphan" technique, this layout aligns every element on a vertical and/or horizontal axis, with at least one other element. The more page components that share such common axes, the more tightly the page is *woven*. Such a page has obviously been planned and the reader relaxes, knowing that he or she is in competent hands.

C means "concentrate." Elements are pushed to the center of the page to create an irregular outside silhouette, pleasing to the reader.

CODFISH FORMULA is demonstrated in this layout from "Inside CNA," CNA Corporation, Chicago. Elements are concentrated to create irregular outer silhouette; there are no orphans; layout is dominated by large picture in center.

(The fallow corners are often more useful when left blank than when filled with type.) But we must avoid *trapped space*, a large area of white, completely surrounded by printed elements. This has the same unpleasant effect as a hole in the middle of a piece of cloth.

As we follow these exhortations, we must keep in mind other requirements of a good layout. One is "Don't be tentative." Whatever the typographer does, it should be done so definitely that the reader knows it was done on purpose. The outside silhouette of a page, as mentioned in the previous paragraph, must be markedly irregular. If elements vary only a trifle, the reader is suspicious that the designer simply missed a measurement or that a cropping knife slipped and cut off more or less than was intended.

A free page is sometimes called a *jazz layout* because it follows the principles of good Dixieland music. The band plays a simple tune once; after that the listener "hears" the melody mentally while the band weaves the harmonics. So with a jazz layout: The typographer suggests,

POOR HEADLINE PLACEMENT can lead eye away from start of story. At top left, eye is brought down into column 2. In top center, heavy display of headline and art draws eye strongly away from POA. So does concentration of display elements in terminal area in example at top right.

In examples below, one at left shows head in cup where it leads eye into column 2. Other two examples require special setting of body type. Center specimen creates ragged-left body type which is always undesirable; example at lower right leads eye away from POA. In both instances, eye is led into body type directly below end of headline.

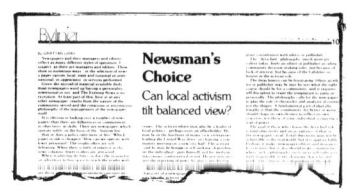

but doesn't define a basic rectangle, leaving it to the reader to fill in the blanks, as it were. To do this, we must *define the margins*. Each of the four margins must be touched by at least one element. One element may define two or more margins; a picture in the corner of the page defines the side as well as the horizontal margin.

We must remember the Gutenberg diagram that defines the reading diagonal. There must be a strong element in the POA of the spread. (Note that there can be more than one POA on a spread. That for the entire 2-page layout is in the top left of the left-hand page. If there are other articles on the same spread, each one will have its own POA.) We must never attempt to make the reading eye go "against gravity." So the placement of the headline is important.

The head should never be below or to the right of, the start of the story. This runs contrary to faddish but malfunctional placements—such as *in the cup*, when the head is in column 2 with body type running high in columns 1 and 3; at the bottom of the page or in the center of the page, especially when body type must be set in a runaround to make space for the head; or in column 3 or even on the opposite page.

To avoid misunderstanding, we note that the head may be anywhere

205

in column 1 if the story starts at the head of column 2, even if the head is physically lower than the start.

The path of the eye from the end of the head to the start of the story must be as short and direct as possible. We've already noted that in discussing newspaper layout; the adage becomes even more important in magazines because the free page allows placements that can create a complicated head-to-text path.

As the editor places the head, thought must be given to the use of a *blurb*. This is a block of display type, usually written in normal body style, that amplifies the head. This can be useful when the head is a teaser but it is used even with summary heads. The blurb is often placed far from the head itself, used primarily as an optional, display device. While the blurb may function primarily as a visual element, its content is important. So it should be placed so that there is not a sharp break in

ORIENTED LAYOUT shown above is diagrammed at right. Notice how pictures a and c are aligned at top margin, and b and d at foot. Modified silhouette b aligns with type on axis 5, point where silhouetting begins. Notice on axis 1, alignment of head is on e of "People" and approximately on stem of r in "Ayer." Picture d doesn't quite align on axis 2, but it is buddied up at its foot. This system is very similar to Swiss grid except that new axes for alignment are created every time element is placed. Consequently there is greater flexibility than with fixed orientation of Swiss grid.

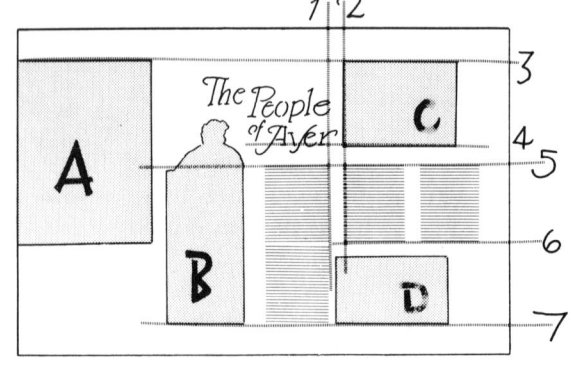

thought as the reader goes from head to blurb and also that the blurb doesn't lure the reader away from the story.

Jumping the Gutter

The editor must *jump the gutter*, tie the two facing pages into a single, attractive area. The obvious cord to tie the two pages together is to run the headline and/or pictures across both pages. This works on the *center spread*, the two pages at the very center of the magazine. But it's the only one that has both pages printed on the same piece of paper; all other spreads are on two separate sheets. And there's the rub! As pages are folded, collated, and stapled, chances for misalignment are constant. A discrepancy of a pica is not at all rare. If each facing page is misfolded by one pica and in opposite directions, the misalignment becomes glaring. Just as bad as the break in a horizontal element is the misfolding at the gutter. As a result, a strip of white may streak through a halftone or a strip of the halftone may fold off the page and mar the one on the other side of the fold.

If a headline must run over the gutter, it should be placed so that the space between words comes at the gutter. If there is misalignment, it is not so obvious. A tripod or wicket may be used with the bimo on the left-hand page and the main head on the opposite one.

Facing pages can best be tied together by horizontal aligning of elements such as the tops of columns of type or of halftones. If they are misaligned, it will not be painfully obvious. The use of a color, if available, can be duplicated on facing pages, uniting them neatly. If decorative initials are in color on both pages, or a duotone is used on each page, or rules are duplicated on each side of the gutter, the facing pages will have a harmony that ties them together.

The center spread of a magazine is the most valuable one. That's because the book naturally opens flat there and the reader sees the whole expanse without the distortion that occurs on other spreads as the pages curve downward toward the gutter. There is no problem of aligning elements on opposite sides of the center spread and the gutter can be crossed mechanically with no danger of misalignment. For these reasons many editors prefer to show, or to start, their major story on these pages.

Picture Placement

Pictures should be placed logically. If we have a photo looking up at a towering tree or building, it will naturally fit at the top of the page. If the camera peered down into a deep ravine, the foot of the page is the logical position for it. Pictures taken at eye level can run at almost any spot.

Bleeds should be used with equal logic. A picture should be bled only

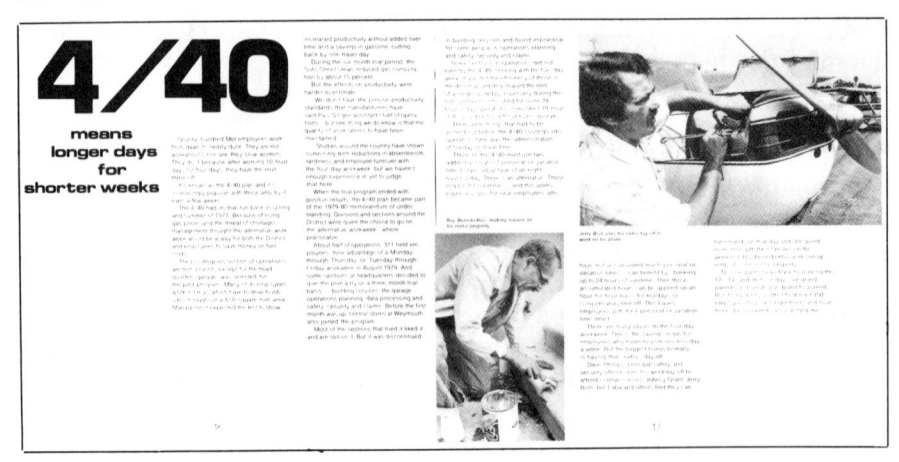

HEAVY HEADLINE in POA dominates this layout in "People" of Metropolitan Water District of Southern California, Los Angeles. Note unusual format: 10-inch-square page.

if it has an expanding composition as discussed in Chapter 7. Pictures should not bleed to the gutter; there is no expanding effect there. And never, never, never should two pictures bleed to the gutter from opposite pages, especially if they touch each other.

When a picture bleeds, a half pica must be added to the dimension of the plate on each side of a bleed. A picture bleeding at the foot of a page will, let's say, be 33 picas deep. But on the printing plate, the halftone must be 33½ picas deep. If a picture bleeds at the side and bottom, it will be a half pica wider and a half pica taller than the printed image. For bleeds are made by printing the picture on a sheet of paper, then cutting it off through the printed image. It's impossible to actually print an image right to the edge of the paper. If the editor succumbs to temptation and bleeds to the gutter, no extra area is required because there the page is simply folded, not cut.

Ornamentation should be used functionally. A major function of ornaments is to contribute to the mood of the article. Various periods in our history are closely associated with specific ornamentation. Art Nouveau decorations connote the turn of the century. Wild West days are recalled by ornate borders and frames, the Art Deco era of the 30s by geometric devices.

Periodically the faddists resurrect a 1940s trick of using large blocks of gray or black for no other purpose than to fill space. Heavy rules, horizontal or vertical, are often injected into a page for just as slight a reason.

Borders around pages are useless and constrictive. They reduce the size of the page; they preclude bleeds, even good ones; they clutter up the landscape.

THE EDITOR AS MAGAZINE DESIGNER   209

Hairline rules that divide a page into a series of boxes have only one dubious virtue; from time to time they are fashionable.

As on newspaper pages, the lines of force in photos will dictate their placement to a high degree. If the lines of one picture carry the eye into an adjacent one and its lines continue a smooth, pleasant curve, the layout will be unusually effective.

Remember that every picture must have caption material (its own, never combined with that of another) and this material should be placed as close as possible to the picture. Never should all captions be ganged in one portion of the page. When that is done, some art and type will be so far apart that it becomes a most difficult job to try to link them together.

A magazine should flow like a book, from page to page. So an article should never be jumped to a distant page. If the reader merely turns the page, as in reading a book, the continuity is not broken. This turn should always come within a paragraph, never at the end of one. Some editors use a pictorial device, an arrow or a pointing hand or even the word "Continued," to encourage the reader to proceed to the next spread. Even if such a device is used, there is no need to say "Continued from previous page."

To tie together a multi-spread article, some editors use a pictorial device, sometimes a portion of a halftone from the opening spread or some kind of ideogram that suggests the content of the piece. Sometimes the headline is repeated in smaller size. An interesting device is the

TABLE OF CONTENTS runs on cover of "Insight" of The Continental Group, Stamford, Connecticut, as does masthead. On this 8½x11 page, bar at top of page and numbers in table are in bright blue.

SCHOLAR'S MARGIN is used by "All Hands" of United States Navy. Headlines are in color. Body type would have higher readability if broken into shorter—preferably no longer than 8-line—paragraphs.

running head. A sentence, in normal English, not headlinese, is written to summarize the article and is set in a display size. It runs across the top of each page of the article, reading from one spread to the other. We seek to break the head into logical subdivisions: "Prospects for coming year/raise optimism among leaders/ as productivity increases/ and absenteeism drops dramatically."

The best device to tie spreads together is, of course, the story itself. If we see a head and picture about airplanes on pages 4 and 5 and pictures on the same subject on pages 5 and 6, even the least perceptive reader will put the two together and come up with four.

If ornamentation or decorative initials are used, they will be a visual binding.

We should let the reader know when the article has ended. In newspapers we have eliminated 30-dashes that indicate the end of a story; for on such a page the end is obvious. But in a magazine, where stories may or may not wrap to another spread, it is a courtesy to the reader to mark the end. This may be any kind of typographic ornament; most frequently it is a square, outline or solid, or a bullet, a big period. Some editors use the monogram or insignium of their organization as the *end mark*. It should be small and unobtrusive; it is placed at the end of the last line of copy. If that last line is completely filled, the end mark goes at the end of a blank line below it.

SCHOLAR'S MARGIN is used as its original form was—for marginal notations. This example is from "Human Ecology" of New York State College of Human Ecology at Cornell.

THE EDITOR AS MAGAZINE DESIGNER   211

An interesting pattern is the *scalloped page*, especially useful when we have a lot of body type and little, if any, art. A headline runs at the top of the page (violating our warnings against such type across the gutter). Body type is set to a measure that gives six columns across the spread. It aligns at the top but the bottom is made deliberately ragged. One leg of type must run down to the foot margin. The others should vary drastically in length. Adjacent columns must vary by at least eight lines of type to give the scalloped effect. Small pictures may run at the bottom of any leg of type or at the bottom margin but generally this pattern is used without any art.

The Grid

Appealing and effective patterns can also be obtained by using the *grid system*, often called the *Swiss grid*. The spread is divided into squares, usually eight across and 10 deep. Headlines must touch at least two grid lines and pictures and body type occupy complete squares. In a

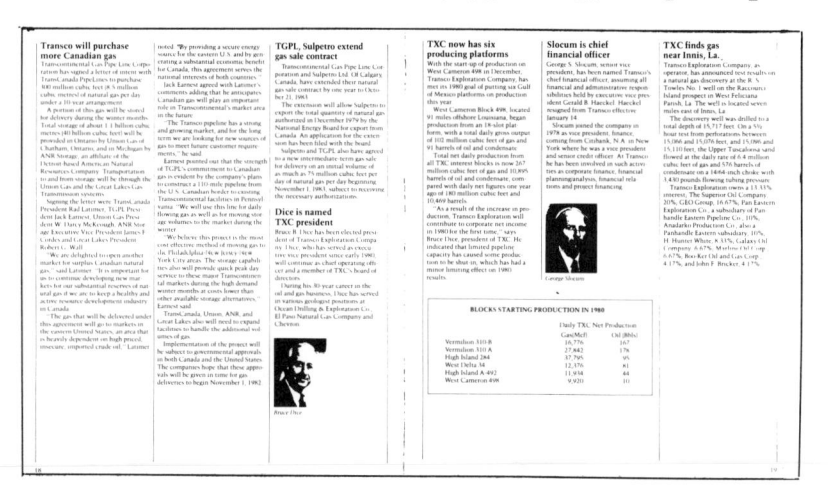

SCALLOPED PAGES add interest to pages where little or no art is available. Above example from "Hot Tap" of Transco Companies, Inc., Houston, shows how photographs may be used at the bottom of columns or boxes. At right is spread from "Baylor Progress" of Baylor University Medical Center, Dallas. Small logo "Miscellany" is in color, heavy bar in black. Note that scalloping is very pronounced and therefore most effective.

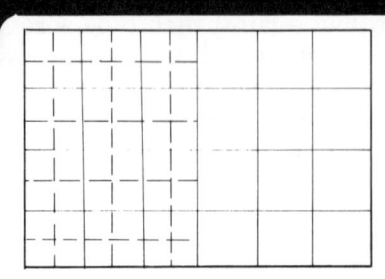

THE SWISS GRID SYSTEM is based on grid such as one above. Here left-hand page at left has 48 squares and right-hand page has 12. There is no set number; editors may choose any grid they want.

Headlines must touch two grid lines, vertical and horizontal. Pictures and body type occupy complete squares. Greater amount of squares in grid, greater flexibility of makeup.

In example below, start of story is shown by asterisk and arrows indicate how body type wraps. Note in second example that body type is set two grids wide.

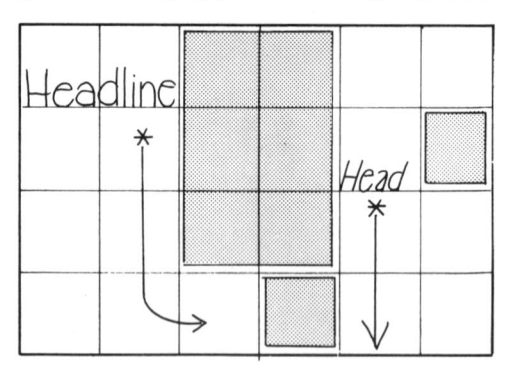

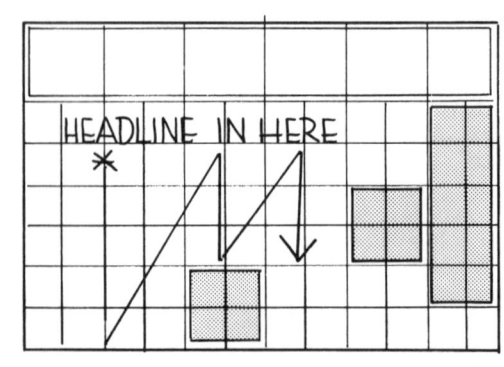

MEMO:

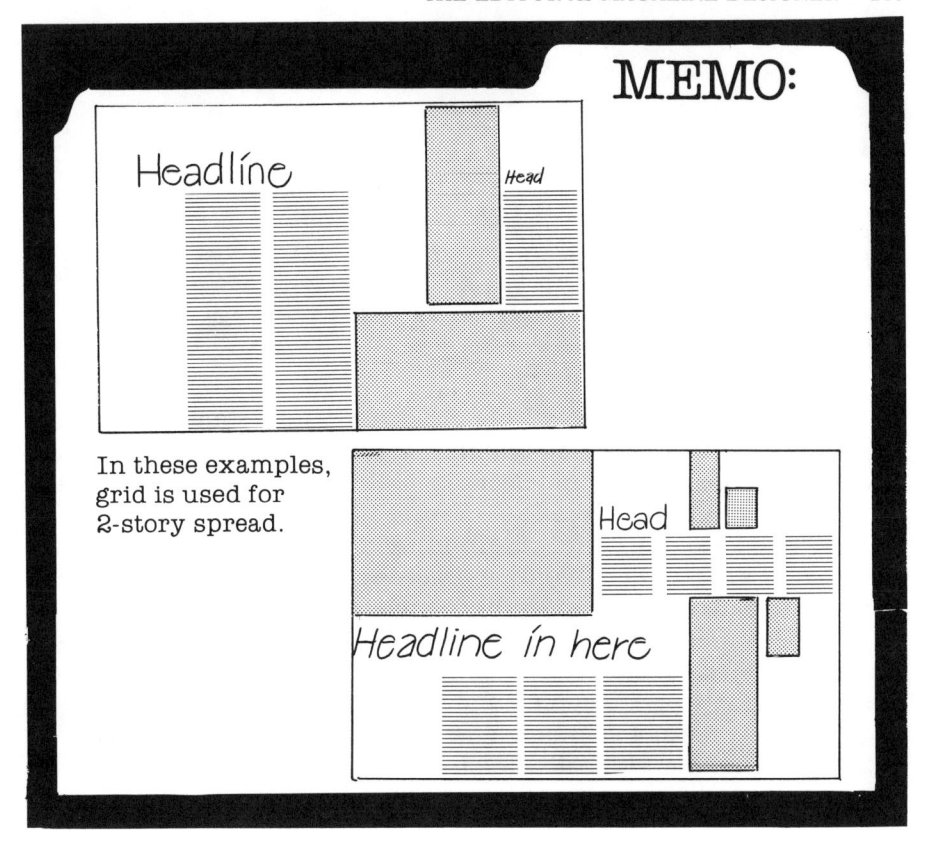

Headline

Head

In these examples, grid is used for 2-story spread.

Head

Headline in here

minor variation, pictures align on at least two grid lines. This system gives us an oriented layout; we must then meet the need to concentrate and dominate.

The greatest challenge to the editor's skill is placing two or more articles on one spread.

There are, of course, almost countless ways of doing this. But the successful ones are almost always based on the same principle. Arrange the smaller article (or articles) into a rectangular area. You may define it with a sideless or full box, or let it define itself. This element is treated as we would an illustration and is placed on the spread as we'd place a picture. The major story then wraps around the subordinate one, conforming to all the principles of easy, logical eye-flow.

If the elements are full-page deep, the vertical separation can be an unusually heavy column rule. It is pleasant—but certainly not necessary—if this rule bleeds top and bottom off the page.

It's particularly important to keep the headlines well separated.

A tint block, either in color or gray, may define an element. Another defining technique is to set the shorter or shortest article in bright type and ragged-right.

SCALLOPED PAGE of type is squared off by interesting line drawings. Notice that all headlines are approximately same optical weight and page would be very static without good art. Example is from "Hartford Magazine" of Hartford Insurance Group, Connecticut.

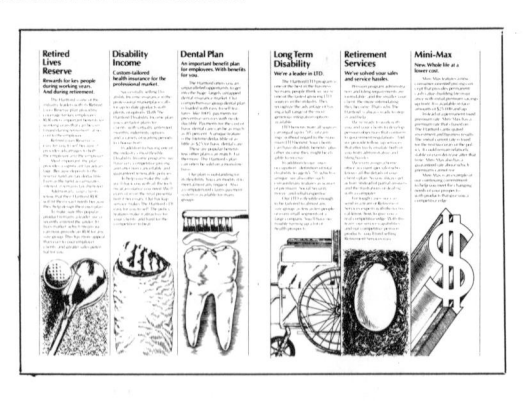

The page or spread should not be divided into equal areas; that creates a static, uninteresting situation. If it is absolutely necessary that divisions be equal, one should be horizontal, the other vertical to create at least an illusion of difference.

The "freedom" the editor has in using display type too frequently becomes just carelessness. Among practices to beware of and—except in the most rare cases—banned from use are:

1. Type running sideways. This is sometimes used for section logos that identify regular departments in a magazine. In this case they become symbols or ideograms and actually not "read." This use is acceptable even if not commendable.

2. Type running vertically. Such type cannot be read; it must be deciphered. Again there may be a rare instance when we want to give the impression of strong vertical shape or direction. A piece with the headline AVALANCHE had that word running vertically, each letter a trifle wider than the one above. The effect of the headline sliding down a steep mountain side was worth the loss of legibility. But opportunities like this are, obviously, not a frequent occurrence.

3. Type running diagonally. Frequently on magazine covers it simulates a ribbon running across one corner. If this must be used, it should be on the POA or the TA so the reader can orient to the type by turning the head to the left, a not-uncomfortable position that most right-handed people assume when writing, anyway. Diagonal type has little use on inside pages.

4. *Bounced* or *wavy-based* type. Bounced letters never align at the baseline. Trying to read it is like riding a pogo stick down a cobblestone road. Type aligning on a wavy line is not quite as disruptive to reading but this technique often creates awkward gaps between letters that decrease legibility.

5. *Stacked* type. In this setting there is no space—or just a trifle—between lines. This style is most often used with all-cap setting. When lowercase letters are used, they frequently overlap; that is, descenders from the top line and ascenders from the lower line extend into a common area, sometimes even touching.

6. Broken words without hyphens. This style is used when the editor wants to use big type in a too-narrow area. Feeling—quite probably—that hyphens in this case would be distracting, the editor simply eliminates them. A typical example is:

CON
NEC
TI
CUT

The fragmentation becomes even more conspicuous when the syllables do not align at the left.

7. Script, Cursive, and many Ornamented typefaces in all-caps. The capitals of many fonts in these classifications are actually not distinguishable by themselves; we recognize them only in combination with more legible lowercase letters. (A Detroit daily once spelled the city name with a Blackletter *V* instead of *D* and no one even noticed it for months, those caps being so close in form.)

To work through a complicated layout problem and get a preview of how it might look, the editor might well use a *page matrix*. This is an entire page filled only with body type. (It's created by pasting up column after column of body type, then making photo copies.) Headlines of appropriate size and form are clipped from any source, usually back issues of the magazine. Halftones are simulated by rectangles of medium gray construction paper. These elements are laid on the matrix and pushed around until a pleasant page pattern and a logical reading path are achieved.

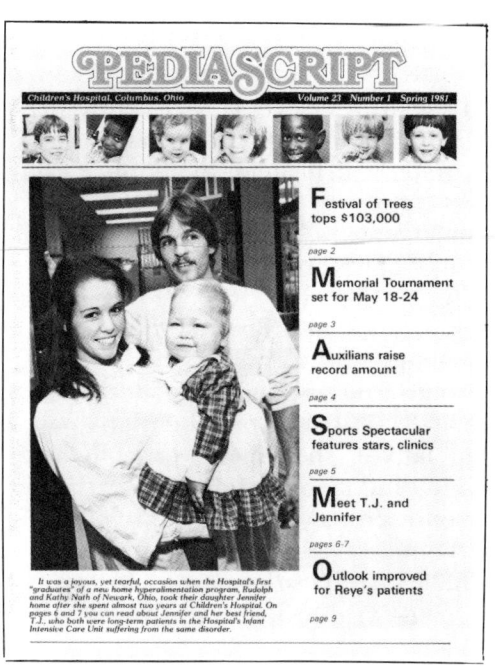

APPEALS fill almost half of this 8½x11 page from "Pediascript" of Children's Hospital, Columbus, Ohio. Picture also refers to an inside story—so whole page really is given to appeals.

216 EDITING THE ORGANIZATIONAL PUBLICATION

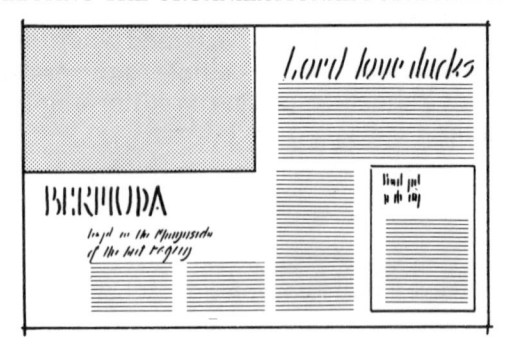

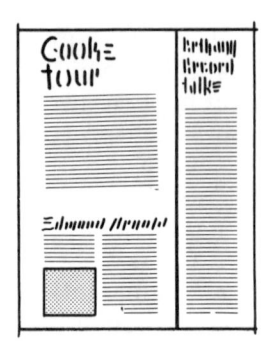

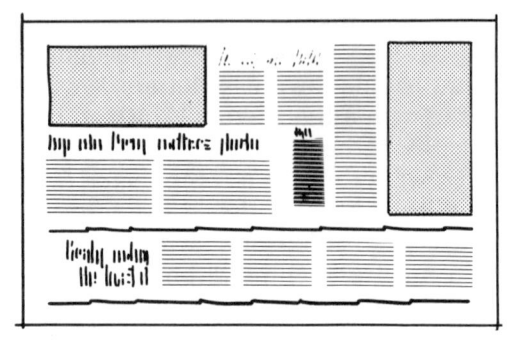

THREE-STORY LAYOUTS are shown for both single pages and double spreads. It is important to keep headlines well separated from each other and to arrange body type with minimum of empty sweeps.

Pagination

Most magazines are printed in signatures, several pages on a single sheet. The editor should have a *pagination* or imposition chart to show the pages on each signature. Such a chart can be made by simply folding a miniature signature.

There is confusion with the term "signature." Some people refer to an "8-page signature" as one where eight pages are printed on one side of a sheet of paper. Others would refer to this as a "16-page signature," counting both the front and back of the sheet. Be sure you and your printer are using the term in the same sense.

Let's assume that you are printing 16 pages on a single sheet, whatever you call the signature. Take an 8½x11-inch piece of blank paper and fold it, first into horizontal halves, then once vertically and, finally, once more horizontally. Holding it so the folds are at the left and top, write the page number on each page without unfolding the signature any more than necessary.

Now, when you unfold it, you have an *imposition chart*. On one side will be, starting from the top left, pages 1, 16, 13, and 4 in the top row,

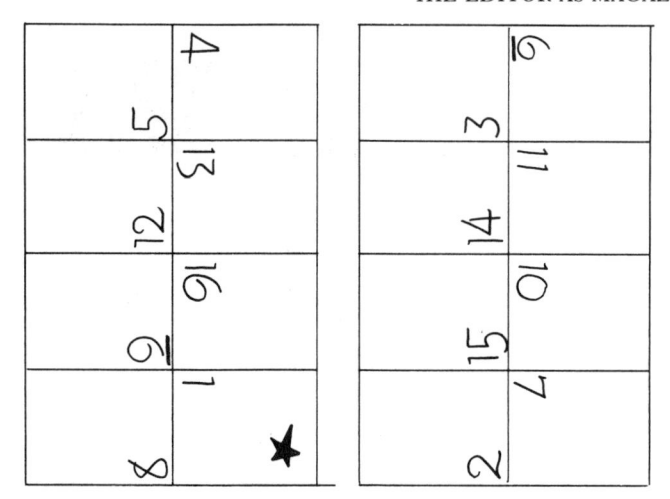

IMPOSITION CHART shows how pages are arranged in signature. If color is planned for cover (shown by star) it is also available on other seven pages on sheet.

8, 9, 12, and 5 in the bottom. The head of each page will be at the fold.

On the other half of the sheet are 3, 14, 15, and 2 at the top, 6, 11, 10, and 7 at the bottom. (When you numbered the pages, 10, 11, 14, and 15 were the ones difficult to do.)

Suppose you can afford color on only one side of the sheet. You'd probably want it on the cover. Then all the other pages on that side—4, 5, 8, 9, 12, 13, and 16—could carry color at no extra charge.

Signatures may be smaller than 16 pages (on rare occasions larger). Two or more signatures are inserted into each other to make a larger book. Then the numbering changes. Suppose we have two 16-page signatures. The first signature is numbered 1 through 8 and 25 to 32. The second signature numbers from 9 through 24, and is inserted at the center fold of the first signature. If you have more than one signature, you might use one extra color in the first signature and another color on the second.

Like the newspaper editor, the magazine editor can use a sketch dummy. But it is best to use a pasteup dummy. Get a second set of proofs from the typesetter or make photocopies of your proofs. Mark them with the proper galley number, repeated on a vertical line right down the center of the galley at intervals of about 3 inches. Then, no matter how we cut up the dummy, each section of it is identified by the proper number. Sometimes we must write the number again on a fragment of the original to make sure the person doing pasteup recognizes it.

Each type element is pasted on a same-size blank page in precisely the proper position. Pictures may be indicated by a drawn rectangle or by a

ALL-TYPE COVER of "Pet Scripts" of Pet Incorporated of St. Louis begins lead article on cover, then continues it on following page. This technique is highly effective if used rarely. Page: 8½x11¾, in blue-gray ink, with nameplate in black, on cream paper.

Pet Scripts Pet Incorporated
400 South Fourth Street
St. Louis, Mo. 63102

PS

Volume 1, Number 1   May 1981

News about Pet's people, products, and performance will be featured in this new publication - Pet Scripts (or **PS** for short). Just as the name implies, this newsletter will capture in print the activities and accomplishments of Pet people and the divisions for which they work. And just like any **PS**, special messages or observations about Pet will be brought to your attention.

PS asked the President. There could be no better way to lead off this new publication about Pet than to communicate the overview of the company as seen from the President and Chief Executive Officer, Boyd F. Schenk. Recently, in an interview, Mr. Schenk assessed Pet's performance over the past year, 1980, and commented on what lies ahead for the current year. Here's what he said.

"The analysis of a company like ours is always a complicated task given the large number of diverse businesses within Pet. This past year is especially complex because Pet was faced with a whole series of adverse external events common to all business - recession, high cost of money, inflation, and the soaring cost of energy that is needed to both produce and distribute our products. *(Continued on following page)*

---

photocopy of the original. If a silhouetted picture is placed, we often will measure to two separate points. We may show, in case we have a human figure, that the top of the head is 3½ picas from the top margin and the elbow is 2½ picas from the left margin. When these two points are properly determined, the silhouette will be in the proper position and will be properly oriented vertically. The point in the photo should be an obvious and unmistakable one.

If there is any doubt at all about the clarity of instructions, the pasteup should be augmented by verbal explanation. Not only do we show a 1-pica space between a head and the blurb, we might well write in the margin "1 pica #" and draw an arrow to where we want that space.

A careful *pasteup dummy* means the printer doesn't have to make editorial decisions. When we draw a sketch dummy, the first column may be one line too long. The pasteup person must then decide whether to steal a little space from around the head or subhead or picture to make room for the last line or whether to move it to the next column.

The opposite may just as readily occur. The column is a line or two short. Where should the extra space be placed, under the head, above the pic, between paragraphs? All these are decisions that only the editor should make. A precisely pasted dummy makes sure that only the editor does.

THE EDITOR AS MAGAZINE DESIGNER 219

S&F SPARK & FLAME is an employee publication of Arizona Public Service Company, an investor-owned utility serving electric and/or natural gas energy to customers in a 50,000-square-mile service territory in Arizona. Comments should be addressed to the editor at Station 1392, Box 21666, Phoenix, AZ 85036.

Editor: **Kathi Hostert**

Manager, Editorial Services
Bill Herr, ABC

Members, Phoenix Chapter, International Association of Business Communicators.

MASTHEAD carries name of publication in same form as on page one. "Spark & Flame" of Arizona Public Service Company in Phoenix subordinates actual name to large monogram. Both on front page and in masthead on last page, monogram and bar are in bright color. Publication uses unusual page size: 5½x11½.

Don't be in too much of a hurry to cut up and paste portions of the galley. Too often, when minor adjustments have to be made, the editor will have to cut and paste single lines of type. This is not only a messy job, but those snippets of paper may become lost, misplaced, or misidentified. Rather, mark off the number of lines that you want to put in the first column, then that which goes in column 2, etc. If slight adjustments must then be made, they can be done before the galley is cut up and pasted down.

As with any layout, the reader's convenience is a major concern. Empty sweeps should be examined closely to assure that the path of the reading eye from one column to another is as short and direct as possible. We should avoid jumpovers because they are more confusing on a magazine page than in a newspaper and we must make sure that captions are kept clearly distinct from body type lest they distract the reader.

While reader convenience should be our first goal, we should also seek to make the pages visually attractive and exciting. While we want to lure the looker into becoming a reader, we must remember that it takes visual allurements to attract the looker in the first place.

But pictorial beauty must always be secondary to the readership of body type. Unless that readership has been attained, the most beautiful magazine or pages therein is a failure.

Chapter 10
The Editor

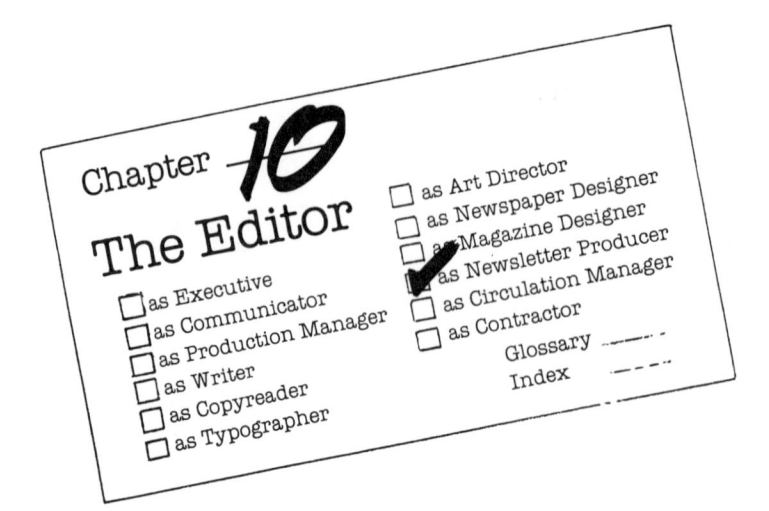

- [ ] as Executive
- [ ] as Communicator
- [ ] as Production Manager
- [ ] as Writer
- [ ] as Copyreader
- [ ] as Typographer
- [ ] as Art Director
- [ ] as Newspaper Designer
- [ ] as Magazine Designer
- [x] as Newsletter Producer
- [ ] as Circulation Manager
- [ ] as Contractor

Glossary
Index

Judges of contests have long complained that many publications entered in the newsletter category are really not newsletters. Some are newspapers, some are small magazines. Many are formally titled "Newsletter" but calling a cactus a rose does not make it a rose. So we must define the term, misty and unofficial as such definition may be.

The newsletter must convey news. It may not be hot-off-the-griddle news, but it must be news to the reader. An organization might send a newsletter to a specialized group who would find the information fresh even though it covered as much as the past three or even six months.

The newsletter must look as if it carries news. Facts, names, specifics must be stressed. Items must be short and pithy.

The newsletter must be designed to be read quickly and to give the impression of such quick reading. It should be very informal, like a personal letter, in content, tone, and appearance.

Many editors, to convey a feeling of immediacy and spontaneity, use typewriter type to suggest that this piece was just dashed off and hustled into the mail with great urgency. This is a common typographic characteristic of newsletters but not necessarily the qualifying one. A newsletter can be typeset and still retain the flavor of a quickly dispatched memo.

Some observers insist that there be no pictures at all in a newsletter. Others will accept simple line art, preferably expository art, but not halftones. This hearkens back to the earliest newsletters which were duplicated on a Mimeograph and just couldn't reproduce halftones.

The newsletter editor must guard against the temptation to make his or her publication too slick. The syndrome is familiar: The publication begins with unjustified typewriter type, then proceeds to justification, to cold type, to a 3-column format, to pictures, and to color. Now we wind up with something that doesn't have a specific name but sure as shooting is no longer a newsletter.

THE EDITOR AS NEWSLETTER PRODUCER 221

over coffee
November 14, 1980

May I help you?

There were four days last month we made lots of people mighty happy.

It was in two Customer Service areas, beginning with the Medicare group on October 21. Special Accounts followed on October 29, 30 and 31.

Every person who called in with a question to those areas those days had his call answered. Every call that came in, did. No hangups, no frustrations. Just answers to questions. All day.

It was the first time for both groups to answer 100 percent of the calls that came into their areas. It paid off.

Constructive criticism

Holding back anger can cause physical and emotional damage.

Try venting your frustrations like this.

Defuse your anger by telling whoever you're mad at *why* you are angry.

Focus your anger on the specific situation instead of the person.

When dealing with others' anger toward you, don't be defensive.

Poncho villa

Our building will be overrun by rain ponchos next week. The company purchased one for each employee.

The ponchos will keep us from getting all wet if we have to leave work in the rain.

"The purpose of having the rain ponchos is for everyone to have them at their work place in case we have a practice or a real evacuation of the building," explained Howard Wertz, manager of Administrative Services.

He said the ponchos resulted from "the company's concern for employees if we have to evacuate in the rain or if we have to evacuate and stay out for a while and it starts raining."

The poncho is made of transparent vinyl. Our company name and symbol is printed in blue on the back of the poncho. It slips over your head, and has a hood to protect your head from the rain. Velcro snaps on the sides close you up into a neat, rain-proof package. One size fits all.

The poncho folds flat and will fit in a handbag, briefcase or drawer of your desk.

If we have an evacuation of the building, carry your poncho with you. If it's raining, wear the poncho.

If you're away from your work station when an evacuation is called, don't go back to get your poncho. Just walk out of the building by the nearest evacuation route.

You can wear the poncho home on rainy days. "Just be sure to bring it back the following day and have it at your work station."

If you lose your rain poncho, you may buy another one at the company's cost of $3.45.

Your manager will give you a rain poncho sometime next week. You may not need it. But if you do, you'll be prepared. It's revolutionary.

Mean machine

Growls and gurgles from your stomach aren't a sign of hunger.

The audible signals result from air and liquid being moved around in the intestinal tract. The higher the pressure in the stomach or intestines, the higher the pitch.

NEWSLETTER in simplest form uses typewritten body and acetate headlines. Only simplest of art work, as at top of column 2, is used. This is "Over Coffee" of Blue Cross and Blue Shield of Alabama in Birmingham.

Content

Emphasis is always on news; sheer feature material is rarely used. Often the newsletter refers the reader to other sources where subjects can be treated at greater length.

Writing should be studiedly terse, even telegraphic. Many editors develop a style that uses many abbreviations and acronyms, often known only to the special readership; "prez," "veep," and "sec" may identify officers. Sentence fragments are frequent; so are simple listings and calendars. Often names are emphasized by capping, underlining, or boldfacing.

However, this style can easily degenerate into an affectation that is downright annoying—and sometimes confusing—to the reader. Frequent underlining or boldfacing can make your copy difficult to read, and the accent value is lost when used too often.

Editors should almost never use abbreviations or acronyms—especially in-house ones—without explaining them, no matter how certain they are that "all our readers will understand that." No matter how unlikely it seems that an "outsider" will read this (and this is an indication of how we underestimate the potential of our own publication!) there's always that possibility. If that reader can understand what you're saying, you may well have gained an interested friend—but if you have used incomprehensible terms, you've just shoved a "strangers not wanted" sign in that unsuspecting person's face.

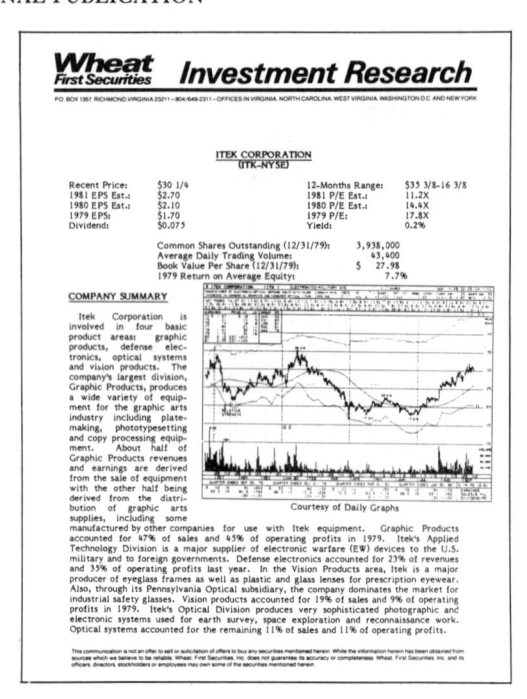

SIMPLE LINE ART, especially expo art, is traditional with newsletters. Here, for "Investment Research" of Wheat First Securities, Richmond, Virginia, body type is done on typewriter.

Format

The simplest newsletter is on an 8½x11-inch sheet designed as a single page that looks much like a conventional business letter. It's folded twice, as a letter is, to fit a No. 10 envelope. The next simplest is that same 8½x11 sheet folded once to make a 4-page folder, with each "page" handled as a separate unit. We might use 8½x14 pages in a 4-page folder.

Then comes a double-fold of the same basic sheet, creating a folder of six narrow pages. This may be a letterfold, the upper and lower thirds folding down upon the middle one, or it may be an accordion fold, when the upper third is folded away from the reader and the lower third is folded toward him or her.

Less frequent formats are a 4-panel accordian fold using an 8½x14½-inch sheet. A most unusual one is when three 3½x8 panels are joined at their narrow edges to create a long vertical strip.

The format depends on three important factors: What size sheet can our press print? Will the sheet "cut to waste"? Can the letter be easily folded to fit a standard envelope?

The first two questions are answered simultaneously in most instances, for press sizes are predicated on standard paper sizes.

THE EDITOR AS NEWSLETTER PRODUCER 223

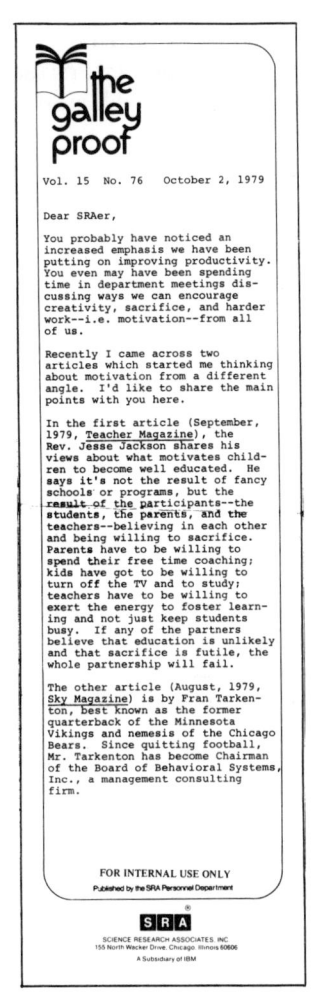

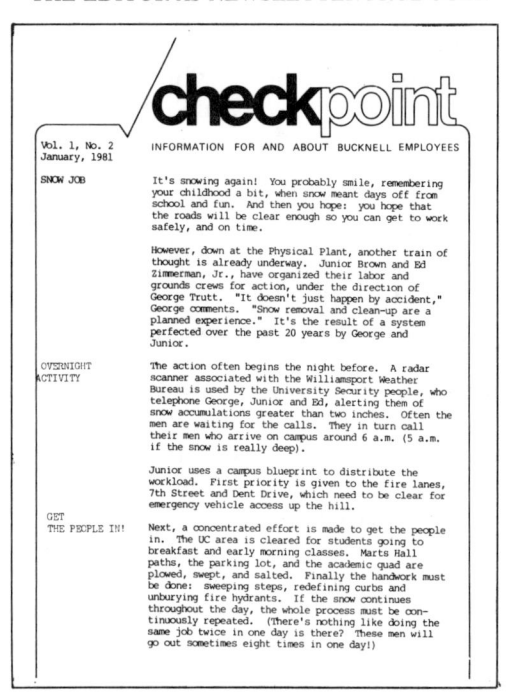

NEWSLETTER of Bucknell University, "Checkpoint," is in simple, conventional 8½x11 form. Nameplate and vertical rules are in dark blue on light gray paper.

"THE GALLEY PROOF" of Science Research Associates, Inc., Chicago, is in unusual vertical form that resembles proofs for which it is named. Page is 4½x14. Often just a single sheet, on occasion it becomes four-pager. Nameplate and rules are in bright green.

Book or *writing* papers, which are used for newsletters, come in sheets of 17x22 inches or 17x28 inches. (These divide into the familiar 8½x11 or an 8½x14 *legal* size.) It's doubtful that a newsletter would be printed on a rotary press but in that case, standard widths of the paper roll are also based on the multiples of 8½x11.

The ordinary stencil duplicator such as the Mimeograph takes a regular 8½x11 sheet or the 8½x14 legal sheet. Simple offset duplicators found in many offices take similar sizes. If a regular printer is used, press capacity will vary considerably and the editor should learn exactly what is available. Generally speaking, smaller *runs*, the number of copies printed, are done on presses with smaller page-size capacity. In almost all instances, presses use sheets based on multiples of 8½x11. Almost every print shop has a press that will easily handle 11x7 sheets which fold down to a 4-page lettersized "booklet," a 17x22 sheet which prints four letter pages on each side of the sheet or a 17x28 sheet which is four legal-size pages.

If the editor chooses an unconventional format, say 7x10, or any square page, the basic sheet will cut to waste—a thin strip must be sliced off the top and side. This sliver will be too small to use for any other purpose; it is sheer waste. Yet the editor must pay for it because paper is sold by the basic, untrimmed sheet. If the press run is not great, it may be reasonable to pay for such waste for the sake of obtaining an unusual shape and size. But in the long run, the editor should try to use every square inch of paper that's been paid for.

If the editor chooses a conventional page size, there will undoubtedly be a press readily available that will handle it. And vice versa. So the first two requisites are met at the same time.

Many newsletters are just that, letters that go through the mail. The editor should make sure that the publication will fit a standard envelope. The most common is the *No. 10 envelope*, 4 1/8 x 9½, which is used for regular business letters. There are many, many other sizes available but for economy of price, constant availability, and ease of stuffing, the No. 10 is probably the best choice.

Many newsletters are distributed internally without envelopes so the problem is nonexistent.

We can also eliminate the need for envelopes—and the process of stuffing them—by using a slightly heavier stock. This can make the piece a self-mailer, one sturdy enough to withstand postal delivery without extra covering. Usually postage costs will not be increased and the savings of envelopes and stuffing labor will pay for the heavier paper.

Printing Methods

If printing is done commercially, it will probably be by offset and the platemaker's copy will be prepared exactly as it would be for a conventional newspaper or magazine printed by that method. Larger organizations may have an in-plant printing department that also requires camera-ready copy.

The editor usually has less choice of method when printing is done right in the office. The stencil method is commonly known as Mimeographing although there are other machines—such as the Gestetner—that use the same principle. Small offset presses that use homemade *paper masters* or commercially made aluminum plates are operated in many offices. The *hectograph* process, also called *spirit duplicating*, is feasible only for a short run.

For the hectograph—commercially called *Ditto*—process, the 8½x11 page is first typed or drawn using a special carbon paper that

TRADITIONAL NEWSLETTER APPEARANCE is maintained although the page-size of "Teller" of Indiana National Corporation, Indianapolis, is 9½x12½. Printing is in dark brown on buff stock.

puts the image in mirror form on the back of the typewritten sheet. This is placed face downward on a bed of gelatin onto which the image transfers. When a piece of printing paper is pressed onto the gelatin, a little bit of the original image lifts off to become the printed, right-reading image. Eventually all of the original image is depleted; this is usually well under a hundred copies. If more are required, a fresh "plate" must be prepared. So this method is feasible only for a very small circulation. It is rather messy to prepare, the gaudy purple color is hardly exhilarating, and there's a tendency for the ink to rub off onto the reader's hands. All in all, this method is far down the list of desirability.

The method of printing dictates the method of preparing the printing elements, and that, in turn, dictates much of the typography of the newsletter.

Typography

Let's assume that we are using a typewriter to "set" type.

The first choice is the size of the face. Regular typewriter faces are either elite, with 12 characters in a linear inch, or pica, with only 10 characters per inch. Because it's larger, pica is a trifle easier to read and therefore is often the choice when a plate is made directly without a photographic process. If a negative is produced and there is, therefore, opportunity to change the size, a good technique is to make the pasteup about 10 percent larger than the plate will be. This reduction helps sharpen the type.

Regular "typewriter" face is a Square Serif. If the editor wants to emphasize the immediacy of the newsletter—that it was just typed up moments ago and rushed into the maws of the postal system—this regular face will best give that impression. (A typewriter face is also available on phototypesetting machines. But we usually use our desk typewriter to prepare our "plates." The economy and the advantage of doing this work in-house are obvious.)

Regular Roman faces are available on some typewriters. They are attractive and adequately readable but do lack the spontaneity of the Square Serifs. Sans Serifs faces are available on almost all typewriters; because of the brevity of items in a newsletter, these Sans have adequate readability.

Scripts and Cursives should be avoided as violently as ice cubes in beer. Their readability is nil and their letterforms are of execrable design.

Conventional typewriters use *constant spacing*; each character is given exactly the same space, whether it's a cramped-up M or W or a beanpole l or i or even a period. While this system riddles words with unwanted gaps around the narrow characters and thus reduces readability, this, too, contributes to the sense of speed and urgency in preparation.

Variable spacing on more sophisticated typewriters fits characters more snugly and enhances readability. It also makes the typesetting look more formal; the editor must weigh that against the loss of the impression of immediacy.

Typewriters that use the "bouncing ball" principle can change faces in a matter of seconds. The editor may then use a second face as bright type or for headlines.

Direct typesetting is used to cut stencils for the Mimeograph or to make paper masters. If plates are made photographically, the editor has a far wider choice of faces for headlines.

Body type is either typed onto a glossy paper and pasted up (just as phototype is for newspapers or magazines), or the typing may be done directly onto the pasteup sheet. Headlines may be either typewritten or acetate. If the latter, only one face should be used, the editor deliberately foregoing the variety of size and slant we seek for more formal publications. (There is a large typewriter face—the equivalent of about 18-point—that's used for manuscripts of speeches. This may require a special typewriter. Because it's available only in Sans, this face is generally used only for headlines.)

MEMO:

Manual✓typewriters✓require two typings to..
justify✓the lines.✓First set✓the desired...
line length (A).✓Come as close as possible.
to this line✓as you type,✓filling out the..
line either✓with periods as has✓been done..
up to here or,✓to prevent✓confusion✓withXXX
punctuation, with X's. Then go back and put
a check mark✓where the extra space is sup-X
posed✓to go.✓The✓best✓place is✓after aXXXXX
period or comma; the poorest, after an l.

If your typewriter✓allows half-spacing,X
you may run over✓the line by an initial orX
two and tuck in that character where you've
indicated✓with a circle. Here just✓beforeXX
or after an i or l is a good place to squeeze   2
in that extra letter. (The number in the mar- 2
gin shows how many extra characters you have.) 3

If you can't half-space✓and you go over.
~~the line, simply cross out that line and type~~
the line,✓simply cross✓out that✓line andXXX
type it over again, shorter.

Stencil Cutting

Let's look at procedures for cutting a stencil. The editor may prepare a simple sketch dummy. Or the story may be typed in the same form in which it will appear printed, creating the equivalent of a paste-up dummy even while writing original copy.

Ready to cut the stencil, we must first clean the typewriter thoroughly. This is such an obvious step that it's almost embarrassing to mention it; but it is consistently overlooked and examples of poorly cut stencils are legion. Some people will clean the type after each page has been cut; others will play it even safer and do it at the end of every column.

General instructions for cutting stencils are given in or on each box of stencils. They show how to take advantage of cushion sheets that will give clean images. While details vary according to the manufacturer, they concern the use of a plastic film covering and a cushion sheet behind the stencil itself. There is spirited debate whether a clearer image is obtained by dispensing with the plastic overfilm. Many editors believe eliminating the film is the best technique.

The stencil is fragile and tender handling is a prime necessity. When typing on the stencil, type one column; then remove the stencil by depressing the paper release. By all means avoid rolling the stencil up or down; this will wrinkle or even tear the stencil.

If you are typing sideways on the stencil, make a little trough of a folded piece of paper to protect the edge of the stencil as you feed it into the machine. If you don't have a wide carriage, you may fit the stencil in one of two ways. You may cut down the gutter of the 2-page spread that you're typing on the stencil. Each page is cut separately and then the two are joined with *stencil cement*. As an adequate overlap must be provided, the actual cut will come, not exactly on the center of the gutter, but moved over 2 or 3 picas. The other method is to cut off the lower portion of the stencil. Then the two pages are kept as a single unit and, after they have been cut, the tail is pasted back on.

Guidelines, printed on the stencil, show the area that can be printed on the machine. Be sure that the margins of type fall within these lines. If characters are on the line, they will not reproduce.

Be sure to set the ribbon control at the "stencil" position.

An electric typewriter, where all strokes are of equal force, usually will produce the best stencils. But a good typist, taking pride and care in the job, can produce an evenly cut stencil on any machine. Always, stencil cutting should be done at a slower tempo than normal typing and with a crisp, staccato stroke. Capitals and other characters on shift position should be struck a trifle harder than lowercase. But care must be taken that the normal stroke is not so hard that it will completely cut out the bowls of such letters as *o, b, p* and *q* or even those semi-bowls like *u* and *c*.

The typewriter used for stencil cutting should be serviced frequently and adjusted so all characters make a consistent and even impression. It is important that this adjusting be done while actually cutting a stencil. Because it's far more convenient to do so using the regular fabric ribbon or film, the serviceman usually chooses this method. The editor must insist on the proper way.

Make corrections as soon as you become aware of them so you don't have to roll the stencil back and forth. The entire page should be proofread once more before printing begins, of course.

If just a letter or two needs correcting, apply *correction fluid* in a thin, even layer. Be sure the fluid has dried thoroughly before typing on it. Drying takes only a few seconds but impatient typists too often create distorted letters by cutting through areas that haven't dried thoroughly. When typing manually, use a lighter touch for the correction letter else it will appear darker than surrounding characters.

If major corrections must be made, it's better to slice out an entire section or paragraph, retype the material correctly on another piece of stencil and paste it into the original. (The frugal editor never throws away a spoiled stencil; fragments of it are used for corrections.) Whenever stencil cement is used, let it dry at least a half hour before printing.

Lettering Guides

Lettering guides are templates cut into a piece of rigid plastic; the stylus or lettering pen runs in the slots to form the letters.

The guide for letters with bowls, areas enclosed by circles or ovals, is usually made in two sections. To make a cap *B*, for instance, the vertical stem is drawn from one portion of the guide; then the guide of the bowl is moved into place and the curved portion drawn. To save space, the guide for the I is often used for the stems of B, P, T, etc. and the template for the upper portion of the B is also used for the P. While using such guides does not require acute skill, it can be done more quickly and precisely after some practice. So it pays to fool around with the guides, using scrap paper, to acquire maximum deftness.

If headlines are cut with such a template, or if drawings are made right on the stencil, these processes take place at this stage, preferably on a light table or Mimeograph *scope*. The heavy backing sheet is folded back so the image can be seen more clearly; a transparent writing plate of plastic is placed between the stencil and the glass. The stencil is kept flat and smooth by means of spring clamps on the scope or with masking tape on a light table.

A T-square is placed so the bottom of the letterguide will rest on it and properly align the heads. The square also prevents wrinkling and tearing of the stencil. A straight *stylus* is used with the letterguide; it has a tiny ball on its end and so is called either a *ballpoint* or a *needle* stylus.

The stylus is always drawn to the intersection of two strokes. To draw an *M*, for instance, the left stroke is drawn upward and so is the second; the third stroke comes downward to meet the second and the final stroke goes upward again. For an *E*, the vertical stroke is done first, then the horizontal ones are drawn to the left, toward that first stroke.

It's best to use several light strokes rather than one heavy one in cutting the stencil. Go over the line until all the wax of the stencil has been pushed aside and the stroke shows up clear and white. Great care must be taken that the stencil isn't torn; pressure on the stylus should be no more than that necessary to remove the wax. Spacing between letters is done by eye. Space between words should be about the width of half the cap M.

Illustrations are now added. The original drawing is placed between the glass and the writing plate. Some editors remove the writing plate and use the drawing as a cushion; but this technique is recommended only for the person with considerable experience in cutting stencils. Excellent results are obtained by cutting through a piece of silk or plastic, placed over the stencil. (The wrapping of cigaret packages is excellent.) A *loop* stylus is used except for the finest detail which may require the ballpoint. Pressure should be even and firm enough to make clear, white lines.

Shading can be added to such line work by placing a *screen plate* of metal or plastic directly under the stencil. When the stencil is rubbed with a flat stylus, the pattern, in relief on the plate, is created on the stencil. A *border stylus* has a tiny wheel which, when rolled across the stencil produces a regular coinedge pattern. These styli are used primarily for borders but can be repeated, side by side, to cover a larger area.

Pre-cut illustrations are available from many sources, especially organizations such as the Red Cross, March of Dimes, U.S. Savings Bonds, and various religious groups. Many of these are little ads for the causes of the sponsors but many are seasonal, pure ornamentation. Before you start typing, mark the area for the illustration on the stencil, with correction fluid, so that it's kept blank. After typing and when all other handwork has been done on the stencil, the rectangle is cut out. The illustration is cut out of the large sheet in which it originally came and is pasted onto the stencil, with stencil cement. A margin of 2 or 3 picas must be allowed all around the cut-out window. The insert is placed on top of the stencil. Then in the printing process, when the stencil is placed face-down on the drum, the larger stencil will be pressed upon the smaller insert and a tight seal assured.

The stencil must be placed carefully on the cylinder of the Mimeograph. Don't over-ink. Keep a stack of scrap paper around so you can run through several sheets—sometimes as many as a couple dozen—to get proper ink distribution before feeding good paper. Be sure to keep the rims of the cylinder clean; excess ink oozing out from the sides of the stencil is the prime culprit in smudging.

EATON Update

Volume 8 • Issue 9
May 15, 1981

For managers, professionals, and technical personnel

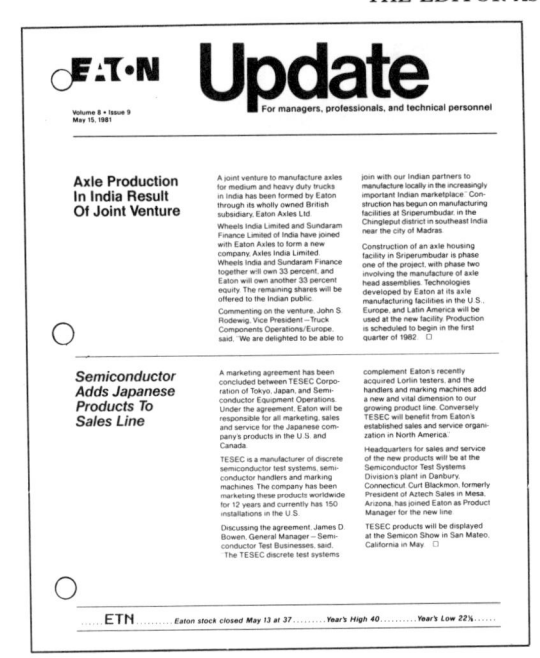

Axle Production In India Result Of Joint Venture

A joint venture to manufacture axles for medium and heavy duty trucks in India has been formed by Eaton through its wholly owned British subsidiary, Eaton Axles Ltd.

Wheels India Limited and Sundaram Finance Limited of India have joined with Eaton Axles to form a new company, Axles India Limited. Wheels India and Sundaram Finance together will own 33 percent, and Eaton will own another 33 percent equity. The remaining shares will be offered to the Indian public.

Commenting on the venture, John S. Rodewig, Vice President—Truck Components Operations/Europe, said, "We are delighted to be able to join with our Indian partners to manufacture locally in the increasingly important Indian marketplace." Construction has begun on manufacturing facilities at Sriperumbudar, in the Chingleput district in southeast India near the city of Madras.

Construction of an axle housing facility in Sriperumbudar is phase one of the project, with phase two involving the manufacture of axle head assemblies. Technologies developed by Eaton at its axle manufacturing facilities in the U.S., Europe, and Latin America will be used at the new facility. Production is scheduled to begin in the first quarter of 1982. □

Semiconductor Adds Japanese Products To Sales Line

A marketing agreement has been concluded between TESEC Corporation of Tokyo, Japan, and Semiconductor Equipment Operations. Under the agreement, Eaton will be responsible for all marketing, sales and service for the Japanese company's products in the U.S. and Canada.

TESEC is a manufacturer of discrete semiconductor test systems, semiconductor handlers and marking machines. The company has been marketing these products worldwide for 12 years and currently has 150 installations in the U.S.

Discussing the agreement, James D. Bowen, General Manager—Semiconductor Test Businesses, said, "The TESEC discrete test systems complement Eaton's recently acquired Lorlin testers, and the handlers and marking machines add a new and vital dimension to our growing product line. Conversely TESEC will benefit from Eaton's established sales and service organization in North America."

Headquarters for sales and service of the new products will be at the Semiconductor Test Systems Division's plant in Danbury, Connecticut. Curt Blackmon, formerly President of Aztech Sales in Mesa, Arizona, has joined Eaton as Product Manager for the new line.

TESEC products will be displayed at the Semicon Show in San Mateo, California in May. □

.....ETN......... Eaton stock closed May 13 at 37.........Year's High 40..........Year's Low 22⅜.....

FILING NEWSLETTERS for future reference is facilitated by prepunching. "Update" is international publication of Eaton Corporation of Cleveland, Ohio, for managers, professionals, and technical personnel who might have long-range use for research material published here.

Become familiar with *head adjustments* that allow changes of the top and bottom margins. Side margins cannot be adjusted.

Uneven inking can be due to several causes. The stencil may be poorly cut and at this stage there's nothing to do except cut a new stencil or sweat out an imperfect job. The ink pad which is placed between the metal cylinder and the stencil may be worn or lumpy. (You can prevent most of this by taking meticulous care to replace the oiled-paper cover on the cylinder whenever it's not in use. This prevents the pad from drying out.) Inspection before starting the job is the only way to prevent this. The stencil may be taken off, a new pad put on, and the stencil replaced. But this is a messy job that usually results in smudged copies; and there is some danger of the stencil tearing. The impression roller that presses the paper onto the stencil may be worn unevenly or dirty. It should be cleaned before starting a new stencil; during this process it can be inspected for wear.

A dirty *impression roller*—one onto which the paper is rolled, then pressed against the stencil or printing plate—will smear the backs of the printed sheets. Or the printed image may set off on the back of the sheet. If this offsetting doesn't cure itself in a half dozen impressions or so, we have to *slipsheet*, placing a sheet of scrap paper between each pair of printed sheets. This must be done by hand and so the machine must be slowed down sufficiently to give enough time for such manual insertion.

Allow ink to dry at least a half hour before *backing up*, printing the reverse side of the paper.

Color with Duplicators

It is easy to use colored ink in the Mimeo process. Assume that you want to use red for ornaments or boxes on a normal black-and-white job. Do your dummy in one color. Lay it under a blank stencil on the light table and mark the areas to be in color with a dab of correction fluid at each corner; do this on two stencils. On the "black" stencil, cut all the regular material, being careful not to encroach upon the color areas. On the "red" stencil, cut the color elements into the proper areas, being equally careful not to invade the black areas unless surprinting is desired. . .which shouldn't happen very often. Now, keeping the stencils precisely aligned at the top and sides, lay both of them on the light table and see that the *register* of the two colors is correct.

The black stencil is printed in the customary fashion. Now a piece of stencil typing film or some other ink-proof material is placed over the ink pad and, over this, a clean ink pad is attached to the cylinder. As the second stencil lies face up on a table, outline the color areas with an ink brush in the desired color. Attach the stencil to the machine but do not remove the backing sheet. As you press the stencil lightly onto the pad, the color areas will be neatly outlined on the pad. Lift the stencil and paint in the outlined areas with the colored ink, working it in so the pad is saturated. Lay the stencil back into position and lock it into place; remove the backing sheet; you're ready to run. On long runs you may have to re-ink; simply lift the stencil, paint on more ink and off we go. You may use the same pad for a third color if the areas are at least an inch apart. An interesting technique is to do a simple piece of line art in two colors at once. The top half is inked in, let's say, blue, and the bottom half in green. As the printing is done, the two colors will blend at the middle into a blue-green area that will expand as the printing proceeds. Obviously this technique can be used only when color need not be separated and is not essential to the design.

To assure proper feeding, paper should be fanned before being placed on the feed bin. A *take* of paper—an inch or so thick—is held firmly in one hand and with the thumb of the other, the curved handful of paper is separated by riffling the ends. During certain climatic conditions, very dry air can help create static that causes paper sheets to cling together tightly. Fanning helps a little bit but more useful is a string of Christmas-tree tinsel (especially the copper kind) stretched across the cylinder where the paper leaves the impression cylinder. Anti-static spray is also available from your duplicator sales organization although it is needed only rarely.

The paper is peeled off the impression cylinder by a set of curved metal fingers, *strippers*. If these are bent or dirty, they don't do their job; the paper may be rolled around for a second impression against the stencil and general chaos sets in. Strippers should be checked at the very first indication that feeding is not smooth.

TYPESET NEWSLETTER retains traditional feeling of spontaneity by avoiding illustrations and using simple display. This is "Independent Investor" of The Fidelity Group of Boston.

When the stencil has been run, excess ink should be blotted off with sheets of old newspapers. The fairly clean stencil is then covered with its original backing sheet and stored in a convenient fairly cool place. Stencils should be kept until you're very sure that a rerun is not necessary. Reruns may be required because many people have asked for extra copies. Or you may discover a major error that will demand running one side with a new stencil. The saved stencil can then be used to run the reverse side and this horrendous situation is only half as traumatic as if you had to re-cut both fore and aft stencils.

Many organizations have machines to cut stencils electronically and in most cities you can have such stencils made commercially. Original copy—either that typed on a pasteup sheet or a conventional pasteup such as is used to make offset plates—is wrapped around a cylinder, scanned by an electric eye. On a corresponding cylinder, the stencil is cut by an oscillating stylus. This method can reproduce fine detail and even do a halfway passable job on photographs.

If a metal offset plate is used on an office duplicator, a pasteup or mechanical is required. Usually these plates are made by commercial platemakers who can reduce the pasteup and who will make genuine halftones of the photographs.

Paper masters are sheets of thin cardboard with a special surface. Using a carbon ribbon, typing is done right onto the master. Headlines may be lettered and illustrations drawn with a special ink. It is probably a little better to do the hand art first, then the typing, to prevent smudging, but this is not vital.

Lettering guides, just like those used for cutting stencils, are also available for use with special pens to prepare pasteups or paper masters. The pen should be held as vertical as possible; if it's tilted, ink may seep under the edge of the guide. No pressure should be applied to the pen; gravity will draw sufficient ink onto the paper. Strokes should be made—like those in cutting stencils—toward the intersection with another stroke.

Having noted how headlines may be made with lettering guides, we ought to note that results are not always happy. It is extremely difficult to create good printing from stencils with traced letters. On masters, the letterforms are also difficult to control and there is constant danger of smearing wet ink as the letterguide is moved into position for the next letter.

If acetate letters are not usable, the best results will probably be from using the typewriter for heads as well as bodies.

The simplest typewritten head is a line or two of all-cap, flush left that rides above the story just like a typical newspaper head does. We know we sacrifice some legibility by going all-cap, but we still use this letterform because we need all the optical weight we can get.

The *inset* head runs in the space that otherwise would be filled with type in the top-left corner of the type rectangle. There should be at least three spaces between the longest line of the head and the start of the body type, which is set flush-left; there should be one blank line of space between the head and the first full line of body type.

The *hanging indent* head is a 1-liner set flush left. The story begins on the same line as the head. The second and all succeeding heads are indented 3 spaces from the left.

When the hanging indent head is set in two lines, both are flush left and the story begins immediately after the head in the second line.

The hanging indent may be set in two flush-left lines with the story starting in the third line, indented 3 spaces as are all the other lines. When the head and the start of the story are on the same line, the style is called *running-in*.

Many editors will underscore these heads for added weight. This practice though, further reduces legibility and the little extra weight that it adds is negligible. With paste-up copy, an interesting effect is to run a heavy rule—about 3- or 4-point—just above and exactly as wide as the head.

The *read-in* head is simply the capitalization of the first word or two, preferably 12 to 18 characters, of the story itself. Both the caps and downstyle matter are on the same first line. This requires a lead with strong and short opening words to be effective.

Stencil printing can be combined with other methods. Some editors will have their nameplate printed by letterpress or offset and do the news matter by Mimeo. When this is done, the nameplate may be in color at no extra cost. Some editors will have nameplates printed in three or four different colors on white paper and use a different color each issue as a matter of differentiation among them. Others will use different colored paper, keeping the nameplate in the same color throughout. This is the least expensive method although the little extra cost of printing the flag in different colors is a good investment. A full year's supply of nameplates must be printed at one time to be economical. You'll note that only the front page need be printed, not all the inside pages as well.

Paper for stencil printing comes in a pleasant variety of colors; the editor should choose clear, bright colors. Colored ink should not be used on paper of a different color. A dark, colored ink on a lighter tint of the same color may make a pleasing combination if the ink is dark enough and there is adequate difference between type and background. Black-on-white is the most readable combination for stencil printing, as it is for any other method. Black on light, clear yellow, or light cream or buff can be attractive and functional.

Page Layout

"The simpler, the better" is the standing formula for a good newsletter. Boxes, rules, dingbats, and more ornamentation are not necessary for a neat job. If rules are absolutely needed, the asterisks, space mark, plus or equal marks may be used to form a division with a little different texture.

On an 8½x11 page, three column-widths can be used effectively. The best is the 20-pica line length used in a 2-column format.

The simplest is a 1-column format; then the newsletter looks like a regular business letter. However, the line will contain about 72 characters and that is a trifle long for easy reading. This setting can be used for an occasional short item, though.

A variation is to use a single column but indent it generously, an inch to an inch and a half on either side. This, too, should be used only occasionally and then for a comparatively short item. This setting is most effective when lines are justified.

Scholar's Margin

An interesting format is the *scholar's margin* based on the design of early books when margins were made unusually wide so the reader could write notes and comments there. This format has a 12-pica column at the left, the scholar's margin, and the regular column is 28 picas wide. The alley between them is 2 picas. The narrow column is usually at the left although it can be used—though not quite as effectively—on the outside of the right-hand page of a spread. So the scholar's margin would go to the right of the regular column only on pages 3 or 5 or other odd-numbered pages. But on page one, the narrow column is always at the left of the page. In the scholar's margin are placed headlines, sometimes pulled quotes, and small illustrations.

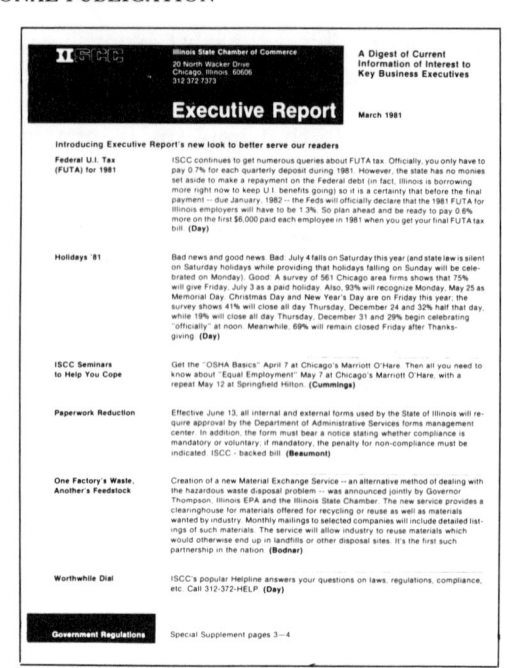

TYPESET NEWSLETTER uses scholar's margin. Nameplate is preprinted in color. This is "Executive Report" of Illinois State Chamber of Commerce, Chicago.

Illustrations can then be used in three widhts: in the narrow column, in the wide column, or clear across the page.

Headlines are often set flush-right although conventional flush-lefts will also work well. Pulled quotes or blurbs are best set flush-right or justified.

If the scholar's margin is at the right of the wide column, it is most effective if that wide column is justified. If justification is impractical, both columns can be boxed; boxing is also pleasant with justified lines. If a picture runs clear across the page, the caption runs in the wide column. For a wide-column picture the caption runs alongside in the scholar's column and when the picture runs in the narrow column, the caption, of course, runs immediately under it.

This format is especially useful when headlines are set on the typewriter because the generous space above and below them, in the narrow column, focuses attention on the type. There is, of course, a "loss" of space; much of the scholar's margin is blank. The editor must determine whether this is actually a loss or whether it's an investment of paper to assure readership. (Scholar's margins are growing in popularity with regular magazines.)

Art

We've noted that some people believe that no pictures should run in a newsletter. Such omission certainly adds to the "letter" flavor. It is possible to reproduce halftones by offset or by stencil printing although the quality is not especially high with the latter method. Original photographs must have good tonal gradation; those the least bit contrasty will emerge as line conversions and, especially for portraits or pictures that must carry fine detail, this can just about ruin the value of the art.

By any printing method, line art reproduces best and seems to enhance the immediacy of a newsletter.

The lack of any art at all need not be a handicap, however, and the editor who can't use pictures need shed nary a tear about it.

Some editors like to use ornamentation, often because it's so readily available. Others use it because they fear the utter simplicity of their typographic resources demands some enlivening. But the true newsletter doesn't need embellishments any more than does a letter from you to a close friend or family. Simplicity gives a sense of immediacy—and even urgency—and enhances the "letter" quality of the communication. And, as with any publication, it is the content which is most important; stark design emphasizes that content.

HEADLINE STYLE for typewritten material.

```
THIS HEAD    When the inset head
IS INSET     is used, there must be
             a generous margin between
the head and the copy. At least three
spaces to the right of the head and
one blank line below it.


HANGING INDENT. This head is actually misnamed.
    For the head is neither indented nor hung.
    It is the body type that is indented,
    About four spaces for this indent gives
    a pleasant effect.


HANGING INDENT
IN TWO LINES. This style builds in an
    effective strip of white alongside
    the headline as well as that created
    by the indenting. It is a pleasing style.
```

```
HANGING INDENT:
NO RUN-IN
    Note that here the story starts on
    a separate line, rather than continuing
    the line of the head.


RUNNING-IN THE HEAD is the way this style
is designated. The headline is actually
a portion of the story set all-caps.


READ-IN HEADLINE IS ANOTHER WAY in which
this same style is designated. Copy must
be written so that appropriate words for
capping begin the story. If the opening
phrase is weak, the head loses most of its
effectiveness.
```

Chapter 11
The Editor

- as Executive
- as Communicator
- as Production Manager
- as Writer
- as Copyreader
- as Typographer
- ☒ as Art Director
- as Newspaper Designer
- as Magazine Designer
- as Newsletter Producer
- as Circulation Manager
- as Contractor

Glossary
Index

The greatest story since the Ark landed on Mount Ararat isn't worth the paper it's printed upon unless someone reads it. And no one is going to read it until the newspaper, magazine, or newsletter is delivered into the potential reader's hands. So the last step in the long and complicated publication procedure—*circulation*—is as vital as any other.

The organizational editor, unlike the editor of a commercial periodical, usually has responsibility for circulation. It is easy to slight this part of the job, partly because there are few guidelines as to proper circulation methods.

On-Site Distribution

The simplest way is to place a stack of the publication where employees can pick up a copy. This has been used successfully by many organizations. The editor must determine the spot or spots where the publication is to be made available. In a small organization, this is relatively simple. A spot near the timeclock is logical and convenient. But when the organization's personnel are spread through a large building or in several widely separated sites, it may not be quite so simple.

The editor, or a savvy associate, should select distribution spots at every site. This should—or must—be approved by people in charge of plant safety and of production so that employees who gather 'round to pick up their copy will not create a safety hazard.

Every building has natural patterns of traffic flow; people prefer to go down Aisle 5 rather than Aisle 6 for no apparent reason. The editor must determine these patterns and offer the publication at points of highest traffic, just as a retailer wants to locate a store on the route most people prefer to take. There are also natural gathering places—the water cooler is just one of them—and they are the very best places to offer the publication. For the bandwagon effect can be pronounced: The employee who observes fellow workers picking up and reading a publication will usually be tempted to do the same. Logical sites can usually be best determined by personal observation of employee habits.

Distribution sites should be out of the path of heavy traffic. A reader involved in a good story may become the victim of a scuttling forklift; too many readers may tie up vital movement of machinery and material. The publication should be protected from dirt of any kind; no one wants to pick up a newspaper under an inch of soot.

The publication has been designed to attract readers and the container in which they are proffered must display these lures properly. When Michigan Bell changed the size of its employee newspaper, it spent several thousand dollars providing new containers; research into the pattern of distribution indicated that it was a good investment.

The circulation manager—whether the editor or someone else—should watch distribution boxes closely the first hours and days when a new issue has been placed in them. A fine line must be drawn between having too few and too many copies at any given point. It is wise to post, conspicuously, notices where back issues may be obtained in case an employee missed an issue because of absence or if someone wants additional copies to send to friends or relatives.

Any unclaimed copies should be picked up in a fairly short—and always consistent—time after publication. Nothing will destroy the image of a newsy and interesting communication more decisively than to allow fly-specked and dog-eared copies to accumulate dust until the next issue appears.

Most copies are picked up very shortly after they're placed in a dispenser. As soon as you learn the pattern, you can determine how many copies to place in each container and also when it is wise to move some copies from one spot to another.

This is, of course, difficult to do in distant locations. Now the editor must depend upon the efficiency of a local surrogate circulation manager. Even more important, the editor must take steps to assure that the publication will be placed at distribution points immediately after arrival at the distant location. There have been instances where an editor discovered many bundles of magazines gathering dust in some obscure corner of a receiving room because no one had taken the time to open the bundle and put the periodical out for the taking. In almost all instances, the publications were not issued at regular intervals, so the prospective reader never established a habit and never noticed the absence of the latest issue.

That is another—and compelling—reason why a periodical must come out at rigidly regular intervals: to establish the habit of looking for it and to make its absence conspicuous enough so potential readers will ask for it and thereby make it impossible to neglect distribution.

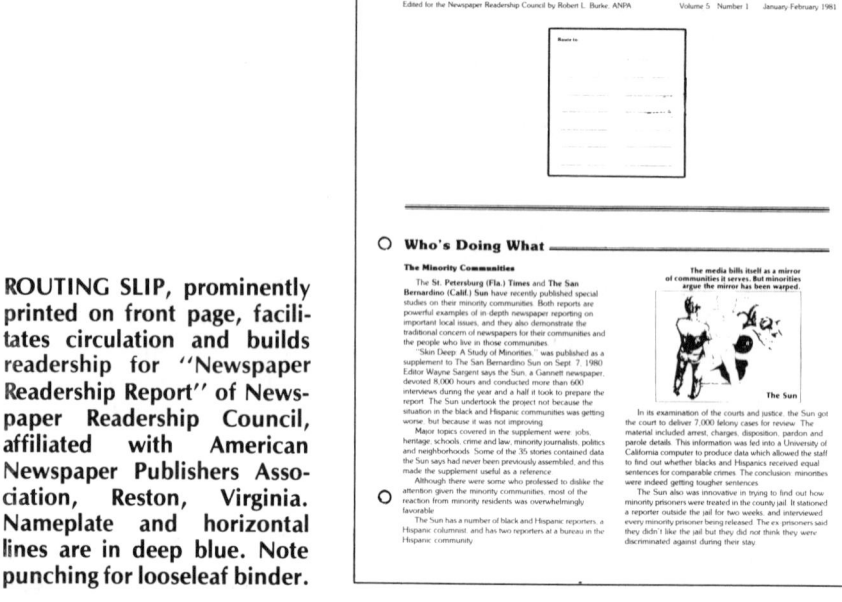

240   EDITING THE ORGANIZATIONAL PUBLICATION

ROUTING SLIP, prominently printed on front page, facilitates circulation and builds readership for "Newspaper Readership Report" of Newspaper Readership Council, affiliated with American Newspaper Publishers Association, Reston, Virginia. Nameplate and horizontal lines are in deep blue. Note punching for looseleaf binder.

Another in-plant system is to address copies specifically to employees and have them delivered through the company mail system. Unfortunately, most manufacturing plants don't have such a service for production workers.

Copies may be distributed along with paychecks. Some organizations deliberately choose a small format so the publication can fit into the regular pay envelope. Others have the distributor hand out the checks with one hand, as it were, and the publication with the other. This is not as difficult as some people would have an editor believe. If top management recognizes the value of the publication and passed the word emphatically, the periodical can easily be delivered by hand to the individual.

Mail Circulation

Perhaps the best way to circulate the organizational publication is to mail it to the employee's home. Advantages are obvious. The editor is reasonably sure that every employee is receiving a copy. More important, the employee's family is exposed to the publication. Personnel experts emphasize that the greater the interest and involvement of the family, the more motivated the employee.

Mailing costs are high, however, and all indications are that postal rates will continue to rise. Second-class postage rates—which theoret-

"PLAIN BROWN WRAPPER" protects regular cover of "Focus" of Mutual Service Insurance, St. Paul, Minnesota. Cover on slick stock and in color is thus protected going through the mail. It is suggested—top right—that the wrapper be removed upon receipt of magazine.

ically provide first-class service at reduced prices—apply only to publications with paid circulation. That eliminates almost every organizational publication. Third-class mail is woefully slow and is often pushed aside for delivery at a time so late that the periodical has lost almost all immediacy.

Presorting by zip code reduces to some extent the price of first-class mailing. While this merely shifts sorting costs from the post office to the editorial office, it's just as easy to set up your mailing list by zip code as any other way and thus effect substantial savings for large circulations. Changes in zip-coding—as by expanding the code from five to nine numbers—may demand a complete and costly overhaul of the entire mailing list and thus change the economic balance.

First-class postal rates approach the exorbitant. Some editors who have used that method for delivering emergency information, complain that it seems that post-office workers handle all obvious publications as casually as they would second- or third-class mailings, no matter how much postage has been paid or how conspicuously they are marked "First Class."

The acute and constant problem with any mailing system is to keep the list correct and up-to-date. Depending, of course, on the number of names on the mailing list, it takes hours, days, and even weeks of continuous work to keep the list clean. For employees, payroll records are the most accurate source for addresses. Organizations with computerized payrolls can usually run off address labels with little trouble or time. But, again, it is necessary to have the complete and expressly stated endorsement of top management to persuade the computer department to take on this job. Too often the editor is solemnly assured that it is just impossible to prepare a mailing list when actually it is just a

MAILING LIST revisions are invited by this postcard bound into "Panhandle Magazine" for Panhandle Eastern Pipeline Company, Houston. Business reply card makes it easy for reader to use this form of communication.

trifle inconvenient to the computer crew.

Most vexatious is trying to keep a clean mailing list which includes retirees, stockholders, members, dealers, distributors, government officials, and news media. It is a major task to decide just how widely a publication should be circulated. While some organizations can afford to have both internal and external publications, many groups must make one publication serve a varied audience.

Most retirees enjoy the organizational publication so much that their gratitude is almost embarrassing. The slight extra cost of supplying the publication is highly justifiable on a humanitarian basis alone. External readers are often very important to an organization. Many newspapers use organizational publications for story tips for their business section and even the regular news staff. Governmental officials find them useful as barometers of public opinion, especially when that public is far from the state or national capital where the official may be.

There isn't, unfortunately, a very good checklist for external circulation. No matter how often the editor may ask, in the publication's columns, for readers to notify him of address changes, not often enough is such information sent in. Most exasperating is to get an acrimonious letter demanding why the editor insists on sending the paper to John Q. Retiree when everybody knows that he left this mortal sphere—3½ years ago! Almost every editor can recount such instances.

There is also much newsroom grumbling in daily newspapers and broadcast stations about mail still addressed to John J. Eyeshade, city editor, years after ol' John—and two or three of his successors—have gone to their reward. It is better to address a publication to the news editor or business editor without any given name, just to prevent outdated titles or outdated names with current titles.

The only feasible validation of a mailing list is one provided by the postal service: It will return undeliverable copies, sometimes with new addresses. But even if no forwarding address is available, it saves the cost of production and mailing of copies that will wind up in the dead-letter office. The cost of this service is substantial but it is worthwhile—and it is the only game in town!

If the publication is delivered by United States mail, the editor must decide whether it will be mailed with or without a protective envelope. (Magazines may use an open-ended wraparound rather than a full envelope.) Envelopes add expense, of course—of the envelopes themselves, sometimes extra postage, and the cost of stuffing.

Newspapers are usually wrapped with a wide strip of paper around their middle. This is as effective as an envelope in ordinary circumstances.

If envelopes are used, they must be so attractive that they are not mistaken for so-called "junk mail" and thrown away without inspection. Completely clear plastic wrappers allow the publication to sell itself in the addressee's home just as it would on a newsstand. Costs are quite high but as insurance, plastic envelopes are cost efficient.

If regular paper envelopes are used, they should be imprinted with attractive, large, and distinctive identification so the prospective reader will instantly recognize it. Color is a most useful device here, whether it is the ink on plain—often manila—paper or whether colored envelopes are used.

If publications are mailed *peeled*, without any wrappers, care must be taken to minimize the normal deterioration of postal delivery. Nothing annoys a subscriber more than to find dirty, tattered publications in the mailbox. And it is usually the editor, rather than the post office, to whom imprecations are muttered.

It may be a good investment in reader insurance to use a stock cover on a magazine. Self-covered ones are far more susceptible to en-route wear and damage. Tabloids are usually a bit sturdier when folded twice instead of just once. Practicality of this depends, of course, on the number of pages and the ability to make the second fold.

The skimpier the "package," the greater the danger of mangling in the delivery. There are newsletters that are sent through the mail without any protective covering, but in most instances they are delivered in shape far from pristine and far from maximum attractiveness. Envelopes are almost mandatory for a piece of printing as skimpy as the typical 4- to 8-page newsletter.

When the editor uses the mails, a constant watch should be kept on the efficiency of delivery, in the time required and in the care with which publications are handled. One copy should be mailed to the editor's home to check time and condition. Other copies should be sent to each of the outer fringes of the circulation area. Usually editors enlist

MAILING INDICIA in top right is combined with masthead in area that takes lower third of back cover of "The Word," Manville Forest Products Corporation, West Monroe, Louisiana.

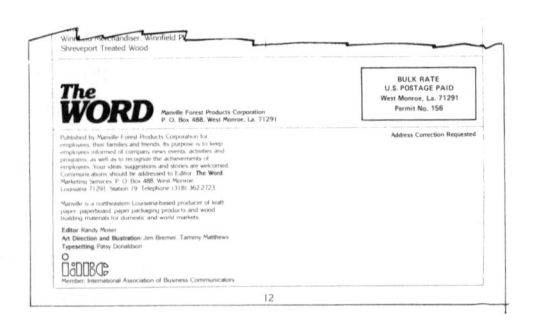

friends to receive the publication, note the time of delivery, and return copies so their condition can be examined.

No matter what the frequency of publication is, the time between the actual printing and the reader's receipt must be minimized. If there is a regular company express service between headquarters and outlying offices, that is the logical method. If other transportation must be used, United Parcel Service is probably the most efficient and reliable. Bus lines offer package service which may be desirable in some locations. Entrusting packaged mailing to the United States postal service almost automatically assures that the publication will be delayed beyond its most effective period.

If delivery is unsatisfactory, the editor should make prompt and vigorous complaint. (It probably won't do much good; postal people have developed rather impervious skins. But it relieves a little of the editor's wrath and may defer the development of ulcers.) First complaints should be made to the local postmaster who may have some practical suggestions on how to hurry up delivery.

Sometimes advancing by only an hour or two the time when the publication is brought to the post office, a whole day or even more in delivery time to the reader's home can be saved. Obviously a mailing at 7 p.m. on Friday will result in a greater total-elapsed-time than one made at 7 a.m. Tuesday. If a matter of a few hours is vital, it would be worthwhile to re-examine the entire production schedule for the publication.

There may be other steps that the mailer can take to speed delivery. If mailing is done in a smaller city, it sometimes is advantageous to take it to a neighboring, larger city. Consultation with the local postmaster or superintendent of mails can often suggest ways of avoiding transfer points where delays normally occur and getting your publication farther along in the mail stream.

If local postal people are uncooperative, or if they convince you that the fault lies elsewhere, complaint can be made to the postmaster where late home delivery is habitual. It is usually politic to make the first representation mild and just-between-us. But repeated complaints ought to have a list of recipients of carbon copies almost as long as the

Congressional Directory. Copies should go to the Postmaster General in Washington and to every Congressional representative in the House and Senate. Even the most obdurate bureaucrat is not entirely unmoved by having shortcomings expressed to influential people.

It is best, of course, to establish relations other than adversary with at least the local post office.

The organizational editor might well discuss problems with circulation managers of newspapers in the area. While dailies are relentlessly cutting down the use of mail, most still have to use the postal system to some extent and are more aware of protection steps than the organizational editor.

To most editors circulation is hardly glamorous. But it is a highly important process that cannot be shunned by a successful publication. There's no point in growing roses where no one can sniff them—or publishing material that doesn't get into the reader's hand.

Chapter 12

The Editor

- [ ] as Executive
- [ ] as Communicator
- [ ] as Production Manager
- [ ] as Writer
- [ ] as Copyreader
- [ ] as Typographer
- [ ] as Art Director
- [ ] as Newspaper Designer
- [ ] as Magazine Designer
- [ ] as Newsletter Producer
- [x] as Circulation Manager
- [x] as Contractor

Glossary
Index

Ben Franklin wrote the copy, set the type, and hand-printed his "Poor Richard's Almanac." So he had complete control over every step in its creation. Today's editors have to rely on at least one, and often several, craftsmen in producing their publications.

Many editors must use correspondents and/or freelance writers as has been discussed in Chapter 2. Others must rely on freelance photographers and/or artists, and we've discussed how to make photo assignments in Chapter 7: Working with freelance artists can be frustrating unless a consistent procedure is used.

First, explain precisely what you want the artist to do. Should this be a light, cartoonish drawing, a loose pencil or pen sketch, or a meticulously rendered wash, watercolor, or oil? If you don't know the technical term for a particular art technique, clip a sample from a magazine or newspaper and say, "This is the style I want."

Then explain the purpose of the art. Should it set a mood for an article? If so, what mood: depression, happiness, excitement; 1860 or 2021 A.D.? Should it illustrate a narrative? If so, what particular aspect should be stressed or which of many episodes should be dramatized?

If the art is to be highly technical, be sure to go over this carefully with the artist or, better yet, have someone from Engineering or Sales or a concerned department sit in with you.

Tell the artist what size the drawing is to be. Usually art is best reproduced when it is about 50 percent wider than the proposed plate will be. Extreme reduction may lose significant detail.

The price should be agreed upon. Usually a flat rate is set for a particular piece of art. On rare occasions the artist is paid by the hour. The latter method can be costly if the artist is dilatory or keeps inaccurate time records. The editor must know the going rate for art work in the city or area. This can best be obtained by calling art or advertising agencies or, even better, fellow-editors.

Establish at what point, if any, final approval will be given. The artist will usually do a pencil rendering—in varying degrees of polish—to show to the editor. After minor changes have been agreed upon, the artist then goes to the final work. Only rarely is a second sketch needed. On highly technical drawings, not only the editor but the involved departments give approval. This is best done when everyone concerned, including the artist, takes part in a general conference.

The reviewers should point out errors; they should make suggestions or specify exactly what bothers them about the sketch. But the details of the final work must be decided by the artist. The observer may say: "The hills behind our new factory seem to be bluer than this sketch shows." But it is not considered "proper" to say, "The hills should be exactly the color of this piece of cloth that I swiped from my wife's sewing basket." Details are always best left to the creator.

A most important specification is the date for the final delivery of the finished art. Freelancers have a notoriously poor reputation for promptness—even though you may be blessed by working with the exception. Of course, you can refuse to pay for late delivery; but that's no help in meeting your own deadlines.

Art agencies are the best insurance. Here a centralized office represents many artists. When the editor needs some work, the agency will show samples of each of its clients. Once the editor has chosen an artist, the agency carries on by insisting on deadlines and by promptly billing for finished work. Agencies handle photographers on the same basis.

Two craftsmen who can be absolutely maddening to the editor—or be heaven-sent allies—are the designer and the printer.

The designer, in most instances, is concerned with the package and, too often, cares little about the content. Designers are generally "picture people" who have little affection and less respect for words. Their major concern is to produce layouts that are pleasing—preferably stunning—to the eye. Often the editor is as bedazzled as the reader might be and defers to the designer, totally abdicating editorial responsibilities.

It must be made clear at the first contact between editor and designer that the editor is in charge. (While this seems so self-evident that to assert it sounds ridiculous, this relationship is not always clear. Indeed there are organizational publications where the art director is listed on the masthead above the editor!)

The editor must have final approval on any layout and cannot shirk the responsibility of invoking a veto on occasion.

As early as possible in the production cycle, the editor should confer with the designer. The objective of the written material should be made clear; the writer may even be called in to contribute opinions. The designer should know the progression of the magazine and all the

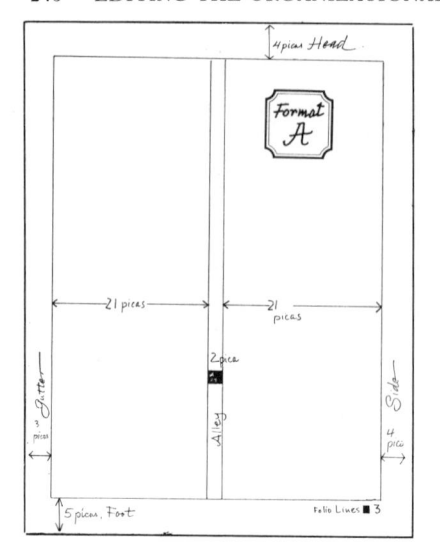

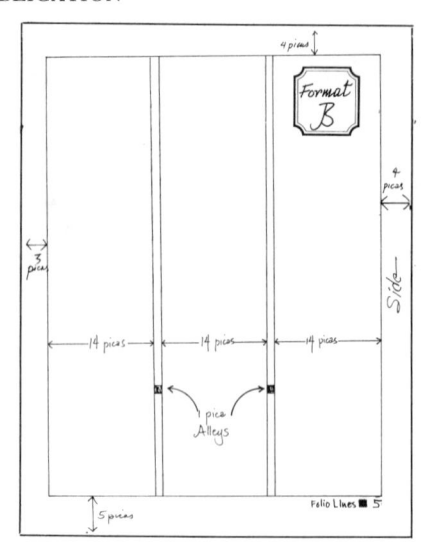

SKETCH DUMMIES show proposed format for 8½x11 magazine, and, if adopted, can be used as page-specification charts. Three page formats are suggested. Format A and B (above) are conventional. Format C (below) provides space for editor's commentary on article that runs in wide measure. Second page of Format C is also shown in detail. If story runs longer than two pages, it continues in format A.

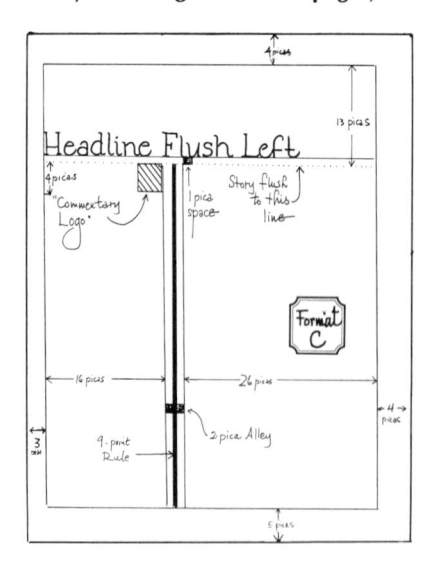

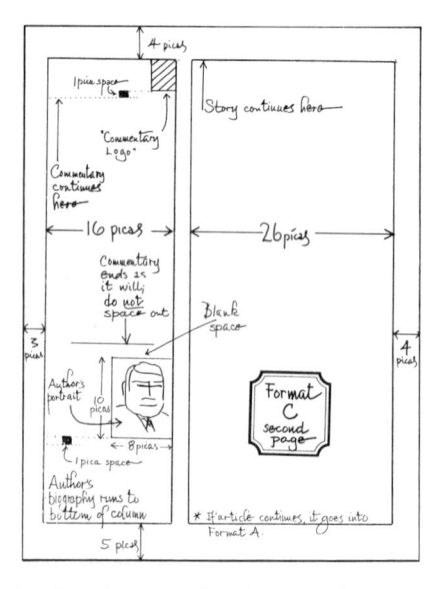

articles scheduled for the issue. For the book must be designed as a whole. We can't take the layouts of, say, a half dozen articles, no matter how good they may be individually, and lump them together into a single, effective whole.

There must be a rhythm in the presentation of a magazine. Long and short articles should alternate as should those heavy or light in content.

There should be a variety in tonal value of succeeding spreads. Yet there must be a consistent harmony from cover to cover.

If at all possible, the designer should read—or at least skim—the manuscripts before they're typeset.

The editor should contribute ideas at this planning session. Most editors have at least a vague idea of the packaging they would prefer.

There will be disagreement between editor and designer on more than one occasion. Each is a creative person and creative people often just don't see eye to eye on specifics. So it is necessary that each have respect for the other's professionalism, and each must be thoroughly dedicated to producing a quality publication. A magazine will never be successful if it is nothing but a showcase for competing egos.

The designer will show rough layouts to the editor for approval. Just how detailed these dummies are depends on how sophisticated the editor's eye is. If the designer need draw only some form of a shorthand dummy to convey the idea to the editor, that will save a lot of time, money, and mental energy for the final job. The editor can sharpen his or her eye by studying early sketches and comparing them with the finished, printed product.

The editor should also practice drawing dummies; this is an effective way to convey ideas to the designer and does not require high artistic skills.

Once the preliminary sketch has been approved, the designer does the finished art work and, in many instances, prepares the mechanical dummy, the pasteup.

But it is essential for everyone concerned to realize and to give wholehearted devotion to the proposition that the editor is the ultimate authority. Certainly the editor must give the final inspection to the pasteup before it goes to the platemaker.

The editor-printer relationship is an even more perplexing one. The editor is the customer, the printer is the supplier. And the customer is—or should be—always right!

But the relationship between many an editor and printer is one of Hitler and Stalin in 1938; "armed truce" is too mild a description. Perhaps this is because the two come in contact too often during times of stress. The editor, unaware of the technicalities of typesetting and printing, often makes unnecessary and even impossible demands upon the craftsman. Too many printers take advantage of the ignorance of the customer to insist that certain things the editor asks are "just impossible" while actually they are only inconvenient. Usually these encounters take place close to deadlines and the pressures of time on already frazzled nerves abrades the relationship.

But the printer is a highly skilled professional. If we enlist him as an ally instead of tolerating him as a forced conscript, we can combine talents to create the best possible publication.

PAGE LAYOUT possibilities are shown in this proposal for the magazine. These suggest possibilities in a 2-column format. Actual layouts, though, should be based on available material. Never should copy and art be forced into preconceived pattern.

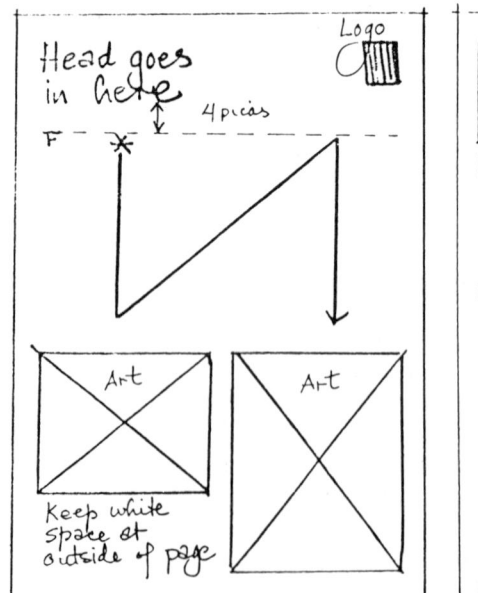

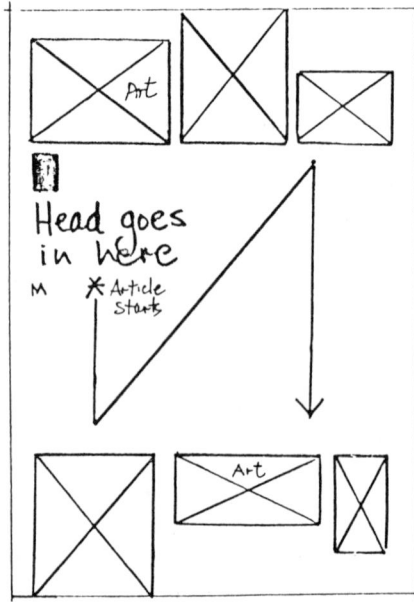

Common complaints printers make about editors can be a checklist for editorial New Year's resolutions:

"They never make deadlines."

"They don't know the cost of what they want, then complain when they get the bill."

"Dummies aren't clear and instructions are garbled."

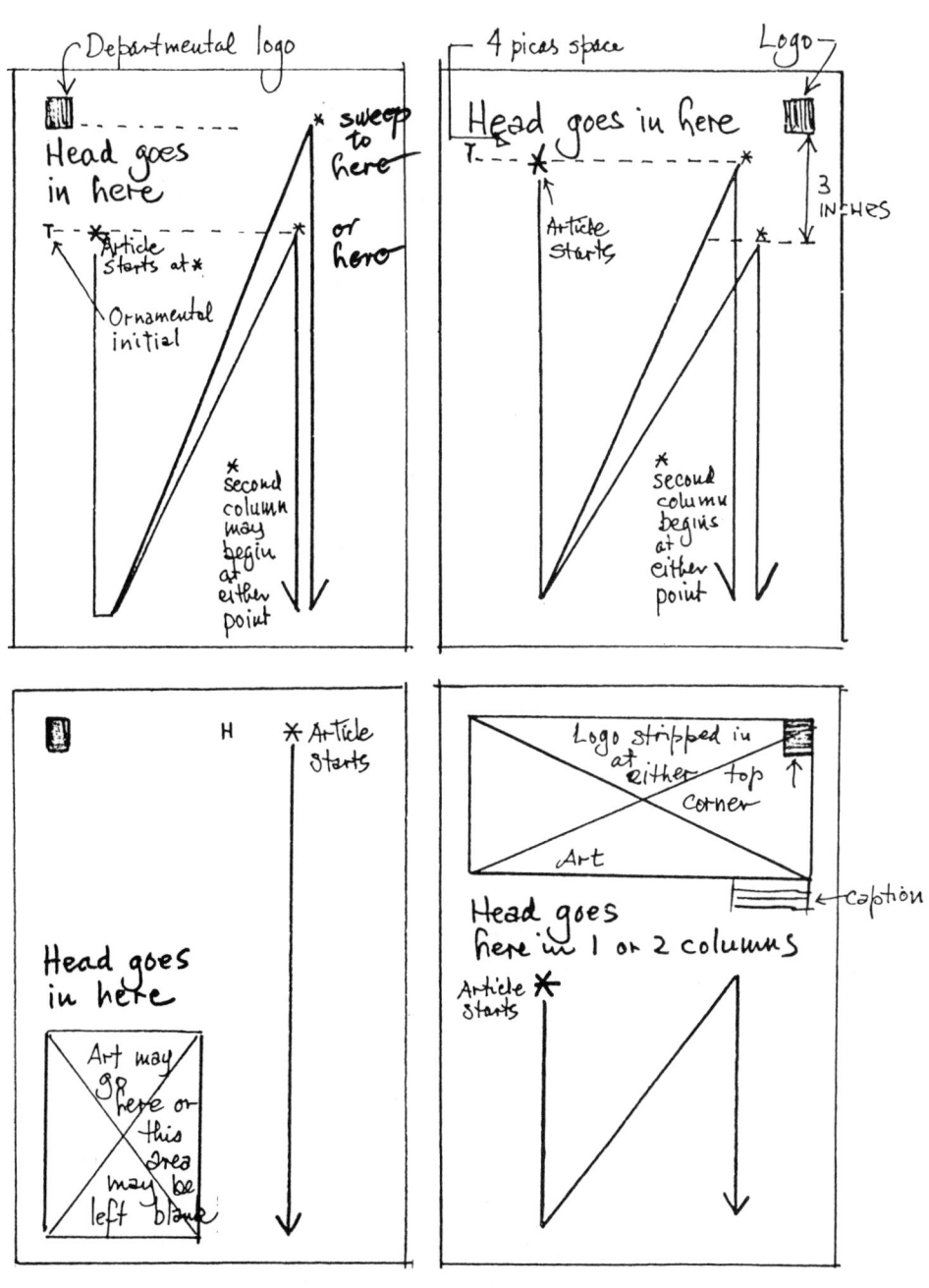

"They know it all; they never take advice."

"They want things that can't be done or can't be done with the available time and budget."

"They change their minds too often."

"They make unnecessary changes."

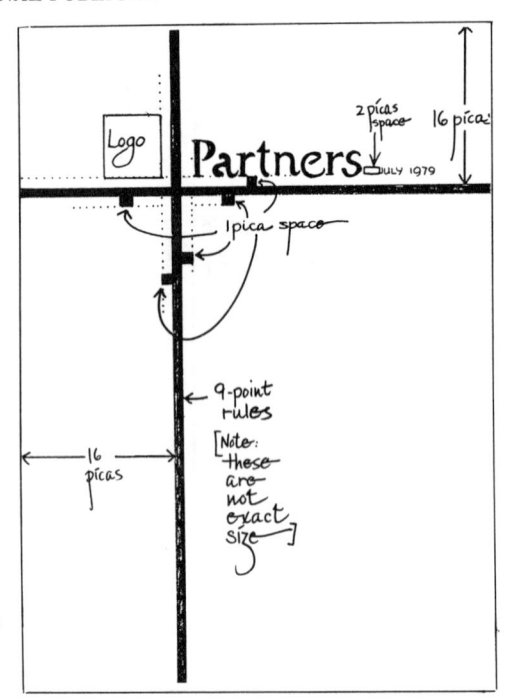

MONDRIAN COVER—based on pattern of rectangles—affords great flexibility in use of cover art and appeals. Sketches on next page show some variations, and details of specifications are shown in dummy at right.

Printers must get paid for the time they spend on the job. If an editor has second thoughts and requires that the entire front page be made over, the printer will be paid for that extra effort. But he won't be happy. For the printer doesn't like hidden costs. Each job a printer produces is an advertisement for that plant. The printer wants every dollar that the customer spends to be reflected—and obviously so—in the product. If too many costs are unnecessary—and their results invisible—it will give the impression that the printer's charges are too high. That's why the printer complains about some editorial practices while the editor wonders, "What's all the griping about? You're getting paid, aren't you?"

A constant complaint of printers is imprecise instructions. (One editor was known to have asked for "24-point agate." As agate is 5½-point size and has nothing to do with letterforms, the request was obviously difficult to fulfill.) So the editor should vow a vow that all instructions will be explicit. . .and possible to follow.

Dirty copy, that with many corrections and changes, is another hair-grayer for the typesetter. Often it's best to have such a manuscript retyped. Even the most competent typist isn't paid as much as a journeyman compositor and it's foolish to have a costly craftsman waste precious time trying to decipher hieroglyphics.

Another temperature-raiser is disregard for deadlines. Printing equipment is very expensive and must be kept running constantly to pay

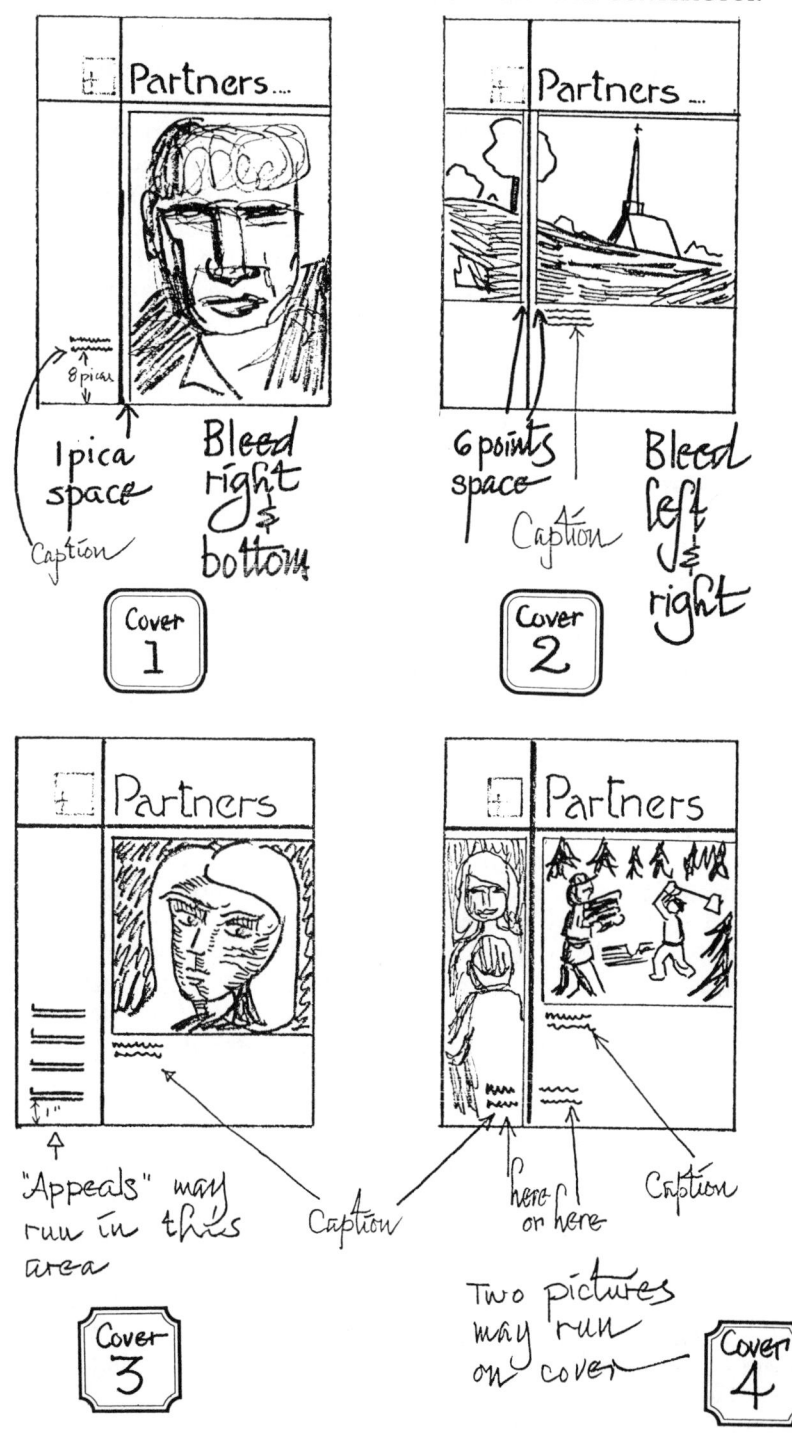

THE EDITOR AS CONTRACTOR

for itself. So highly detailed charts are commonplace in printing plants; they show each machine and the jobs that are allocated to it, hour by hour.

Suppose your publication is scheduled on the press from 10 to 11 a.m. Tuesday. You get your final proofs back 30 minutes late. The printer couldn't keep the press standing idle for that period—it's too expensive, and would throw the next customer's job off schedule. So that following job is put on the press at 10 o'clock. But it's a long job that will keep the press running until closing time tonight. That means your job won't be run until tomorrow and the 30-minute delay has mushroomed to 24 hours.

A realistic schedule must be established and then adhered to religiously. Depending on the size of the publication and the amount of timely news it carries, a good schedule will usually call for three deadlines on copy. Anytime material comprises the first batch; regular copy is due a day or two later; a small amount of late-breaking copy can be accommodated much closer to press time.

Handling of proofs must be done on a strict schedule. The printer is committed to delivering them at specified times; the editor must return them on a schedule just as rigid. That schedule must be drawn so that there's time to read proofs thoroughly and without overtime or weekend work. It's foolish and/or masochistic to accept proofs at 4:45 Friday afternoon and commit yourself to having them back by 9 Monday morning.

The revising of schedules to accommodate holidays should also be written out plainly in the basic timetable.

No other single factor in production is as essential as a good set of deadlines. They should be drawn up with thought and care and observed zealously by all concerned.

There is a running debate, loud but inconclusive, on the commercial relationship between editor and printer. For larger publications a formal contract is executed. Smaller ones may use a *letter of agreement*, a simple order form, or even just an oral agreement. It is wise, though, no matter what the formal document, that all details of the relationship be spelled out in writing, if only in a memo initialled by both parties.

Formal contracts will specify times of payment. For large publications this might call for a percentage of the total charges after type has been set and the rest after printing is complete. Smaller publications usually are billed on delivery.

In many instances type is set by one contractor and printing done by another. Some editors even have camera work—screening halftones and separating color—and platemaking done by yet a third supplier. Some editors even buy printing paper on their own and then deliver it to the press.

There may be advantages in distributing the job among more than one supplier. They must be toted up on individual bases. But there are obvious disadvantages. When deadlines are not met or quality falls off, it's too easy for the pressman to blame the platemaker, who blames the camera operator, who blames the pressman, ad infinitum. If the job is let to only one printer—even though some tasks may be subcontracted—the responsibility is clear and nontransferable.

Acting as your own general contractor also takes a lot more time than you ever anticipated when you first got this idea. You have to talk to two or three suppliers on the phone instead of one. You have to process two or three invoices. You have to keep track of where your job is at any given moment.

More important, it's much more difficult to keep a job on schedule when it's being done in pieces. If the typesetter is a day late sending back your type, you may well have lost your place on the press, as we've already noted. When, in a single-shop operation, delays do occur, the supplier will try hard to make up the lost time in the next step of the process, often going to extreme lengths. But there is no such compunction when one supplier's tardiness louses up another's schedule—you go back to the end of the line and no apologies.

More and more organizations are acquiring in-house typesetting and/or printing facilities. This is a mixed blessing to the editor. It eliminates long trips to the print shop and the editor can scoot down and immediately nip incipient emergencies in the bud.

On the other hand, the printing facility probably is in another department and the editor's authority may be challenged or tested by subtle heel-dragging. The editor and his or her immediate superior should confer with the people from the other department, set up ground rules, and put them in writing.

A major problem is when the printer lays aside the publication to produce a rush job for another department with more clout. This is where those written deadlines must be invoked, politely but with great firmness.

(Many editors take over the pasteup process, whether type is set in-house or commercially. This, too, is mostly a blessing but with enough bane thrown in to warrant a second look before long-range commitments are made.)

Another standing difference of opinion is whether an editor should seek a flat price or a cost-plus billing. A fixed price makes budgeting easier, of course, and protects the editor against wildly fluctuating prices. (Even on a fixed-price basis, there is often a clause that subjects the editor to higher paper costs because that price has risen so greatly and so unpredictably during the entire period of current inflation.)

But every equitable fixed price must have built into it some cushion for emergencies. When an emergency arises with a cost-plus job, the editor pays for it in a one-shot sum instead of having it prorated over a year of fixed-price invoices. But, one way or other, the buyer must contribute to the contingency fund. Of course, if there are no emergencies, the editor enjoys the fixed-price blessing.

On a cost-plus basis, the editor is encouraged to avoid those quasi-emergencies that he himself has caused. Failure to meet deadlines, dirty copy, excessive author's alterations that extend typesetting time, and inordinate amounts of unusable overset are quickly reflected in a higher bill. While actually any customer pays for such costly lapses, in a fixed price they are hidden. When they are apparent and painful, as they are on a cost-plus basis, there is genuine incentive to amend sinful ways.

In a similar debate, editors differ on whether a contract should be automatically renewed at the end of a year or whether bids should be solicited from other printers. In some organizations, there may even be pressure to look around more often than yearly, to get the best price and/or service.

Printing is a highly competitive business and when a job is up for bids, suppliers may figure with an extra sharp pencil. That sharpness depends on just how good or how poor the general market is in that area. Many printers will offer to do the job at a minimal profit just to meet the payroll in a very tight market or to get a foot in the door for future business.

Scheduling can have a big effect on price. A printer who has nothing scheduled for a certain press may give you a very low price simply because it's better than incurring downtime on expensive equipment. But that price may apply only for a short time, maybe only for that particular job. Printers who produce many periodicals may consistently have a slow day or week. Often an editor can take advantage of that by shifting the publication date just a little forward or backward and get a better price.

One editor says, "I intend to stay with my present printer but I put the job out for bids just to keep him honest." That is an unethical practice that most editors will shun. It costs money to make a bid. Prices aren't pulled out of a hat; they are derived after long and painstaking calculations of costs and prognostications about expected increases in wages, materials, and other costs during the life of the contract. It is sheer larceny to take this time away from a purveyor who does not have an honest chance to win the contract.

If a bid is unusually low, it should be inspected carefully. The editor must make sure that there is no hidden opportunity to substitute inferior and lower-priced materials or methods just to obtain that lower cost. Competitive prices can be evaluated only when the end product is identical in every case.

Many editors prefer to work with a printer who is familiar with the publication. The typesetter and platemaker who know the style of a publication can catch many an incipient error before it develops into a costly one. Editors and printers who have worked together for a long time can discuss problems over the phone while people who don't know each other so well may require face-to-face conversations to assure mutual understanding.

Most printers, even when not bidding competitively, will offer a fair price. They know that they must have repeat business and that that comes only from establishing a reputation for fair pricing and good workmanship over a long period.

But the editor must still have a fairly good knowledge of the going prices for graphic-arts services in the area. Most of this knowledge will come from speaking with salespeople. (Even the busy editor will take time to talk with salespeople for they can provide much highly useful information, not only about prices but about new methods, materials, and machinery that may well affect the editor's own job.) Other pricing information will come from fellow-editors. That's why membership in professional organizations is so valuable. It gives opportunity for informal but invaluable shoptalk.

Past performance is the best indicator in choosing a printer. That doesn't mean that a newcomer into the field should be eliminated automatically; but the record book of an established company is still a compelling competitive factor.

Convenience is another factor in choosing a printer. While it is possible to conduct a great deal of business via the postal system, the steady deterioration in that service makes many an editor hesitant to consign manuscripts and dummies to its tender mercies. Sending material to and from the printer by taxi or messenger service is expensive, driving it over yourself takes too much time. Depending on the size of the city involved, the savings of time and transportation costs by doing business on "our side of town" becomes constantly more decisive.

The editor should find out, before choosing a printer, what facilities are available for working in the shop. Press proofs must be checked at the printer's and often page or galley proofs have to be read on site. It's useful to have a pleasant, convenient office placed at the editor's disposal. Parking space or a lack thereof should not be overlooked in making a decision on a printer.

An important factor is the unionization of a printing establishment. Some organizations demand that all their work be done in union shops; some even insist on the *bug*, the union label on all printing.

In a union shop, all "work" must be done by union members. And in the interpretation of "work" may lie complications. Sometimes, in cases of labor-management tension or simply because some overly zealous shop steward wants to flex muscles, the whistle is blown (literally) and work stops if the editor so much as touches a piece of pasteup paper. This is embarrassing, often costly, and always irritating. An editor certainly need not be anti-labor to look into general conditions in a shop and avoid one where it becomes complicated for the editor to work with the pasteup personnel. For, especially on a newspaper, it is almost essential to be able to give instructions right at this final step.

Finally, there should be personal compatibility between the editor and the printer or the employees with whom the printer will work. It's easier to transact business—face to face or by phone—with a friend than with a stranger. And, because the two will have to work under conditions of stress on frequent occasions, the lubrication of mutual liking and respect can keep the wheels whirring smoothly.

Printing Specifications

Details to be spelled out in the contract or letter of agreement include:

1. Size and number of pages of a "standard" issue, and the cost if the number is changed.

2. The number of pictures in a typical issue and whether they will be charged on a flat basis or by number or area.

3. The number of galleys of type and the cost of author's alterations. From past experience, the printer will know pretty well how much typesetting and negative screening is required for a publication of a given size, and often sees no need to break down costs in this way. But it is still worthwhile to specify these charges.

4. Method of delivery should be spelled out. Does the printer deliver the publication to us? If so, where? The loading dock, the receptionist's desk, the editor's office? Or will the editor pick up the publication at the printer's? This detail is more important than it sounds. Too often a new deliveryman may casually dump the bundle at the receiving room while the editor tears hair at the front door.

5. The kind of paper and how substitutions may be made. This is far from last in importance and is placed here on the list just because it requires the considerable explanation which follows:

Paper

Two kinds of paper are customarily used for periodicals. *Newsprint* is the lowest quality and is relatively—but only relatively—the lowest in price. It varies by weight and degree of whiteness. Book paper, used for some newspapers and most magazines, is of higher quality and price. There are many variations the editor must consider. *Weight* is the foremost. It is a major factor in the *opacity* of paper and also in comfort and pleasure during the reading process. It's not at all pleasant to attempt to read a publication that seems to collapse in your hands like a wet wash cloth.

Paper is designated by size and *substance* (a measure of weight). A typical specification might be: 25x38—60M. That means that a thousand sheets of that size weigh 60 pounds. This system is used even when the paper is on a roll instead of in sheets. (Note that printers use M—with a horizontal line through it—to designate a thousand. This can be confusing as there is a growing use of M to designate a million.)

Book paper is *uncoated* or *coated*, the latter being that which most of us recognize as "slick" paper. (Indeed, magazines are often classified as "pulps," those printed on coarse paper and considered as low in editorial quality and content, and "slicks," such glossy—in paper and content—magazines as *Vogue* and *People*.) Highly shiny paper should be avoided; its high reflections irritate the reading eye.

The smoothness of paper affects the fineness of halftone screens that can be used. On newsprint, 100-line screens are about par, with variations from 85- to 120-line. Coated stocks—the coating is a talcum-fine clay—can use up to 150-line screens and in some instances those as fine as 200-line. An uncoated stock called *super-calendered*—which has been "ironed" by hot, smooth steel rollers—can use up to 133-line.

Offset papers are *sized*, coated with a glue-like solution so that the water used in the printing process will not soak into the paper and wrinkle and distort it. As virtually all organizational publications are printed by offset, it is not necessary to designate this characteristic when specifying paper.

High opacity is desirable. The *show-through* on lightweight paper is annoying at best and in many instances can spoil or destroy the effectiveness of art.

The final decision is on color. Plain old-fashioned white will assure the highest legibility of type and clarity of illustrations. But even white comes in variations, from a very faint bluish tint to the slightest bit on the yellow side.

A very pale cream is pleasant but other colors, generally, should be avoided. Some editors print special seasonal issues on colored stock, the most horrendous being red or green for Christmas—especially when the opposite color is used for ink. Sometimes there is advantage in printing a section of a magazine in colored stock. A report on a new health insurance plan, for instance, could be presented on four pages of a different-colored paper at the center of the book and the reader urged to remove it for permanent reference. But such occasions are rare, of course.

Newspapers are best on white stock. Newsprint has the advantage not only of lower cost but of its association with the timeliness of the daily press. Many editors, though, prefer book paper for their newspaper, believing that the finer halftone reproduction and the more substantial tactile appeal will enhance readership.

Final decision on paper can realistically be made only by examining, by seeing and feeling, samples of proposed varieties. The printer

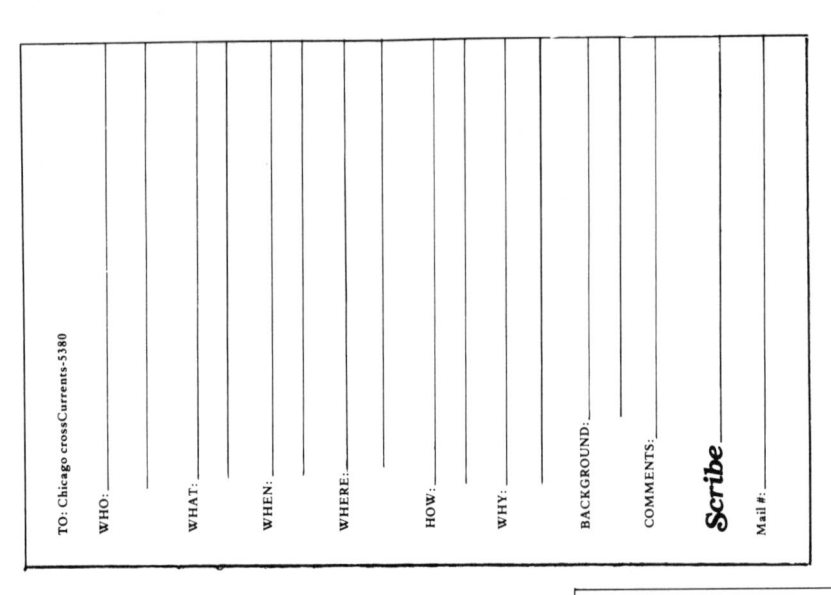

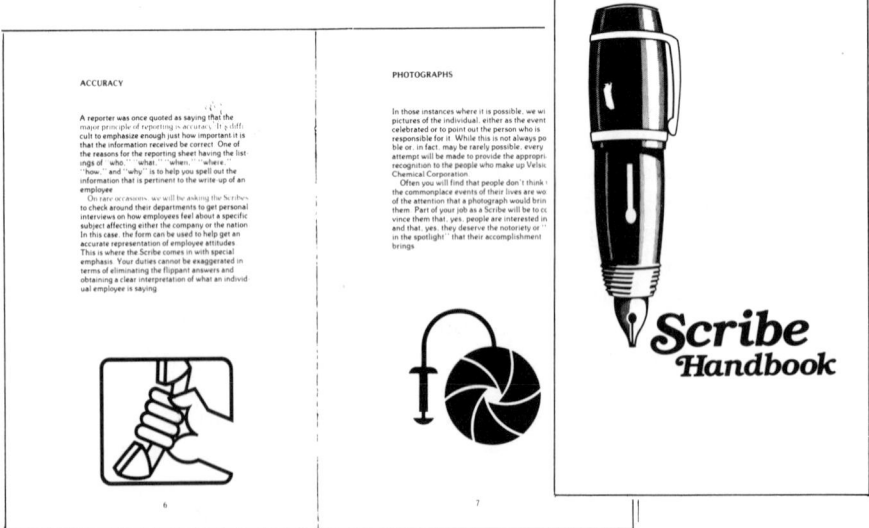

CORRESPONDENTS' HANDBOOK is attractive in black and white with terra cotta illustrations. This is produced for stringers of "Cross Currents" of Velsicol Chemical Corporation, Chicago. One page of book is form whereby correspondent reports salient facts for rewriting by regular staff. These forms are also printed on regular copy paper and widely distributed. In this example, only "Scribe"—honorary title given to correspondents—is in black; other material is in terra cotta.

should, of course, be consulted to assure that the chosen paper will run well on his presses.

Paper is specified in the contract by trade name: "Chippewah Book, 50 pound; or equivalent." Because the paper industry has been endemically plagued by strikes and shortages, it is not always possible to buy the exact paper desired. Often the editor has no choice; use a substitute or don't print.

The word "equivalent" defies precise meaning: Is Coca-Cola the equivalent of Pepsi? Are blue jeans the equivalent of brown gabardine? The editor usually has to depend on the integrity of the printer when substitutions are necessary. The good printer will seek specific approval of the editor when a different stock must be used, whether or not this approval is specified in the contract.

If a magazine uses a stock cover, each of these decisions must be made separately for that element, for there is as much variety in cover stock as in book paper.

Binding

Binding generally consists of *stitching*, metal staples. For magazines up to about 60 pages, two staples are adequate; larger books may require three. The weight of the paper is a major factor in this decision and the editor ought to inspect examples of similar publications before reaching a decision.

Tabloids and magtabs are sometimes fastened by a thin strip of paste in the gutter. This gives a feeling of permanence that is often desirable especially when a high quality book paper is used.

In working with these professionals, it is essential that the editor be treated by them as a professional. It is wise to learn the jargon of their craft, the standards of a good job, and the general procedures.

The editor must—gracefully yet forcefully—resist attempts at "hazing" that too often occur in studios and print shops and at all times remind everyone concerned that the editor is the customer and the boss. When this relationship sets in, people with different talents and responsibilities can function as a well-coordinated team and produce the best possible publication.

And so we close this examination of the organizational editor's job on the same note that we began it. The editing process is a long and complex one. It demands close teamwork among people of many and disparate talents and skills. But also it demands that the editor be the director who blends all the many processes into an effective channel of communication.

But perhaps the pressing demand is that the editor *think* about every journalistic task. While instinct may direct the editor to a happy solution to a problem, it must always be tempered by rational planning.

MEMO:

OBJECTIVES OF NEWSLETTERS

1. To inform employees of news at our facility such as new products and accounts, personnel changes, how the plant is doing, problems, earnings, activities of individuals and departments, service anniversaries, birthdays, achievements of individuals and the plant.

2. To influence employees to promote efficiency, prevent waste, cut costs, promote sales, reduce tardiness, absenteeism and reduce personnel turnover, to increase productivity, combat rumors, promote the flow of communication between management and employees, reduce resistance to change.

3. To inspire employees to have a pride in their job, in their company, to encourage teamwork and an esprit-de-corps, employee good will and morale, confidence in and loyalty to management, personal initiative and drive, to have a competitive urge and a desire for personal improvement.

4. To educate employees on changes in company policies, procedures or benefits, about health and safety, good citizenship, the benefits of the free enterprise system, the economics of business and the importance of the company and its activities to America.

5. To entertain employees with human interest items, social news, humorous comments and tell about unusual personalities and employees with unique talents, hobbies and avocations as well as those participating in sports and recreational activities.

"THE CHARTER" of "CCA Today" is spelled out and made available to all staffers as well as management personnel. Container Corporation of America is headquartered in Chicago.

There is no room for Pavlovian reaction, no escape in "We've always done it this way."

The editor must always be aware of the ultimate goal: transmitting information that will benefit the organization. The goal must always be on record. This may be as formal as the document reproduced on this page, drawn up by Margaret Tresley of Container Corporation of America to set the course for its "CCA Today." Or it may be completely informal, something that the editor uses as an occasional reminder to check the publication's compass. Whether it's in writing or remains oral, goals should be articulated, not remain just tenuous thoughts floating vaguely among our brain lobes.

The editor must build a staff. It may be one formalized by the payroll; it may be a completely voluntary group of correspondents. Often it's a combination of the two. In any case, the editor must maintain control over the staff—by conventional managerial authority over paid employees, by cajolery over volunteers. Again it pays to articulate duties and, especially, standards such as the handbook shown on page 260, prepared for the reporters for *Cross Currents* of Velsicol Chemical Corporation of Chicago by Bill Cunnea.

The editor must be well familiar with the mechanical processes of converting information into a printed piece. This knowledge becomes constantly more essential as electronic word-processing gives to the editor much of the responsibility of typesetter and compositor.

The editor must be aware of new conditions that affect the interests of readers. As the Puritan work ethic erodes, the editor plays a substantial role in motivating employees by persuasion and education: Educating them to realizing that "What's in it for me?" is actually and only "What's in it for the organization."

Finally, the editor must share the ever-building body of knowledge about communicating and editing. Membership in professional organizations, attendance at conferences, workshops and seminars, constant reading in professional and technical journals, all these must be melded into a planned and on-going midcareer educational program.

And what are the rewards for an editor's good work? Well, monetary compensation rises steadily; disparity between male and female editors' income is being whittled down almost as steadily. Proximity to the seat of power is an advantage in any organization...and the editor certainly has that. Entry into the chain of command is easier and at a higher level for an editor in many organizations.

But there are other compensations that are attractive to the creative person: a chance to express oneself, the thrill of converting an idea into a tangible, the satisfaction of contributing to an organization, indeed to society.

Best of all, perhaps: The editor's job is fun. The better the editor knows his or her job, the more fun it is. And the better the results. The more fun the editor has in creating a periodical, the more fun it is for the reader.

So again, in full circle, we come back to where we started this discussion: The editor's job is to satisfy the reader. Then communication is at its best.

Chapter — The Editor

☐ as Art Director
☐ as Newspaper Designer
☐ as Magazine Designer
☐ as Newsletter Producer
☐ as Circulation Manager
☐ as Contractor
✗ Glossary
☐ Index

☐ as Executive
☐ as Communicator
☐ as Production Manager
☐ as Writer
☐ as Copyreader
☐ as Typographer

anytime, time or evergreen, material with no compelling time factor to dictate its use.
A/O, axis of orientation, vertical line at left margin of series of lines of type to which reading eye automatically returns to begin successive line.
appeal, matter on cover of magazine luring reader to inside article.
armpit, jamming of heads by running narrow one immediately under wider headline.
art, all illustrative material, lettering, and ornamentation prepared by an artist. Also, original copy for platemaking.
art heading, ornamented label head.
Artype, trade name for widely used acetate material.
ascender, letter with portions that rise above meanline such as b, d, f, h, k, l, and t. Also that part of the letter which projects.
attention compellor, element of strong visual appeal.

a

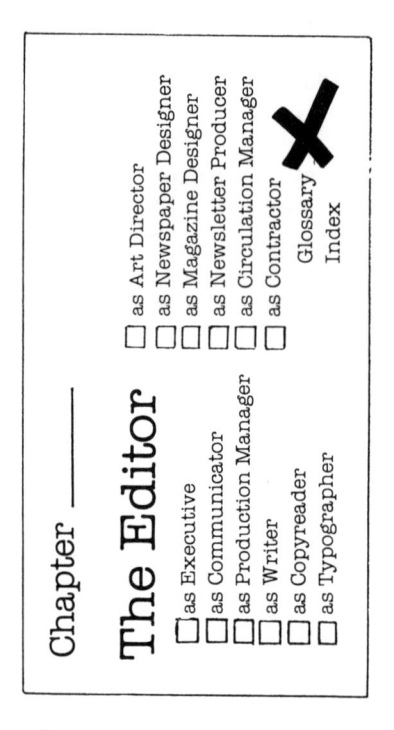

AA, author's alteration, any change in type not required to correct error of typesetter.
accent face, headletter in markedly different form from regular headline type.
acetate material, letters, ornaments, and screens printed on clear plastic for transfer to camera copy. Includes stick-on and transfer material (*which see*).
advance story, one announcing future event.
agate, 5½-point type. Also, any type used to set tabular matter such as classified ads, box scores, market reports, etc. Also, copy to be set in that size.
alley, thin strip of white separating columns vertically.
American, ethnic group of Square Serifs in which serifs are heavier than regular monotonal strokes of letterforms.
anchor, placing strong display element in every corner of newspaper page, especially lower one.

b

backgrounder, article giving general information to facilitate understanding of current happening.
backslant, letterform slanting to left.
back up, to print second side of sheet of paper.
ballpoint stylus, needle-like instrument used to cut fine lines on mimeograph stencil.
bank, one line of headline. Also that area in composing room where typographic material is stored prior to pasteup.
banner, main head on front page of newspaper, especially one extending clear across page.
baseline, that imaginary one on which bottom of primary letters align.
basement, lower half of newspaper front page.
bastard measure, any odd line lengths not used regularly by a publication.
bay mortise, rectangle cut out of side of halftone so picture surrounds three sides of opening.

Ben Day, system named after inventor of adding dot or line patterns to line art to give effect of gray tone. White patterns are laid on black areas to lighten tone, especially when used in color as tint block (*which see*).

b.f., boldface, letterform of normal form and width but with all strokes heavier than those of normal form.

big on slug, typeface so designed that ascenders and descenders occupy relatively little of vertical dimension, leaving more room for bowls and primary letters.

bimo, (pronounced buy-moe) short for bimodular, headline with two separate portions such as kickers, hammers, wickets, and tripods (*which see*). Also, the subordinate element of such a headline.

bio block, biographical material about writer, usually run at end of article.

BL, body line, increment of measurement—height of one line of body type—for dummying pasteups.

Black Letter, Text type race (*which see*.)

bleed, picture that runs off edge of paper.

blow up, to make printing plate larger than original art, especially when done to make halftone dots highly conspicuous for decorative affect.

blue line, photocopying method used for proofing cold type.

blurb, block of type larger than body size and smaller than most headlines, used to amplify or explain head in magazine.

body type, that of comparatively small size used for articles and stories as contrasted to display type used for headlines.

book, a magazine, especially that part enclosed in a stock cover (*which see*).

book method, technique for correcting proofs, using two marks for each error, one intratype, the other marginal.

book paper, that of high quality and smooth surface used for printing most magazines.

border, plain or ornamented frame used to make boxes. Borders are usually wider and more ornate than rules used similarly.

bowl, round portion of letters such as a, b, c, d, etc.

box, typographic element surrounded on four sides—or top and bottom only—with border or rules.

bracketed, serif joined to main stroke by a curve, as in Old Style Romans.

breaker head, divider, large subhead, usually at least 14-point, used to relieve large masses of body type.

bright, short, interesting, often humorous editorial feature.

bright type, body type different from normal text face and often set ragged right, used for accent effect.

broadsheet, newspaper of conventional size, about 15 x 22 inches.

broken rule, coinedge (*which see*).

brown line, photocopy used for proofing cold type.

buddy system, oriented layout (*which see*).

bug, asterisk. Also, union label on printing.

bullet, large period used for typographic decoration.

bump, to jam, to place a headline, picture, or box so it is immediately adjacent to another such element.

burn in, to darken area of photograph by darkroom manipulation.

burnish, to smooth acetate material so it adheres tightly to camera copy.

busted head, one too long to fit into allotted space.

by-line, that at beginning of article that identifies writer.

C

calligraphy, beautiful writing, technically all hand lettering but commonly that in Script or Cursive form, usually with many swashes and ligatures. Often used for nameplates, headings, etc.

Canadian wrap, system of subdividing longer story into series of 2-leg units under 2-column breaker heads.

canopy, headline that runs across picture and horizontally adjacent story.

captions, explanatory matter accompanying pictures. Most commonly used for magazine; in newspaper usually called cutlines.

caret, upside down V used in proofreading to indicate point where omitted material must be inserted.

catchline, line of display type between picture and caption matter.

center spread, two facing pages at very center of newspaper or magazine.

chart, visual display showing specifications of publication such as margins and spacing.

checkerboard, effect produced by running many lines of identically shaped and sized pictures, especially portraits.

chimney, series of heads and/or pictures of same width stacked to fill entire page depth.

circulation, distribution of publication to readers. Total number of each issue of copies produced and distributed.

civil libel, non-criminal printed defamation causing injury to an individual rather than to society as a whole.

classified, want ads, that advertising set in identical body type and with small or no headlines, then grouped by subjects.

clip book, one containing art, usually classified by subject, ready to use in pasteup.

closeup, sign like parenthesis lying sideways, placed above and below two words or portions thereof that are to be brought together with no space between.

coated paper, that covered by thin layer of finely ground clay to create very smooth printing surface.

COD, codfish formula, one in which all layout elements are concentrated toward center of area, oriented by common alignment of elements and dominated by strong visual element.

coin-edge, broken rule, one made up of small, parallel lines similar to milling around edge of coins.

cold type, matter produced by photo-typesetting although commonly used to designate strike-on and paste-on matter, also.

collage, single piece of art created by pasting together two or more individual pieces, commonly but erroneously used to refer to montage (*which see*).

color separation, breaking down full-color original art in three pictures, each showing only one primary color in the original.

color, typographic, overall tone or density of type face or printed page. Also, typographic devices to alter such page tone.

column, vertical subdivision of page. Also, regular feature in newspaper or magazine.

column-inch, area one column wide and one inch deep, used to measure editorial and advertising matter.

column rule, thin vertical line that separates columns of type.

combination, combo, two or more related pictures grouped as single unit.

combination plate, one including halftone and line in single plate.

commentary, article which gives writer's opinion or evaluation of event or situation.

common diagonal, system of scaling pictures on principle that all rectangles of same proportions have diagonals at same angle from horizontal.

compensatory damages, money paid to victim of libel to cover actual loss of income caused by defamation.

comprehensives, comprees, cutlines so detailed that no accompanying story is necessary. Also, highly detailed dummy for pasteup of complicated page.

concentric circles, special halftone screen creating image by varying thickness of circles on common axis.

Condensed, letter with normal height and weight of strokes but narrower than usual form.

connotative head, teaser head (*which see*).

constant, element such as nameplate or masthead that appears in every issue of a publication.

constant spacing, that on a typewriter which allows the same space for every character, regardless of its width.

continuation line, that which indicates story is continued from a previous page.

continuous tone, photographic or hand art such as oil paintings, watercolors,

GLOSSARY 267

etc., in which gradations of hues or grays are subtle and cover entire area.

cool colors, those on color wheel from yellow-green through blue with no red components. Those that seem to recede from viewer.

copy, all original material to be converted into type or printing plates but especially editorial content of publication.

copyfitting, determining by mathematics how much space a piece of copy will occupy when set in a specific face and size of type.

copy log, record of all copy sent to typesetter or platemaker.

copyright, exclusive right by law to make copies of literary and other creative works.

correction fluid, one used to cover error on Mimeograph stencil.

correction line, one pasted over original one to correct typographic error.

counting a head, assigning numerical value to each character, then determining whether total length of headline will fit in predetermined width.

cpp, characters per pica, used in copyfitting method.

credit line, that identifying the maker of a photograph appearing in a publication, especially if not a staff member.

criminal libel, one that inflicts injury on all society and is thus punished as a crime.

crop, to eliminate unwanted areas of a photo by actually cutting or, more frequently, by indicating them by marginal marks.

crop marks, marginal indicators that show which portion of a photograph is to be used for platemaking.

cropper's Ls, two L-shaped pieces of paper or plastic laid so they form a rectangle and used to find most advantageous area within a photograph.

cursor, tiny dot of light on the screen of a video display terminal which indicates where typographic changes are to be made in copy.

cutlines, picture captions, especially those in newspapers, set in body type.

cutoff rule, thin, horizontal dividing lines in newspaper page. Often "rule" is omitted in conversation.

cut to waste, designating page size for publication, brochure, etc., which results in large areas of unusable paper trimmed from standard-sized sheet.

cyan, blue-green hue used in process-color printing.

d

dateline, opening of news story showing city of origin. Erroneously used for folio lines (*which see*).

deck, portion of headline set in one type size and style.

decorative initial, large letter, usually of a different font, used to start first word of occasional paragraph, to add typographic color to large masses of body type.

decorative rule, printing elements that produce horizontal lines in form more ornate than simple monotone.

define the margin, layout technique in which at least one element touches each margin.

definitive head, summary head (*which see*).

delete sign, medieval form of lowercase *d* used as proofreader's mark to indicate removal of unwanted element.

descender, letter with projection below the baseline. Also that part of the letter that projects as on g, p, q, and y.

dirty copy, that with many corrections, making it difficult for typesetter to read accurately.

dirty proof, one with many typographic errors.

display, to arrange typographic elements to make them conspicuous and appealing to reader. Also, type used in larger sizes than body as for headlines, initials, etc. Also, advertising that uses large type, pictures, and areas of white space.

Ditto, spirit duplicator, where thin layer of original copy is transferred to another sheet of paper to make duplicate copies.

dogleg, portion of body type protruding from what would otherwise be a simple rectangular area.

dominant head, heaviest one on page, which acts as nucleus for page pattern.

dominant picture, one used in combo, at least 50% larger than any other in the group.

double spread, two facing pages, especially of a magazine.

downstyle, system of capping only first word and proper nouns in headlines.

dummy, drawn guide that printer follows to produce page pattern designated by editor. Also, to draw such a guide.

duotone, color-printing technique, using plates made from single black-and-white photograph, which creates single image from two impressions, one in light, one in dark, ink.

Dutch wrap, continuation of body type to column not covered by headline.

e

editorial, article of comment representing opinion of publication as a corporate entity. Also, all matter in a publication that is not advertising.

editor's note, explanatory material about article or author that runs before beginning of story.

Egyptian, ethnic group of Square Serifs, in which serifs are of same weight as that of monotonal letterform.

8-on-9, 8-point type (commonly used by newspapers) placed in an area 9 points deep.

electronic editing, that done on copy in tape or disk form as displayed on VDT screen (*which see*) instead of by hand on typewritten copy.

e-line, expo or expository, second line of picture caption that gives very brief explanation of subject. *See i&e-line.*

elite, small typewriter face which has 12 characters per linear inch.

em, blank space in square of size of type it is used with. Called mutton or mut to avoid confusion with en. Commonly but erroneously, synonym for pica.

empty sweep, path of eye when it is not reading, as from end of line, column, or leg of type to start of next one.

en, vertical half of em space. Called nut to avoid confusion with em.

end mark, visual device to indicate end of story or article.

error line, that in which typographic error has been found and over which correction line is pasted.

ethnic, second division of type races, such as Old Style and Modern in Romans.

evergreen, anytime, editorial matter without compelling time factor that dictates its use.

expo line, e-line (*which see*).

expository, expo, art, maps, charts, graphs, and diagrams.

external publication, one published by organization for audience other than employees or members.

f

face, style of type, identified by family name.

fair comment, defense against libel that permits evaluators to give opinion of performance of people in public pursuits, such as politicians, actors, athletes, etc.

fallow corner, top right and lower left corner of ad or, especially, of page.

family, major division of typefaces, after races and ethnic groups.

feature, story with greater human interest than of news significance.

first revise, proof after first corrections have been made.

5 Ws, elements necessary for complete news story: who, what, where, when, and why.

flag, nameplate, name of publication, especially of newspaper, in display form on first page or cover. Erroneously called masthead (*which see*).

flat color, spot color, that used for printing in any form other than process color (*which see*).

flat-out, 1-up technique (*which see*).

floating flag, newspaper nameplate narrower than full width of page, dis-

GLOSSARY

played in position other than at top of page.

floppy disk, flexible plastic plate, like small photograph record, on which is stored material for electronic editing or actuating typesetting machine.

flush left, type set so all lines are even at left margin.

flush right, type set so all lines are even at right margin.

folio lines, technically, page numbers, but in common usage also include date and name of publication. On front page of newspaper they include volume and number and place of publication.

font, collection of type in one size and face.

foot, bottom margin of page.

formal page, one in which entire area is filled with typographic elements and white space is incidental.

format, general appearance of page of publication, especially page size and number of columns.

4-across-5, 1-up technique (*which see*) in which four columns of type, set at regular measure, occupy five columns of space.

free page, one in which type and pictures are not arranged in conventional columns and which uses large areas of white space as display elements of the page pattern.

fresh air, white space on printed page.

front, first page of any section of a newspaper. *See* section page.

full box, border around four sides of a block of type.

full format, newspaper of about 15x21 inches using six to nine columns.

functionalism, philosophy of typography that reminds editor to give adequate coverage both in future stories and in reports.

functional layout, one designed for maximum communication with minimum effort by reader and producers.

g

galley proof, first impression or photocopy of type, made to detect errors.

gatekeeper, person, such as writer or editor, who anywhere in the path of communications decides which facts shall be printed.

ghost, to lighten background of photo without obliterating it entirely.

gimcrack, typographic ornament.

golden rectangle, area in proportion of about 3x5, considered by ancient Greeks to be most pleasant of such shapes.

Gothic, ethnic division of Monotonal type race, with letterforms of equal strokes, usually cramped curves, often pinched where bowl meets stems and without serifs.

graf, abbreviation for paragraph.

grid sheet, pasteup sheet (*which see*).

grid system, Swiss grid (*which see*).

guideline, proofreading method in which marginal correction is linked to intratype error by a written line.

gutter, both margins between facing pages.

h

hairline, thinnest rule used for separating elements horizontally on newspaper or magazine pages.

halftone, technique for reproducing continuous-tone original art by pattern of dots or lines of various sizes and proximity. Also, any picture so reproduced.

hammer, reverse kicker, short one-line head, twice as large as main head which is below and a little to the right.

hand art, any nonphotographic illustration material.

hanging indent, style of setting type so second and each succeeding line is indented same amount at left. These glossary entries are so set.

hard copy, strike-on matter produced simultaneously with photocomposition or Teletype tape as guide for editor or for proofreading.

hard news, that of major significance as opposed to feature material or news treated in a lighter style.

hard wiring, direct electrical connection between various typesetting machines, thus eliminating need for tape to actuate them.

head, abbreviation for headlines. Also, margin at top of page.

head adjustment, manipulation on stencil-printing machine such as Mimeograph to vary width of head margin at top of page.

heading, simple label used on regularly appearing departments of newspaper or magazine.

headletter, type used for headlines.

headline, display type that seeks to lure reader into body type, usually by summarizing story.

headline schedule, hed sked, all headline forms used by a publication, usually grouped by column-widths.

hectograph, gelatin process for duplicating limited copies of material written, drawn, or typed on paper master, then transferred onto gelatin surface for setting-off. Ditto is trademarked name of such machine in common use.

hen-and-chicks, layout built around dominant element.

hood, small bottomless box around headline but not story.

horizontal layout, system in which body type is disposed of horizontally instead of vertically.

human interest, matter of small news value but of high readership because of personal empathy.

i

identification and exposition, I&E lines, picture identification in which first (ident) line gives name of subject and second (expo) gives terse explanation of news interest.

ident line, name of person under photo, usually portrait.

imposition, placing of several pages on single sheet of paper so they will appear consecutively after folding and cutting of signature (*which see*).

impression rollers, cylinders on printing press that push paper against plates.

incised, intaglio (*which see*).

index, table of contents for newspapers.

indicia, legal data about publication especially required for second-class mailing privilege.

inferior character, one that aligns below baseline, such as in formula such as H_2O.

initial, first letter of word set in larger or more decorative face. *See* inset and rising initial.

inline, style of type in which white line runs down center of main strokes of letter.

inquiring photographer, feature, usually carried regularly, in which individuals chosen at random are asked views on current question, which then run with photos of persons.

insert, sandwich (*which see*).

inset head, headline occupying area blank in top left of copy block.

inset initial, large letter occupying area left blank in top-left corner or mass of body type.

inside spread, two facing pages at exact center of newspaper or magazine.

intaglio, method of printing in which lines incised into metal plate are filled with ink which is then deposited onto paper. Commercial form is rotogravure.

interlocking mortises, pictures, each with corner area removed, fitted closely together.

internal publication, one for only members and/or employees of publishing organization.

internal mortise, opening, usually rectangular, completely surrounded by halftone, in which is placed caption material.

internal silhouette, tint block (*which see*) which is cut out so that black image it surrounds is printed on white paper rather than on colored area.

interpretive reporting, that which adds to basic facts with explanatory matter and often opinions of writer.

in-the-cup, headline placed in second column of story with first column of body type running as high as top of head.

inverted pyramid, style of writing news story so most important element is at beginning and others are in descending order of importance. Also, head-

GLOSSARY 271

line form in which centered lines are progressively narrower.

issue, all copies of a newspaper or magazine printed on a given date. Revisions of newspaper issues create editions.

Italic, form of Roman type slanting to right. Used widely but erroneously for right-slanting letters of all races.

itemization, reporting style in which series of facts are listed, often as sentence fragments.

Itlax, Itlx, Ital, X, abbreviations for Italics.

j

jam, to place headlines so they touch each other. *See* tombstone, armpit.

jazz layout, one in which rectangular area is suggested but not defined by typographic elements.

jim-dash, hairline or 2-point rule, usually 3 ems wide, used to separate items within a story.

jump, to continue story from one page, usually the front, to another. Also, story so continued.

jump head, headline on portion of story continued from front page.

jump line, one that instructs reader to continue story from one page to another.

jumpover, placement of barrier within column of body type that then continues below barrier.

jump the gutter, layout technique tieing together facing pages into single oriented composition.

justify, to set type so left and right margins align. Also, to make all columns on page of same length.

k

keyline drawing, simple outline of forms in accompanying halftone, labelled for easy identification.

key plate, basic printing plate, usually for black, upon which is registered areas of spot color. Also, drawing from which such plate is made.

kicker, small head, usually underscored, above and slightly to left of larger main head.

l

label, headline without verb, actual or implied. Also, unchanging headlines, consisting of only a word or two without art.

layout, pattern of elements in printing form. Also, written diagram which instructs pasteup person how to prepare such form. Also, in two words, act of producing such pattern.

lazy S, proofreader's symbol in form of such letter lying on its side, enclosing words or letters to be transposed.

lc, lowercase, small letters.

lca, lowercase alphabet length, that, in points, of line consisting of all small letters of specific font.

lead, (pronounced ledd) originally thin metal strip used to increase space between lines of type; now extra interlineal spacing. Also, the act of increasing such space to enhance readability or justify column.

lead, (pronounced leed) first part of news story which usually gives all major information in summary form. Also, main story or article in issue or on page.

leader, leeder, row of dots or dashes connecting two or more columns of tabular matter such as name of team and its standing in competition.

leg, vertical unit of body type arranged in several columns.

legal size, 8½x14-inch paper.

legibility, characteristic which makes it easy for reader to see and comprehend comparatively few printed characters such as in headline.

lemon, yellow hue used in process-color printing.

letter of agreement, written document, less formal than contract, stating conditions of business transaction such as printing publication.

lettering guides, templates (*which see*) for tracing letterforms.

letterpress, relief printing in which raised characters capture ink and deposit it on paper. That kind of printing referred to when no adjective accompanies word.

libel, printed defamation, usually used to refer to that based on untruth.

libel, civil, that which damages victim yet does not constitute criminal violation.

libel, criminal, that which is damaging to community and is prosecuted as a crime.

libel per quod, that which plaintiff must prove was damaging under specific conditions.

libel per se, term so commonly accepted as defaming that plaintiff need not prove that damage was sustained.

library, all typefaces available for use by editorial staff.

light table, one with all or part of surface made of translucent material over which is placed material for pasteup.

line, single horizontal unit of headline. Also, banner (*which see*). Also, art.

linear definition, line conversion, line reproduction made from continuous tone original without use of halftone screen.

lithography, planographic printing method based on principle that oil and water will not mix.

logo, (abbreviation for logotype), name of publication—its nameplate or flag —or of advertiser—signature cut—in distinctive form. Also, identification of page or section of publication such as sports or family pages.

loop stylus, instrument for writing or drawing on Mimeograph stencil.

loose register, design of elements for color work that does not require precise placement.

lowercase, lc, small letters of alphabet.

lowercase alphabet length, lca (*which see*).

m

magapaper, tabloid-sized publication using magazine layouts rather than formal pages of newspaper.

magazine, publication issued periodically, usually bound and often with cover of heavier or different paper. Also, that layout style that utilizes large areas of white space and often with elements not in regular column increments.

magenta, purplish-red used for process-color printing.

magnet, optical, typographic element of strong visual appeal, such as photographs, boxes, color elements, and large headlines.

magtab, publication with magazine cover that unfolds to regular tabloid size.

mailing indicia, legal identification of publication entitling it to second-class rates.

makeup, general style in which elements are arranged on pages of publication. Also, in two words, to produce forms or pasteups from which printing plates are made.

man on the street, collection of answers to topical question posed to people picked at random. (*See* inquiring photographer.)

marker art, halftones to which have been added hand art to point out elements in picture, e.g., X marking spot of event.

masthead, collection of information including name of publisher, editor, time and place of publication, etc., usually on editorial page of newspaper or index page of magazine. Erroneously used to refer to nameplate.

meanline, that which marks top of primary letters.

measure, length of line of type.

mechanical, pasteup of cold type used to make printing plate.

mechanical separation, copy for making plates for spot color prepared by artist as contrasted to optical filtering (*which see*).

mezzotint, special halftone screen giving effect of coarse crayon drawing.

minimum line length, shortest measure that can be set for effective reading.

model's release, formal permission in writing given by subject of photograph for use of picture, especially in advertising.

Modern, ethnic division of Roman type race; face with thicks and thins of marked difference, swelling curves, and thin, straight, unbracketed serifs.

modified, silhouette, halftone reproduction in which subject is partially outlined and with one or more straight edges.

Monotonal, type race including Gothic and Sans Serifs, made up of strokes of equal weight and without serifs.

montage, single photograph made from two or more negatives. Often used erroneously to refer to collage (*which see*).

morgue, reference library of publication, especially of clippings from periodical itself.

mortise, to cut area out of halftone plate so that type or other matter may be inserted. Such opening cut out of corner is notch. Opening completely surrounded by halftone area is internal mortise; that surrounded on three sides is bay.

mutton quad, space as wide as point-size of letters it is used with.

n

naked column, one without picture or headline at its top.

nameplate, flag, logo, name of publication in display form as it appears on cover or front page. Erroneously called masthead.

needle stylus, pointed instrument used to prepare stencils for machines such as Mimeograph.

news budget, all material, verbal and pictorial, available for a given issue of newspaper or magazine.

newsletter, publication usually of 8½x11-inch pages, carrying news of immediate interest, with few if any illustrations and small headlines, often only those produced on a typewriter.

newspaper, publication usually printed on newsprint whose major content is news more immediate than that carried in magazines.

newsprint, coarsest and comparatively lowest priced paper commonly used for printing, especially for newspapers.

N-format, broadsheet pages arranged in eight or nine columns and tabloids in five or six columns.

90-degree triangle, three-sided plastic drawing tool, one of whose corners is a right angle.

N-matter, (for "narrow"), material set in narrow columns of 11 picas or less and illustrations made in increments of such columns.

no-orphan technique, oriented layout (*which see*).

notch, mortise (*which see*) that removes rectangle from one corner of halftone plate.

Novelty, ethnic group of Ornamented type race in which letterforms are drastically changed.

No. 10 envelope, one that accommodates 8½x11-inch letterhead folded twice, 4¼x9¼ inches.

nut-and-nut, style of setting type indented one en at each side.

nut quad, blank space whose width is one half of height of type it is used with.

o

Oblique, letterform that slants to right. Erroneously called Italic; term is correctly applied only to slanted form of Roman.

offset lithography, planographic printing process in which image is lithographed to rubber blanket, then set off onto printing paper.

Old English, family in Text race often erroneously used to designate race itself.

one-theme issue, one in which each story and picture explores some facet of single subject.

1-up technique, one which uses one more column of space than of type; also called flat-out.

op (optimum) format, one with five or six columns on broadsheet, four columns on tabloid page.

opacity, density of paper affecting resistance to show-through.

opaque, to remove from negative unwanted flaws such as shadows of pasted-on material, dust specks, etc.

optical center, point 10% above mathematical center of page.

optical filter, colored transparent material used to block out all but one primary color in making plates for process-color printing.

optical magnets, typographic elements of strong interest to readers.

optimum line length, that which is easiest to read, at higher speed, with lower fatigue and with maximum comprehension.

organic, layout which develops logically from message, medium in which it is printed, and conditions under which it is expected to be read.

oriented layout, buddy system, no-orphan technique, one in which all elements are studiedly aligned on common horizontal and vertical axes.

Ornamented, race of type in which decorative additions are made to face or where letterform is drastically changed.

overlay, sheet of transparent plastic material on which are drawn those areas to be printed in color or on which are written instructions to platemaker.

overline, title of picture in display type and above illustration.

overset, type in excess of what can be used for specific given issue and too timely to be held for future use, thus must be discarded unused.

Oxford rule, border consisting of heavy and light rules in parallel pairs.

p

page matrix, newspaper page completely filled with body type in regular column, onto which can be pasted headlines and art to visualize proposed typographic changes.

page proof, first impression of whole form used to find and correct errors.

page spec chart, one showing all specifications of elements of and on page; margins, alleys, placement of folios, etc.

pagination, sequence in which regular features appear in a magazine.

panel, wider-than-normal column at outside of tabloid page.

paper master, offset plate made of heavy cardboard.

paper page, dimension of sheet on which page is printed as contrasted to type page (*which see*).

paragraph starter, decorative device such as star, square, bullet, etc., to mark beginning of paragraph, with or without customary indent.

parallel line, special halftone screen which creates image by varying thicknesses of adjacent parallel lines.

pasteup, mechanical dummy (*which see*).

pasteup dummy, guide to craftsman showing elements on page by affixing photocopies of them onto sheet of paper.

pasteup sheet, gridded cardboard on which are affixed all the elements of a page and from which printing plate is made photographically.

peeled, publications sent through mails without protective covering.

pepper, small elements used to inject typographic color into page.

Perpendicular, conventional, upright letterform. Erroneously called Roman, which applies only to perpendicular of that race.

perforated tape, paper strip carrying holes punched in coded clusters and used to actuate computer or typesetting machine.

personals, small news items concerning only single or very few individuals.

photocopy, reproduction of type, illustrations and whole pages made by reflected light and chemical development.

photograph, image produced on paper or metal by action of light on sensitized surface.

photo lithography, offset (*which see*).

Photostat, trademarked name for photocopying machine. Also, photocopy so made. Also, erroneously used as generic term for all such machines.

phototype, cold type, images of letterforms placed photographically on film or paper, as opposed to 3-dimensional metal printing elements.

pica, unit of printer's measurement, 12 points or 1/6 inch.

picture, photographic communication, used to distinguish it from photograph which may be purely ornamental.

pinched, stroke of Gothic narrowed as curve meets straight stem so that void is adequate for legibility.

plagiarism, appropriation of another's creative work, especially writing, and representing it as one's own.

planographic, lithographic (*which see*), printing process in which printing image is neither raised from nor cut into bearing surface.

plastic plate, relief printing element made of photosensitive polymers.

platemaker, worker who produces printing plates, usually by photography.

PMT, Velox (*which see*).

POA, primary optical areas (*which see*).

point, unit of printers measurement, 1/72 of inch. Also, any punctuation mark.

porkchop, half-column portrait.

poster makeup, style in which tabloid front page carries only large photo and one or two headlines.

precede, (accent on first syllable) **preseed**, explanatory matter that runs before start of article or story. Also, spelled phonetically, preseed.

prepack, technique of making up editorial matter in specified rectangle or space, free from normal column increments and well in advance of intended use.

primary letters, minuscules with neither ascenders or descenders.

primary optical area, POA, top-left corner of page or any subdivision thereof, where reading eye first enters.

printing element, any relief, incised or planographic plate that places printed image on page. Any matter such as heads, pictures, body blocks, rules, etc., so printed.

privilege, legally specified defamatory matter such as public records which may be printed free of libel restrictions.

process color, system of printing three primary colors to reproduce full spectrum of nature.

progression, order in which sections of newspaper or magazine commonly appear in each issue.

proof, rough print of type or plate used to detect errors. Also, hastily made photoprint to show content of negative. (*See also* repro and galley.)

proofreader, person who examines rough impression of type to detect errors and instruct how to correct them.

proofreading, examination of printed matter to discover and correct errors before actual production begins.

proportional scale, scaling wheel (*which see*).

prove (usually perverted to proof), to make rough impression or copy of type to detect errors.

pulled quote, quotations or interesting sentence, pulled at random from copy, set in display type and placed at random to provide typographic color to large masses of body type.

punitive damages, punishment for libel that is paid to victim rather than to state.

q

quad, quadrat, formerly piece of metal less than type-high, used to provide space between words on metal 3-dimensional type. Today intratype space, especially between words.

r

race, primary division of typefaces.

ragged right, unjustified type.

raw tape, idiot tape, tape that will not set justified lines.

readability, characteristics which make it easy and comfortable to read large masses of body type.

readability range, longest and shortest lines of body type which can be read with comfort and efficiency.

read-in, style of headline in which display type is opening of sentence continued in body size.

reading diagonal, broadly defined path of reading eye on page from top left to lower right.

reading gravity, constant pull on reading eye downward and to right.

record shot, photograph to preserve actual event despite lack of pictorial interest.

reefer, line or two of type, set into news story, that refers reader to associated material elsewhere in newspaper.

register, to align color images precisely

in relation to those of another hue in process-color printing.

register mark, device usually consisting of circle and cross, used to align color elements.

reliability tolerance, expected variance in accuracy of statistical findings.

relief, printing, letterpress, method in which characters, raised from bearing surface, capture ink, then deposit it on printing paper.

repro, reproduction, proof, impression of 3-dimensional printing elements, type taken with great care and used as copy for platemaking.

retouch, to correct errors or strengthen weaknesses of photography before platemaking.

reverse kicker, hammer (*which see*).

reviews, critical report on recent book, play, performance, etc.

rising initial, first letter of word, in large size and/or ornamented form that aligns with first line of body type and projects above type block.

river, unwanted strips of white space within blocks of body type resulting from excessive spacing between words.

Roman, type race characterized by thick and thin strokes, modulated curves, and serifs. Also, perpendicular form of this race as contrasted to slanting Italics. Erroneously used to designate perpendicular form of all type races.

roundup, collection of small news items on similar topic combined into single story or running under single headline.

rub-off type, transfer type (*which see*).

rule, element that prints line or border lines simpler than those of conventional borders.

run, unit of production by printing press.

runaround, body type set in various measures so an opening is formed into which may be inserted picture or other type.

running dummy, rough plan for arranging pages of publication (usually newspaper) prepared before all material is available and consequently often revised.

running head, one which continues from spread to spread of magazine.

runover, Dutch wrap (*which see*).

S

salon cover, one on magazine displaying attractive picture that has no relation to any specific story inside.

same size, s/s, instruction for platemaker.

sandwich, very short copy, usually enclosed in rule top and bottom, dropped into body type, calling attention to related story and/or pictures on another page.

Sans Serifs, ethnic division of Monotonal type race, usually with curves more graceful than those of Gothics and usually with no pinching of curved bowls into stems.

scale, to determine size of plate to be made from artwork of different size.

scaling wheel, slide rule in circular form used for picture scaling (*which see*).

scalloped page, pattern in which all legs of type align at top but vary drastically in length.

schedule, headline, hed sked, all headlines used by newspaper or magazine.

scholar's margin, layout pattern for magazines with one wide column and narrow column at outer margin.

scope, translucent drawing surface for cutting stencils.

screen, device used to reduce continuous-tone art to halftone plate. Also, designation of halftone so produced, e.g., 110-line screen designates 110 lines of dots in each vertical or horizontal inch. Also, to reduce tone of black areas of art or type by superimposing pattern of white dots in printing surface.

screened negative, one from which halftone plate is made.

Script, ethnic division of written type race in which characters are connected.

section page, break, split, front, Z, first page of any section other than first.

self-contained picture, wild picture, one that runs without accompanying story or article.

self-cover, magazine or booklet whose cover is same paper as all other pages. (*See* stock cover.)

semi-tuck, placement of type legs aligning at top and running under both picture and rectangle of space at left in which is placed headline.

separation, color, method of using chromatic filters for making plate for printing each primary color in process color reproduction. Also, negative or photoprint that shows only one primary color in exact value as it appears in full-color original.

sequence, series of pictures taken at short intervals to show consecutive action.

series, subdivision of family of type.

serif, small finishing stroke at end of main stroke of letter.

set off, transfer, usually undesirable, of ink from printed page to facing sheet of paper. In offset lithography, deliberate transfer of printed image from rubber blanket to printing paper.

sexn, abbreviation for section and, especially, section page.

shade, value of color obtained by adding black to hue.

Shaded, ethnic of Ornamented type race with alteration made to face of character.

Shadowed, ethnic of Ornamented typeface with additions outside of strokes of characters.

sheet-fed, press that prints on individual pieces of paper rather than from roll, as in web-fed.

shoot down, to make printing plate smaller than original copy.

shotgun head, single head from which read out two or more stories, each with or without its own deck.

shoulder, normal space below a letter that provides interlineal spacing.

show-through, undesirable image on reverse side of sheet visible from front.

sidebar, closely related story subordinate to main account.

sideless box, decorative rule or border at top and bottom only of area.

sideline, one or two lines of display type below picture and immediately to left of cutlines.

signature, group of pages printed on single sheet of paper prior to folding and cutting to make individual pages.

silhouette, silho, halftone from which entire background has been removed.

silver line, photocopy used for proofreading.

singleton, one-line caption, usually in type smaller than catchline but larger than cutlines.

sized, paper coated with glue to prevent absorption of ink into fibers.

sketch dummy, miniature diagram instructing pasteup craftsman how to arrange elements on page.

skyline, material, especially headline, running above nameplate on page one.

slash head, bimodular one consisting of two lines each of a small and a large headletter separated by a heavy diagonal rule.

slip sheet, piece of blank paper inserted in press after each printed page to prevent set-off.

slug line, significant word or two that identifies story or article throughout processing.

soft news, that of little consequence or that written in feature style.

solid, body type set with no extra interlineal spacing.

spacing chart, one showing proper separation of typographic elements such as between head and story, picture and caption, etc.

special screen, one creating halftone plate by means other than regular pattern of dots.

spirit duplicator, Ditto (*which see*).

splayed letter, one in which normally straight strokes such as legs of M and W are bowed.

spot, ornamental typographic device or small drawing.

spot color, flat color, any use of hues other than in process color.

spread, double spread (*which see*).

square halftone, rectangular one with 90-degree corners.

Square Serifs, type race in which serifs are at least as heavy as strokes of basic monotonal letterforms.

S/S, same size, instructions to platemaker.

stacked, type set with no space at all

between lines.

standing head, those which are used repeatedly without changes.

stapling, fastening magazine pages together with wire.

Stat, abbreviated for Photostat, photocopy of type or art used for dummying or proofing.

stem, vertical stroke of letterform, especially that which meets curved bowl.

stencil cement, adhesive used to fasten cut-apart Mimeograph stencils.

stet, abbreviation for Latin let it stand, proofreader's instruction to disregard inadvertently made changes in type.

stickful, rough measure of composition, about 2 column inches, also used to designate length of story to be written.

stick-on, acetate type alphabet characters printed on clear, self-adhesive plastic for arranging into cold-type composition.

stickup initial, rising initial (*which see*).

stitching, stapling (*which see*).

stock cover, one of paper heavier than rest of magazine.

stock photo, one used from files or purchased from agency instead of being taken currently or of specific event.

straight matter, body composition as contrasted to display matter.

streamer, headline full page wide.

strike-on, composition produced by typewriters or similar machines.

stringer, part-time writer for publication.

strip in, to combine two or more negatives in making printing plate. Especially to surprint headline on halftone background.

stub, material in left-hand of column of tabular matter.

style, consistent optional literary or typography usage established for specific publication.

stylebook, collection of guides for consistent literary usage of optional forms.

stylus, instrument for cutting images into Mimeograph stencil.

subhead, short centered line of body type set in bold caps.

substance, weight in pounds of 500 sheets of 8½x11 or 17x22 printing paper.

summary head, definitive head, one that gives brief condensation of its story.

sunken initial, inset initial (*which see*).

super-calendered, paper which has been smoothed by pressing between polished metal rollers.

superior character, one that aligns at meanline rather than base line, e.g., 15^2 or 17^n.

surprint, matter printed over halftone or in color area.

survey, story on readers' views obtained by random interviews.

swash, decorative, elongated stroke of letterform. Also, letter so decorated.

Swiss grid, layout system in which area is covered with vertical and horizontal lines and all typographic elements are placed at intersections.

t

TA, terminal area (*which see*).

table of contents, list of all articles and features in magazine.

tabloid, tab, newspaper format with pages approximately 11x15 inches. Also, journalistic approach featuring frothy content and flashy display.

take, small quantity of paper copy, type, etc. into which a large job is divided for one or more workers for convenience and efficiency.

tape, narrow ribbons of paper with perforations in coded patterns that actuate typesetting or computer machines.

tearsheet, single page of newspaper or magazine removed from original package for filing, proof of ad publication, etc.

teaser, appeal (*which see*).

teaser head, one that piques interest of reader rather than summarizing story.

tempera, poster paint used to retouch photographs.

template, pattern cut out of plastic sheet to form letters by tracing.

10:30 formula, method for laying out newspaper page by beginning in top left corner and continuing in clockwise spiral to place elements.

terminal area, TA, lower right corner of printed page or any subdivision thereof.

Text, Black Letter, type race with letter made of thick and thin straight strokes, narrow voids and sharp corners. Erroneously called Old English which is a family in the race.

30-mark, typographic element used to indicate end of newspaper or magazine story.

3-digit code, one used for identifying headlines.

thumbnail, small, sketchily drawn dummy, usually for advertisement, of major elements. Also, single quote mark or apostrophe.

time material, (short for anytime), feature copy that does not demand immediate use.

tint, value of color created by adding white to original hue.

tint block, area of color over which is printed type and/or art.

title of courtesy, Miss, Mrs., Ms., Mr.

tolerance, percentage of error in statistical findings depending on number of responses.

tombstone, bumped headlines running side by side.

tone, value, relative darkness of page or block of type or photograph.

tower, chimney, arrangements of same-width elements filling complete column or columns of newspaper page.

transfer letters, those printed on transparent plastic which adhere to drawing paper when burnished.

trapped space, unwanted area of white completely surrounded by typographic elements.

tripod, headline form with single short line of large type immediately to left of two longer lines of smaller type.

tuck-in, arrangement of type in which story begins under headline then continues under related picture in column(s) to right.

turn, to continue story to another page.

type, originally metal block from which projects character or line of characters in relief. Also, such blocks collectively. Also, similar piece on a typewriter. Also, printed characters. Also, negatives of such characters used to produce phototype.

typeface, face, particular style or design of type.

type library, all typefaces, rules, borders, and ornaments available for use by a publication.

type page, area filled by typographic elements and not including margins of paper page.

typo, typographic error (*which see*).

typographic color, density of gray effected by mass of type.

typographic error, mechanical one made by typesetter.

typographic style manual, codification of all approved uses of type by a publication.

typography, basic philosophy regarding use of printing elements.

U

u&lc, upper-and-lowercase, style of setting type so first letter of each word is capitalized.

uncoated paper, that which has not been given a special coating to achieve a smooth surface.

underscore, to give added weight to typographic elements, especially headlines, by running rule immediately beneath them.

unit count, method of determining if headline will fit given area by assigning and totalling variable widths of letters.

uppercase, capital letters.

V

value, tone, depth of color, type masses or photographs compared to darkness of comparable grays.

Van Dyke, photocopy used to prove cold type.

variable spacing, typewriter which assigns different widths to characters rather than giving each the same as on conventional machines.

Varityper, strike-on machine for producing justified columns.

VDT, video display terminal (*which see*).

Velox, PMT, photoprint with image in halftone-dot pattern rather than continuous tone.

video display terminal, VDT, tube, electronic machine for writing or editing story in which copy appears on cathode ray tube in back of and above keyboard much like that of electric typewriter.

visibility, ability of typographic element to be seen by contrast between it and background. *See* legibility and readability.

void, counter, blank areas within type characters such as O and bowl of b.

volume, all issues of newspaper or magazine published within one year. Volume thus indicates age of periodical.

W

warm colors, those on red half of color wheel.

wave rule, one with undulating line.

web, strip of paper feeding off roll and winding through rotary press.

web-fed, press which prints on continuous roll of paper rather than on individual sheets.

weight, relative weight of strokes that make letterform. Also, standard for measuring 500 sheets of paper in basic size.

well, narrow area for type and pictures at one side of page area which then carries columns of wider measure.

wicket, headline form with two short lines of small type at left, then longer line of larger type.

widow, short line of type at end of paragraph, usually less than half full.

width, basic variation of letterform that results in Condensed or Extended versions.

wild picture, stand-alone, one that is not related to story.

word processing, electronic system for editing and converting typewriting into set type.

woven, page design in which each alley is crossed by at least one multicolumn element.

wrap, to continue type in column to right of that in which headline runs.

Written, type race with letterforms resembling those of casual writing.

writing paper, variety coated with sizing to prevent absorption of ink.

X

x-height, distance from baseline to meanline of type.

Z

Zip-A-Tone, trade name for shading sheets (*which see*).

Z-page, first page of any newspaper section after the first.

Chapter — The Editor

☐ as Executive
☐ as Communicator
☐ as Production Manager
☐ as Writer
☐ as Copyreader
☐ as Typographer

☐ as Art Director
☐ as Newspaper Designer
☐ as Magazine Designer
☐ as Newsletter Producer
☐ as Circulation Manager
☐ as Contractor

Index

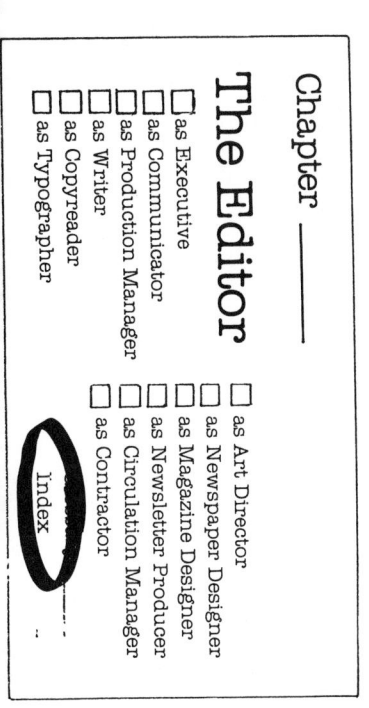

A

accent face, 135
accreditation, 6
accuracy, 94
acetate material, 135
advance stories, 70
advocacy journalism, 97
agreement, of introduction, 106
  of subject and verb, 102
Agrifacts, Indiana Farm Bureau, 30
Alcoa News, Aluminum Company of America, 199
All Hands, United States Navy, 210
American Newspaper Publishers Associations, 240
amputation effect, 158
anchor the corner, 187
anytime material, 42
appeals, 28, 215
armpit, 188
art agencies, 247
art, sources of, 170
  stencil, 237
ascenders, 120
attention compellor, 186
attribution, 107
author's alterations, 48
axis of orientation, 123

B

backgrounder, 69
Bank Notes, Toronto Dominion Bank, 196
basement, 189
Baylor Progress, Baylor University Medical Center, 211
billboards, 34
bimos, 140
bio block, 125
bleeds, 208
blue line, 61
blurb, 206
body type, 120
book method, 49
Boston, Chamber of Commerce, 169
bowls, 120
boxes, 193
  sideless, 131
brights, 70
broadsheet, 8
brown line, 61
Bulletin, Portland State University, 177
bullets, 126

C

California Local Government, 57
captions, 160
Caring, Southwest Alabama Medical Center, 174
catchlines, 161
CCA Today, Container Corporation of America, 262
Celanese World, Celanese Corp., 30
checkerboard effect, 167
Checkpoint, Bucknell University, 223
Children's Hour, The Milwaukee Children's Hospital, 175
chimney, 189
classified ads, 25
clearances, 44
cliches, literary, 111
  pictorial, 149
clip art, 171
codfish formula, 203
collaboration, 118
collage, 160
Colonial Williamsburg News, 168
color, duplicator-produced, 232
  flat, 179
  process, 179
  spot, 179
  separation, 179
colors, cool, 183
column rules, 191
combination plate, 169
combo-picture, 167
Comline, Raytheon Data Systems, 181
comma faults, 100
comment, 114
commentaries, 70
common diagonal method, 156
Compass, Northwestern Financial Corp., 174
compensatory damages, 113
concentric circle screen, 167
connotative letterforms, 146
constants, 173
content, magazine, 21
  newspaper, 23
contents chart, 40
copy control, 55
copyfitting, 55

copy log, 55
copyreaders' marks, 88, 93
copyright, 115
correction line, 48
correspondence, 16
cost analysis, 15
counting heads, 143
covers, 33
critique sessions, 13
crop marks, 153
cropper's Ls, 153
cropping, 153
Cross Currents, Velsicol Chemical Corp., 260
Currents, Hawaiian Electric Company, 13
cutoff rules, 191
cut to waste, 10

D

damages, punitive, 114
dates, 110
decorative initials, 127
define the margins, 205
descenders, 120
dirty copy, 252
display advertising, 25
  type, 120
Ditto, 224
dogleg, 193
dominant heads, 195
dominant photo, 167
dummy, pasteup, 218
  sketch, 52
Dutch wrap, 197

E

Eagle, Anheuser Busch Co., 71, 175
Echo, Polysar Limited, 34
editing process, 84
editorializing, 110
editorials, 27
electronic editing, 83
Elizabethtown Magazine, Elizabethtown College, 178
Emhart News, Emhart Corporation, 54, 78, 81
empty sweep, 53
Entre Nous, l'Association des enseignants franco-ontariens, 179
error line, 48
evergreen copy, 42
Executive Report, Illinois State Chamber of Commerce, 236
expository art, 165

F

fallow corner, 185
features, 68
Fensch, Thomas, 119
filler words, 105
Five Ws, 66
flag, 173
flat-out, 133
floppy disk, 83
Focus, Mutual Service Insurance, 241
folio lines, 175
formal page, 199

282 EDITING THE ORGANIZATIONAL PUBLICATION

fresh air, 140
future book, 41

G

Galley Proof, The Science Research Associates, Inc., 223
galley proofs, 47
gatekeepers, 77
ghosting, 153
good taste, 98
graphs, 165
grammar, 72
gravure, 62
grid sheet, 52
    system, 211
guideline method, 49
Gulf Oilmanac, Gulf Oil Co., 24
Gunning's Fog Index, 99
Gutenberg Diagram, 185
gutter, jumping the, 207

H

halftone art, 148
hammer, 140
hand art, 148, 164
hanging indent head, 144
hard news, 65
hard wiring, 83
Hartford Magazine, Hartford Insurance Group, 214
headings, 176
headletters, 138, 139
headline placement, 205
    schedule, 142
    specifications, 137
    stencil, 234
headlines, bumped, 188
    jammed, 188
hectograph, 224
HFH Review, Henry Ford Hospital, 38
hood, 188
Hot Tap, TRANSCO Co., 136, 211
house organs, 3
Human Ecology, 210
Human Ecology, New York State College of Human Ecology at Cornell, 134
human-intrest stories, 68

I

IABC News, 26
identification, picture, 160
i&e lines, 160
imposition, 61
    charts, 216
Independent Investor, Fidelity Group of Boston, 233
indicia, 175
Ingalls Today, Ingalls Memorial Hospital, 151, 182
initials, rising, 127
    stickup, 127
    sunken, 127
    inset, 127
Inquiring-photographer, 69
inset head, 144
Inside CNA, CNA Corporation, 203
Inside, Southern Company Services, 68

Insight, Continental Group, 209
instruction tab, 155
interpretive reporting, 69
inverted pyramids, 65
Investment Research, Wheat First Securities, 222
itemization, 127

J

job descriptions, 12
jump head, 144
jumping the gutter, 207
jumps, 189
justification, 123

K

keyline drawing, 162

L

label head, 144
layout, functional, 202
    invisible, 202, 203
    organic, 202, 203
leading, 121
legibility, 134
letter of agreement, 254
letterpress, 63
lettering guides, 229
libel, 113
    criminal, 113
    civil, 113
    per se, 113
    per quod, 113
Life, Touche Ross, 128
light table, 57
linear definition, 166
line art, 148
line conversion, 166
line length, 121
lithography, 62, 63
Log, The International Paper Co., 33
Lord Facts, Lord Corp., 173
lowercase alphabet length, 121

M

magapaper, 9
magazines, 8, 28
magazine progression, 28
magtab, 9, 32
    layout, 196
    progression, 32
mail circulation, 240
mailing list, 241
    indicia, 175, 244
man-on-the-street, 69
manuscript preparation, 82
maps, 165
margin setting, 200
marker art, 167
marks of apposition, 104
masthead, 173
mechanical dummy, 56
    separations, 180
Meidinger News, Meidinger Corp., 55
mezzotint, 166
Miami Herald, 95
Mimeograph, 64
minority references, 92

misplaced modifiers, 103
Mobil World, Mobil Oil Corp., 194
mockup page, 55
modified silhouette, 159
Money Tree, AVCO Financial Services, 128
morgue, 73
mortises, 158
    interlocking, 158
Mt. Lebanon, Pittsburgh, 29

N

nameplate, 173
National Arthritis News, 11
Neill, Rolfe, 35
news budget, 184
newsletter, 10
    content, 221
    format, 222
newspaper, 31
    progression, 31
Newspaper Readership Report, Newspaper Readership Council, 240
newswriting, 64
notch, 158
NUS Employee Bulletin, NUS Corp., 69

O

offset, 62, 63
Off-the-cuff, Harleysville Insurance Co., 177
1-theme issue, 24
one-up, 133
on-site distribution, 238
opaqueing, 62
op format, 123
opinion page, 28
    reporting, 18
optical center, 190
    magnets, 185
optimum line length, 121
oriented layout, 206
Over Coffee, Blue Cross & Blue Shield of Alabama, 221

P

page layout patterns, 250
    proofs, 49, 61
pagination, 216
Panhandle Magazine, Panhandle Eastern Pipeline Co., 178, 242
paper, 258
    masters, 224
paragraph starters, 126
parallelism, 106
pasteup, 52, 56
    dummy, 218
    sheets, 57
Pedia Script, Columbus Children's Hospital, 215
peeled mailing, 32
    publications, 243
People, American International Group of New York, 183
People, Metropolitan Water District of Southern California, 208

INDEX 283

perforated tape, 83, 35
periodicals, 3
personal news, 68
personals, 70
pepper, 126
Pet Scripts, Pet Inc., 218
PG&E Life, Pacific Gas & Electric Co., 168
Philadelphia News, 35
Phoenix Quarterly, Institute of Scrap Iron & Steel, 175
photographs, 148
pica, 120
picture placement, 207
    self-standing, 191
    wild, 191
plagiarism, 116
plastic plates, 63
POA, 184
point, 120
polls, 35
    readership, 38
posters, 28
prepacks, 194
Preservation News, National Trust for Historic Preservation, 53
primary optical area, 184
printing methods, 61
    specifications, 25B
privilege, 114
process color, 179
production chart, 42
    check list, 58
Profile, IBM Canada Ltd., 178
progression, 28
proofreading, 47
publication, external, 17
    frequency of, 11
    internal, 17
Publishers Auxiliary, National Newspaper Association, 190
pulled quotes, 129
Pulse, Zurich-American Insurance Cos., 133
pump primers, 75

Q
Q&A, 80
quotations, 95
quotes in headlines, 142

R
Radford, Radford College, 128
ragged-right setting, 124
readability, 120
    gauge, 99
    range, 42, 123, 124
reading diagonal, 185
    gravity, 185
reefers, 130
reference libraries, 73
reliability tolerance, 36
relief printing, 62
repetition, 108
Reporter's Report, 16
Research in Action, Virginia Commonwealth University, 129
retouching, 152

reverse, 125
    kicker, 140
reviews, 70
rivers of white, 124
roundup, 70
rub-off letters, 136
runarounds, 125
running head, 210

S
Sarnia Division News, Dow Chemical of Canada, 193
scaling, 156
scaling wheel, 156
scalloped page, 211, 214
scholar's margin, 210, 235
School & Home, St. Louis Public Schools, 174
screen negatives, 60
second designations, 87
    reference, 110
self-cover, 28
sentence fragments, 109
sexism, 111
sidebars, 190
sidelines, 162
signature, 61
silhouettes, 158, 159
silver line, 61
sketch dummies, 248
slash head, 141
soft news, 65, 68
spacing chart, 42, 43
    guide, 198
Spark & Flame, Arizona Public Service Co., 219
special screens, 166
spirit duplicating, 224
splayed letters, 134
square halftone, 168
stacked type, 202
staff evaluation, 14
staff recognition, 12
Slater, North Carolina, 29
stencil cutting, 228
    printing, 63
stickon letters, 135
stock cover, 28
    photos, 170
story count, 189
strikeon composition, 225
    justification of, 227
stripping-in, 60
surprinted type, 136
surprinting, 125
style, 84
    books, 12, 85
stylus, 229
subheads, 129
surveys, 35, 69
    self-administered, 37
swash letters, 145
Swiss grid, 211

T
table of contents, 29, 178
Tablet, University of Chicago Hospitals and Clinics, 177

tabloids, 8
taboos, photo, 151
tabulation, 127
Talktime, Mother Church of Christian Scientists, 177
taped interview, 80
tearsheets, 176
teasers, 34
Teller, Indiana National Corp., 225
Tempo, St. Joseph Hospital & Medical Center, 191
tense, headline, 141
10:30 formula, 184, 187
terminal area, 185
30-bars, 192
3-digit code, 142
Tielines, Michigan Bell, 25, 197
Timberline, 28
time material, 42
tint blocks, 125, 182
titles, 85
    of courtesy, 87
tombstones, 188
tower, 189
transfer letters, 136
tripod, 141
truth, 114
turned story, 144
Turpin, Dr. William, 84
type, bad usage of, 214
    classification, 143
    terminology, 140
typewriter type, elite, 121
    pica, 121
typographic errors, 48

U
UMA Update, University of Mid-America, 9
union label, 257
Union Tabloid, Graphic Arts Union, 7
unit count, 143
Update, Eaton Corporation, 231

V
VanDyke, 60
Velox, 60
Veritas, University of Miami, 192
video display terminals, 52
visibility, 125

W
Week at Southwire, Southwire Co., 64
wicket, 140
widows, 126
wild pictures, 191
The Wood Manville Forest Products, 8, 244
word-processing equipment, 52
Writing & Editing, Associated Press Managing Editors Assn., 95
WVU Report, Western Virginia University, 177

X
x-height, 120

EDMUND C. ARNOLD

was named a "Distinguished Teacher in Journalism" by the Society of Professional Journalists/Sigma Delta Chi. Literally thousands of his peers might second that motion. For he has appeared before more journalists—in workshops, seminars, and speeches—than any other person. He has conducted more than 200 seminars at the American Press Institute and has appeared in every mainland state and Canadian province as well as in several Central and South American countries and Germany.

A native of Michigan, he began his career at the age of 17 and worked for several newspapers there. He was editor and copublisher of the storied *Frankenmuth News*, one of the country's most famed weekly papers. He was editor of the influential *Linotype News* in New York, then joined the faculty of the Syracuse University's School of Journalism. Since 1975 he has been at the School of Mass Communications of Virginia Commonwealth University in Richmond where he has been named an outstanding professor by the School of Arts and Sciences.

He has written 19 books and more than 2,000 articles; is a contributing editor of the *Ragan Report*, *Reporter's Report*, *Speechwriter's Newsletter*, *Publisher's Auxiliary*, *Canadian Printer & Publisher*, *Random House Dictionary*, and *World Book*. He was a columnist for *Editor & Publisher*.

He was a combat correspondent with *Stars & Stripes* in World War II, decorated for service in France and Germany. He has also been twice honored since then for service to military publications, the latest the Army Medal for Outstanding Civilian Service.

He has won the prestigious George Polk Memorial Award, the Journalism Pioneers and George Washington Medals and many other citations. He was given an L.H.D. by Hartwick College and a Litt. D. by Wagner College.

As a consultant in newspaper design, he has worked with such outstanding newspapers as *Christian Science Monitor*, *Today*, *National Observer*, *Boston Globe*, *Chicago Tribune*, *Kansas City Star*, and *Toronto Star* as well as papers in Iceland, Scotland, and New Zealand.